"Anderson provides fresh insights into dynamics of secession that changed the path of the nation in the mid-1800s. The book's original research carefully details the growing estrangement of Southerners and especially the South Carolina radicals who tested – and ultimately crossed – the frontiers of national loyalty. By exposing the fatal mixture of federalism and polarization that paved the way to national tragedy, Anderson holds up a distant mirror to today's turbulent politics."
—David Brian Robertson, *University of Missouri – St. Louis*

"This book makes important new contributions both to the general theory of federalism, secession, and stability; and to the issues of American stability and disunion in the years leading to the Civil War. Focusing on the critical state of South Carolina, Anderson explains the forces generating this state's leadership in the Southern movement to protect slavery and, ultimately, in the path of secession from the United States."
—Barry Weingast, *Stanford University*

Federalism, Secession, and the American State

One important tradition in political science conceives of the Civil War in the United States serving as the functional equivalent of the English and French Revolutions, bringing with it the victory of liberal democratic industrialism over aristocratic agriculturalism. From this perspective, the Civil War is notable for its impact on the American state. Surprisingly however, little attention has been paid to the distinguishing features of this historic rupture in American politics.

Through primary source research and the re-analysis of the rich historical literature about the antebellum era and the causes of the Civil War, Lawrence M. Anderson explores the relationship between federalism and the movement for secession in the United States during the pre-civil war era. Focusing primarily on South Carolina, Anderson carefully revisits theory on institutional analysis of political development to expose what caused secession in the United States

Lawrence M. Anderson is an associate professor of political science at the University of Wisconsin-Whitewater. He teaches mainly in the area of American politics. His research interests include federalism and secessionism.

Routledge Studies in North American Politics

1 **Political Institutions and Lesbian and Gay Rights in the United States and Canada**
   Miriam Smith

2 **Black Women, Cultural Images and Social Policy**
   Julia S. Jordan-Zachery

3 **How Courts Impact Federal Administrative Behavior**
   Robert J. Hume

4 **State Failure, Underdevelopment, and Foreign Intervention in Haiti**
   Jean-Germain Gros

5 **Mexico-United States Relations**
   The Semantics of Sovereignty
   Arturo Santa-Cruz

6 **Federalism, Secession, and the American State**
   Divided, We Secede
   Lawrence M. Anderson

Federalism, Secession, and the American State
Divided, We Secede

Lawrence M. Anderson

Taylor & Francis Group
NEW YORK   LONDON

First published 2013
by Routledge
711 Third Avenue, New York, NY 10017

Simultaneously published in the UK
by Routledge
2 Park Square, Milton Park, Abingdon, Oxfordshire OX14 4RN

First issued in paperback 2014

Routledge is an imprint of the Taylor & Francis Group, an informa business

© 2013 Taylor & Francis

The right of Lawrence M. Anderson to be identified as author of this work has been asserted by him in accordance with sections 77 and 78 of the Copyright, Designs and Patents Act 1988.

All rights reserved. No part of this book may be reprinted or reproduced or utilised in any form or by any electronic, mechanical, or other means, now known or hereafter invented, including photocopying and recording, or in any information storage or retrieval system, without permission in writing from the publishers.

Trademark Notice: Product or corporate names may be trademarks or registered trademarks, and are used only for identification and explanation without intent to infringe.

Library of Congress Cataloging-in-Publication Data
Anderson, Lawrence M.
  Federalism, secession, and the American state : divided, we secede / Lawrence M. Anderson.
    p. cm. — (Routledge studies in North American politics ; 6)
  Includes bibliographical references.
  1. Federal government—United States—History—19th century.
  2. Secession—United States—History. 3. States' rights (American politics)—History—19th century. 4. Nullification (States' rights)—History—19th century. 5. United States—Politics and government—19th century. 6. South Carolina—Politics and government—1775–1865. I. Title.
  JK311.A63 2012
  320.473'049—dc23
               2012010857

ISBN 978-0-415-51832-1 (hbk)
ISBN 978-1-138-84907-5 (pbk)
ISBN 978-0-203-09566-9 (ebk)

Typeset in Sabon
by IBT Global.

"As it is, we have the wolf by the ears, and we can neither hold him nor safely let him go. Justice is in one scale, and self-preservation in the other."

—Thomas Jefferson, on slavery

"Our Federal Union—it must be preserved."

—Andrew Jackson

"The Union—next to our liberty, most dear."

—John C. Calhoun, responding to Jackson

"The only question . . . is can the Union and Slavery exist together?"

—William Henry Trescott

"I believe this Union and slavery cannot stand together."

—Armistead Burt

"Whom the gods would destroy, they first make mad."

—Euripides

For JZAB
It wouldn't be any fun without them

Contents

	List of Figures and Tables	xiii
	Chronology of Events	xv
1	Introduction: The Problem, the Method, and the Outline of the Book	1
2	The American State and Early Challenges to Central State Authority	9
3	States' Rights in South Carolina: From Nullification to the First Secession Crisis	22
4	South Carolina Secedes	57
5	The Path of Secession in the Three Souths	105
6	The Past and Future of Federalism and Secession	134
	Notes	141
	References	165
	Index	179

Figures and Tables

FIGURES

2.1	Free state representation in the House of Representatives.	13
3.1	Slave population as percent of total population in slave states in 1860.	24
3.2	Percent of (white) families owning slaves in 1860, by state.	24
3.3	Percent of seats held by planters in southern legislatures, 1850 and 1860.	24
3.4	Percent of seats held by planters in secession conventions (or state legislature), 1860–61.	25
3.5	Slave state representation in the House of Representatives.	30
3.6	Population of states in 1860.	31
5.1	Percent of seats held by non-slaveholders in secession conventions (or State Legislature), 1860–61.	117
5.2	From the collections of the South Carolina Historical Society.	132

TABLES

3.1	Free State and Slave State Additions to the Union	45
4.1	Popular Vote in the 1856 Presidential Election, by State	58
4.2	Popular Vote in the 1860 Presidential Election, by State	75
5.1	Per Capita Value of Manufactured Goods Produced in 1860, by State	126

Chronology of Events

November 1832	The South Carolina state convention nullifies federal tariffs
August 1846	The Wilmot Proviso is introduced. It passes the House of Representatives; it never passes the Senate.
February 1848	Mexican cession adds more than 500,000 square miles to U.S. territory.
September 1850	California is admitted as a free state, permanently tipping balance (16 free/15 slave).
April 1852	The South Carolina secession convention affirms right to secede.
May 1858	Minnesota is admitted to the Union as a free state (17 free states/15 slave states).
February 1859	Oregon is admitted to the Union as free state (18 free states/15 slave states).
October 1859	Abolitionist John Brown conducts his raid on Harper's Ferry, Virginia (now West Virginia).
January 1860	Christopher Memminger leads South Carolina's failed mission to Virginia.
February 1860	Alabama Legislature votes to call a convention if a Republican is elected president.
April 1860	The Democratic Convention is held in Charleston, SC. The Convention and the Party splits along sectional lines.
June 1860	John C. Breckinridge and Stephen Douglas are nominated to the Northern and Southern Democratic tickets.
October 1860	Governor Gist sends letters to governors of the Deep South, attempting to discern their reaction to the probable Republican presidential victory.
5 November 1860	The South Carolina legislature convenes to choose presidential electors.
6 November 1860	Abraham Lincoln is elected president.

7 November 1860	Federal Judge A.G. Magrath of South Carolina and other federal officers resign their positions.
10 November 1860	James Chesnut resigns his seat in the U.S. Senate.
10 November 1860	The South Carolina legislature calls for a state convention to meet 17 December.
11 November 1860	James Henry Hammond resigns his seat in the U.S. Senate.
3 December 1860	James Buchanan gives his final annual address. He claims to have no authority to coerce a seceded state back in the Union.
6 December 1860	South Carolina elects convention delegates; separate state secessionists win.
20 December 1860	South Carolina secedes from the Union, unanimously adopting an ordinance of secession.
9 January 1861	Mississippi secedes from the Union.
10 January 1861	Florida secedes from the Union.
11 January 1861	Alabama secedes from the Union.
19 January 1861	Georgia secedes from the Union.
26 January 1861	Louisiana secedes from the Union.
1 February 1861	Texas secedes from the Union.
February 1861	The seceded states meet in Montgomery, AL. The Confederate States of America (CSA) is formed.
4 March 1861	Abraham Lincoln is sworn in as the 16th president of the United States.
12 April 1861	South Carolina initiates the shelling of Fort Sumter, which is held by the federal government. Sumter falls soon thereafter.
15 April 1861	President Lincoln calls up 75,000 troops to quell the Southern insurrection.
17 April 1861	Virginia secedes from the Union. The western counties remain in the Union, eventually forming West Virginia.
6 May 1861	Arkansas secedes from the Union.
6 May 1861	The legislature of Tennessee passes an ordinance of secession.
20 May 1861	North Carolina secedes from the Union.

1 Introduction
The Problem, the Method, and the Outline of the Book

> "Should federal encroachments persist, South Carolina may be forced to calculate the value of union."
>
> -Thomas Cooper, President of South Carolina College, 1827

> "We've got a great union. There's absolutely no reason to dissolve it. But if Washington continues to thumb their nose at the American people, you know, who knows what might come out of that."
>
> -Rick Perry, Governor of Texas, 2009

In South Carolina, in December 1860, a political revolution was undertaken in order to avert a social revolution.[1] This state needed to withdraw from the Union lest its political, social, and economic freedoms were to be put at risk.[2] The withdrawal of this one state from the Union was the result of a calculated risk undertaken by the political elite of that state. As a result of the secession of South Carolina, other states of the Deep South seceded. Then, as a result of the first altercation of the Civil War, the states of the upper south seceded. The Border States never left the Union. The calculated risk paid off, for the most part. In obtaining its political revolution, South Carolina managed, for a short time, anyway, to avoid the social revolution.

Political challenges to central states have always been common. What distinguishes the U.S. from other stable, democratic countries is the long history of the territorial-based challenge to the central state. While secession movements abroad have become almost commonplace, they are a relatively recent phenomenon, a function of a new focus on the meaning attached to national self-determination. Contrast this with the U.S.: secessionist challenge to the territorial reach of the American Union have a long history, beginning before the American Union was founded and leading up until today.

South Carolina was neither the first nor the last state to suggest calculating the value of union, but it was the first to secede. Using the considerable institutional resources of state governments in early America and using a sequential exit strategy devised by the state's secessionists, South Carolina unilaterally seceded from the Union and helped to form the Confederate

States of America. The movement for secession and the war that followed it signaled a crucial transformation in the American political economy: the victory of liberal democratic industrialism over aristocratic agriculturalism.[3]

In this book, I explore the institutional and strategic determinants of secession in the American South. How did it come to pass that secession became the preferred method of redressing grievances? Why did secession take place when it did, rather than earlier, later, or not at all? Why did secession occur in each individual state rather than all at once? Why was South Carolina the vanguard state, initiating secession and compelling secession in most of the other states of the slave South? This project looks at this very old and often-told story in a new light, reflecting also on what this old story can tell us about federalism and secession in other contexts. This book situates this case, first, in the literature on the institutional design of states, second, in the literature on dynamic models of political mobilization—in this case, secession—and third, in the literature on the paradox of federalism—the contradictory finding that federalism can both inhibit and encourage secession.

I explore the political and institutional context of the antebellum period and the political strategies of the landed elite and the political class in South Carolina; I do so because secession, in this case, occurred in a particular sequence and was guided by a particular strategy—with radical South Carolina acting first and alone, thereby forcing the hand of the remaining Southern states. Were it not for the strategy used by this vanguard state, the creation of a Southern Confederacy would not have happened.

I also hope to contribute to the solution of an interesting puzzle in American political development: Why did South Carolina secede, why did some states follow, and why did others refuse to follow? In answering this series of questions—interesting in themselves—this book can also lay claim to answering one of the most puzzled-upon, enigmatic, and controversial questions in all of American history and politics: What precipitated the Civil War?

In fact, the answer to this question is quite simple. The Civil War was precipitated by the secession of most of the Southern states of the Union and the refusal of the new Lincoln administration to allow these states to "depart in peace." The puzzle that must be explained, then, is not what precipitated the war, but secession.

In the simplest terms, secessionism was the result of a perception of a serious threat to slavery experienced by the political class of South Carolina and the Deep South. Secession was, moreover, accomplished by the honing of a proper strategy over time to bring it about. This threat culminated in the election of Abraham Lincoln to the presidency in 1860, which was made possible by a series of economic and demographic changes in the antebellum Union that contributed to a relative decline of the political power of the South. That said, the contours of secession of the Southern states of the Union cannot be explained simply by reference to the threat to slavery, although that threat does provide a sufficient terminological abbreviation for the grievance felt by the Southern states.

Without slavery, there would have been no secession and no Civil War. However, secession in the Southern states had its roots in the very structure of the American state. The institutional design of the American state (i.e., federalism) assured the existence of vastly different political, social, and economic institutions at the state level. This design meant that the separate states of the Union could and did have economies and interests based on fundamentally different organizing principles, and it gave each of the states a high degree of state capacity. An aggrieved constituent unit was more likely to see secession as politically feasible under these circumstances than if the state had been designed according to different principles—such as the principles of the unitary state. Some have cautiously argued that adopting federalism could mute the centrifugal forces of secession.[4] This project demonstrates how this "solution" may end up contributing to the very movement it is designed to prevent.

GRIEVANCE, STRUCTURE, STRATEGY, AND SEQUENCE

This analysis provides compelling new insight into the dynamics of secession. I focus on grievance, because grievance played a central role in mobilizing support for a change to the *status quo*—in this case, secession.[5] Most analysts of secession locate the origin of the pursuit of secession in a desire to avoid or end economic exploitation or hardship and improve the economic position of the seceding group relative to other groups within the borders of the host state; others locate the origin in a group's fear of cultural and political domination by out-group members. Groups that lack political power within their host states are most vulnerable to these economic and cultural threats.[6]

There is a central problem in these conventional explanations to secession. Grievance cannot be the only source of the motivation to secede. Grievance is common; secession is rare. By their own measures, South Carolina and the South were aggrieved for more than a generation before secession took place. Yet, secession did not take place until a set of circumstances lined up to convince South Carolina's elites to take a chance. Grievance is likely a necessary condition of secession, but it is not sufficient for secession to take place. To understand secession, we need to situate that grievance in a wider political, institutional, and strategic context.

Thus, I focus on the structure of the state within which this grievance developed. The federal structure of the American political union played a central role in the development, failure, and eventual success of secession in the South. This institutional design of American federalism, which provided the rules of the game governing political strategies, grievance development, and grievance remediation, both complicated and enabled radical political mobilization. For reasons related to institutional design, some states are more prone to secession than others. The American state was designed (and interpreted) in a way that placed secession on the agenda and made it a viable remediation strategy for those dissatisfied with the *status quo*—especially when that dissatisfaction is territorially bound. Grievance and an institutional structure that is conducive to secession is only part of the story.

This research builds on the new wave of federalism research.[7] One central question of this research agenda asks whether it is possible to design federal institutions that are stable over time.[8] The stability of federalism over time is complicated by the paradoxical impact of the institutions of federalism. Some have found federalism to be a panacea for secessionist conflict.[9] Others regard federalism with a great deal more caution, finding that it has features that contribute to secessionist pressures. Federalism offers a territorial mixed bag, at best.[10] This project is able to provide insight into understanding the paradox of federalism.[11]

The paradox is in operation in the American case. The institutions of federalism in the American Union helped to prevent secession for a long time after secession became the stated desire of South Carolina's elite. This project gets inside the dynamic to explore *how* federalism calms and encourages secessionism.

Institutions matter, but so, too, does strategy. Only once South Carolina got the strategy right was the state able to use the institutions of federalism to bring about secession in the other states of the South. In this case, the right strategy was the right sequence. Secession occurred dynamically and sequentially, not all at once, with South Carolina leading and (some of) the other states of the South following.

South Carolina's actions were decisive in the secession of the states of the Deep South and the creation of a Southern Confederacy.[12] This is not simply a case of South Carolina being willing to secede first—clearly, it was. Once this state was out of the Union, the Union was less hospitable to the institution of slavery. This dynamic continued as more states seceded (i.e., once South Carolina *and* Alabama were out of the Union, the Union was even less hospitable to the institution of slavery, changing the choice-environment for other states, thereby making the withdrawal of subsequent states more likely). South Carolina also changed the choice-environment for the Upper South states. By seceding and orchestrating a conflict with the federal government over Fort Sumter, which lead to Lincoln's proclamation calling up troops, South Carolina pulled the states of the Upper South out of the Union. The secession of South Carolina didn't just make secession more likely: it made secession necessary for most of the other states of the South, but at different times and for different reasons.

In most cases of secession, the sequence is a process of political mobilization within a single compact territory or region. The elites and mass public of this *single* territorially-demarcated population interact with each other and with agents of the central state to achieve secession. In my analysis,

I do not assume that all secessionist units will secede simultaneously. In fact, I assume that secession will occur dynamically, with more radical regions leading the charge of secession, convincing or compelling less radical regions to secede from the host state, sometimes for reasons that are very different from the initial seceder. Secessionist leaders are always at pains to muster support for secession, but there are dilemmas (and benefits) of mobilization peculiar to a region that includes multiple semi-sovereign entities with conventionally recognized political boundaries.

In the case at hand, the sequence and strategy were enormously affected by the jurisdictional complexity of the American Union. In particular, there was no one political voice or political institution that spoke for the South. Had there been a single institution that could speak for the South, it almost certainly would have rejected secession. Was the South willing and able to speak with a single voice, secession might have been unnecessary. In the case at hand, however, this ended up being a significant advantage. It meant unanimity on secession was impossible. It meant the states of the South would have varying degrees of support for secession. It meant the creation of the Southern Confederacy would be a multi-step and multi-stage process that occurred in a very particular order. It meant South Carolina had no incentive to moderate its position and that its position was not diluted by a moderate South. Because the *South* could not secede (and would not secede, even if it could) South Carolina (or some other lone Southern state) would have to be willing to take a calculated risk to secede unilaterally and try to force of the hand of the remaining Southern states. South Carolina was willing to do so—and was the *only* state willing to do so.

Here is one of the profound ironies of this era: a South in the Union that was as monolithically attached to slavery as South Carolina would not need to secede—it could set (and limit) Union policy with respect to slavery by virtue of its monolithic and unquestioned support of slavery. But a South that was divided on the question of slavery—in particular, its future and what was needed to maintain it—needed secession to save it.

METHODOLOGY

Through process-tracing in a single case, this work is able to provide a "moving picture" image of the movement for secession in South Carolina.[13] I explore how South Carolina, working within the complex jurisdictional environment of American federalism, came to prefer secession to other grievance remediation strategies and develop a strategy for achieving it in a way that would encourage secession among other states of the South. I explore how the strategic decision-making of the political elite in South Carolina successfully brought about this unlikely outcome.

This project focuses on three episodes in South Carolina that describe the process of political mobilization for secession. Without the steps and missteps taken in these episodes, and the lessons learned from them, secession in 1860 would have been unlikely and the creation of a Southern Confederacy might not have happened. During the nullification crisis of 1832–33 South Carolina forcefully reiterated the concept of state sovereignty through its nullification of federal tariffs. South Carolina was hoping to sound the first trumpet of the creation of a new, assertive South, but South Carolina was abandoned by a South that refused to adopt such a radical stance (especially given passage of the compromise tariff). South Carolina was forced to back down. During the first secession crisis of 1852, following the passage of the Compromise of 1850 in the U.S. Congress and the failed conference of Southern states, South Carolina approached the point of secession, but again backed down. During this crisis, seeing that there was no will in the South to take radical action, the state convention of South Carolina anemically affirmed of the right to secede, the existence of which few in this state (and in the South as a whole) doubted by 1852. Here, we see elements of South Carolina's strategy developing. First, secede before compromise can be created. Second, secede at the state level, not at the level of the "South," which was nothing more than a political construction.

Finally, in 1860 with the election of Republican Abraham Lincoln, the political class of South Carolina (the planters) believed that the political standings of their state and the South within the Union were in a steep and irreversible decline. In this single most important moment of choice, palpable fear of the consequences of Lincoln's election, in conjunction with the lessons drawn from the past, led South Carolinian political actors to pursue a strategy that assured the secession of their state and was likely to pave the way for the secession of the other radical states of the Deep South and, eventually, force the hand of most—if not all—of the remaining Southern states.

This methodological approach necessitates the examination of these three episodes from a number of different perspectives. First, I examined the changing strategies of secessionist entrepreneurs. I examined the strategy of unilateral secession, which was used by political elites in South Carolina to force the issue upon their own state and the remainder of the South. Here, I relied on a rational choice approach to American political development.[14] Second, I situated these actors in their capacity as political leaders within the institutional structure of the American state. In so doing, this project utilizes elements of the "new institutionalism" to explain how the institutions in which these entrepreneurs were situated impacted their strategies.[15] From the formal institutional design of the state proceeded a variety of formal and informal institutions, or a "set of shared understandings," within the American Union that "affect[ed] the way problems are perceived and solutions are sought."[16] This institutional context meant, in the presence of a powerful grievance, secession would be sought at the expense of other means of redress.

The data explored in this project comes by and large from an examination of primary sources. For each episode, I consulted state records of South Carolina and the federal government. This includes an analysis of official documents of the three state conventions South Carolina held in the antebellum period. I also studied the records of the Nashville Convention of 1850. Perhaps most importantly, I examined the personal papers of the central actors in South Carolina, including—but not limited to—U.S. Senator John C. Calhoun, governor of South Carolina William Henry Gist, U.S. Senator Robert Barnwell Rhett, and U.S. Senator James Henry Hammond. Equally important are certain South Carolinian newspapers and periodicals, as well as pro- and anti-secessionist pamphlets, as these documents both reflected and shaped political opinion and events in this state. Of particular importance are the Charleston *Mercury* and the pamphlets of the "1860 Association," which outlined the strategies and rationale for secession in South Carolina and the rest of the seceding South.[17] I also explore objective measures of the shape and trajectory of the Union found in census data, congressional apportionment, and the patronage power and influence of the presidency. (After all, the event that precipitated South Carolina's secession was the election of Abraham Lincoln to the presidency. Either South Carolina was looking for an event that would allow them to justify secession or the state was sincerely concerned about the consequences of a Republican in the presidency.) I also consulted selected election results for South Carolina, the rest of the seceding South, and the entire Union.[18] Finally, a re-examination of the secondary work on the secession of South Carolina proved to be immeasurably important in the successful completion of this project.

CHAPTER OUTLINES

The chapters of the book are organized in the following fashion: The second chapter explores the concept of the state, origins of the American state, and early challenges to central state authority and the territorial integrity of that state. The third chapter takes up the development of South Carolina as the vanguard state in the defense of Southern rights. It offers an explanation for radicalism in South Carolina and explores the nullification controversy and the first secessions crisis, both of which were crucial moments for the development of positions and strategies that South Carolina would use in the final crisis with the center. The fourth chapter explores the decision to secede in detail: Why, when, and how did South Carolina secede from the Union? I elaborate upon the grievances precipitating secession, the actors involved, and the institutional context that helped to make secession politically feasible, as well as the political strategies used to accomplish secession and the sequence by which it was accomplished. The fifth chapter extends my analytical horizon to include other states of the slave South. I examine the rationales behind secession (or non-secession) in the states that followed South Carolina out of the Union early, in the states that followed South Carolina out of the Union only after the shelling of Fort Sumter and Lincoln's proclamation, and in the states that never seceded from the Union. In the sixth and concluding chapter, I summarize the findings of this study and point future avenues of research in the link between federalism and secessionism. This study can help clear a path to understanding the territorial-political consequences of federalism in other contexts.

2 The American State and Early Challenges to Central State Authority

There is a tendency to see the South as *the* threat to the scope of the federal government and the territorial integrity of the American Union. Looking only at the antebellum era, it is easy to see where this perception came from. Taking a longer view, however, makes it clear that threats to the scope of the federal government and to the territorial integrity of the American Union were not unique to the South and did not originate in the South. Challenges to the territorial reach of the federal government were and are a unique and seemingly permanent feature of the American Union.

If we are to understand the origins of secession in the U.S., we must understand how the American state was put together. The state created by the American Founders was fundamentally different from the industry standard state that existed in Europe at the time of the formation of the American Union. Where European states were created as highly centralized resource-extractors and war-makers, the American state created by the founders was highly decentralized. This is at least partly a function of the political-military environment of Europe compared to North America. Europe was a zone of war; survival depended upon the ability of a state to extract resources from the population in order to engage in war or provide adequate defense from enemies that were literally at the border. The U.S., while created out of war, was fortunate insofar as it did not have competing state challengers in the neighborhood. Given this, the American founders were free to design a state that was different from the European standard. The founders were free to adopt federalism—a nod to the continuing independence of the constituent states and the need to have *some* centralization of state functions.

While there were no significant state challengers in the neighborhood, there were salient divisions between the states. Federalism doesn't eliminate pre-existing divisions between constituent units, but federal institutions do channel divisions and conflict in particular ways, sometimes providing an escape-value for these regional conflicts, preventing them from spilling over into other regions or threatening the center.

Challenges to the authority of the central state were common in the early Union. It was the New England states that issued the first organized, but veiled, threat of secession. How is it, then, that the secession threat and challenges to central state authority, more generally, came to be associated with the South? This can be explained by a changing political-economic dynamic within the Union and this changing dynamic's interaction with the institutions of federalism. Over time, Southerners, especially those in South Carolina, realized that an ascendant North was a threat to slavery, which dominated the political economy of Southern states. In order to meet this threat, the South challenged the authority of the central state, using principles of state's rights and state sovereignty that had been developed much earlier in all sections of the Union.

This chapter traces the origins of challenges to central state authority from the founding of the American Union to the 1820s. It does so to, first, demonstrate the extent to which such challenges were built into the Union itself and, second, to demonstrate how, over time, challenges to central state authority came to be associated with the Southern states of the Union and with South Carolina, in particular.

Originally, disunion was a warning—something undesirable, something to be avoided, not a path to follow. As time went on and the position of the South within the Union became less and less tenable, disunion became a proposal, a plan to follow. South Carolinian elites and those in most of the rest of the Deep South purposely and strategically sought it.[1] This transformation in conceiving of disunion is extraordinary. However, if we understand secession as the ultimate challenge to central state authority, as the ultimate states' right, this transformation becomes understandable. Moreover, despite claims to the contrary, using the threat of disunion to obtain concessions from the central state and to reveal sincere preferences has a long tradition.

South Carolina and the rest of the seceding South were the first and last in the U.S. to exercise the right of secession, but they were not the first to invoke it. Other parts of the U.S. had previously challenged the authority of the central state and the territorial integrity of the Union. Past confrontations with the central authority of the Union, inside and outside South Carolina, constitute South Carolina's learning curve on the road to secession. Without the steps, missteps, and lessons learned from the past, secession would have continued to remain improbable. This chapter examines the central moments in which the meaning, authority, and territorial reach of the Union were challenged. First, I offer an overview of the history, rationale, and design of the American state. I briefly examine the Kentucky and Virginia Resolutions, the institutional significance of the election of 1800, and New England's secession threat at the Hartford Convention. These early episodes provide the historical context in which South Carolina's movement toward independence is best understood. Most importantly, the secession tradition in the U.S. was not limited to the South alone.[2]

THE EUROPEAN AND AMERICAN STATES

The central and novel proposition that I make in this exploration of secession is that the institutional design of the state plays a central role in shaping grievance and the strategy and sequence of secession. Given the centrality of this institution to my argument, I would first like to offer a definition of the state. I define the state as the "organization with a comparative advantage in violence, extending over a geographic area whose boundaries are determined by its power to tax constituents."[3] State formation describes the process by which (and the context in which) a state is constructed. The process of state formation in the West is defined as "constitution making, involvement in wars, electoral democratization and bureaucratization."[4] The institutions that arise from the process of state formation differ according to the context in which the state's formative moments occur, accidents of history, and the intentions of those designing the state.

There is a consensus in the field of political science that the exigencies of war-making were the primary motivating factor behind state formation in Europe.[5] This means the origin, development, expansion, and strengthening of the state can be traced to the cycle of interstate competition and war among the proto-states of Europe. Every war-making advance made by one state had to be duplicated and improved upon by all the others. Implementing and improving upon these advances to remain militarily competitive required a substantial and regular source of revenue. Regular taxation of the inhabitants of these political units provided such a source. Bureaucracies formed or were rationalized in order to facilitate the regular collection of taxes. In Europe, this cycle of conflict was exacerbated by the geographic contiguity of competing states. From these beginnings a strong, functionally differentiated, territorially bounded, centralized, and unitary state came into being.

This state was confronted with a number of challenges. On one hand, there was the ever-present threat of war, which meant that every state was at risk of being conquered by neighboring state-competitors; on the other hand, this state was confronted by internal threats (what J.P. Nettl called "anti-system" movements).[6] These internal threats were primarily threats to the state's regime. That is, after the threat of being conquered by a foreign power, the most common threat to this state concerned the domestic political ordering of the regime, but not the territorial integrity of the state itself.

The European state was and is characterized by a high degree of "stateness," or state "saliency,"[7] which refers to the *extent* to which the institutions of the state are centralized, differentiated, and autonomous from society. "Stateness" also encapsulates the capacity and autonomy of state institutions, which refers to the ability of actors within state institutions to turn their policy preferences into reality, and to do so independent of social forces within the state. "Stateness" also includes a territorial element: The state is not only the centralized, differentiated, and autonomous institution that taxes, protects, and makes war; it is also, in one fundamental respect, the territory itself. Michael Mann wrote, "The state is indeed a *place*—both a central place and a unified territorial reach."[8] Thus, a high degree of stateness assumes a stable territorial reach within which state institutions extract resources and provide services. In Europe, the states that emerged typically had a clear center of sovereignty and clear boundaries. To alter Tilly's familiar formulation: War made a state that was centralized, rationalized, territorialized, and unitary, and *this* state made war.[9]

The circumstances surrounding the formation of the American Union were distinct from the pattern of state formation in Europe in a number of critical ways, which helped to contribute to the unique institutional design of the American state: In North America, there was no history of absolute monarchy and centralization; there was a lack of extensive experience with interstate war;[10] and there were no significant regional competing state-challengers. Furthermore, the creators of the American state were familiar with the pathologies of the European state and state system, and they purposely set out to avoid them.[11] Without the imperative to create a strong state to protect citizens and territory from external predation, the founding fathers created a federal state in which sovereignty was divided between the states of the Union and the federal government and in which the authority of the central state was limited.

The unique design of the American state meant that this state would be characterized by relative "statelessness." Nettl claimed "no truly federal regime can incorporate any adequate notion of the state, since both functions and powers involved in this concept are—by almost any definition—coordinated with the regional units, and the necessary overall superordination of sovereignty does not therefore exist."[12] One scholar of the American state put it this way: prior to the Civil War, "*there was no state.*"[13] This claim may be exaggerated, but it does help us to understand the institutionally and jurisdictionally complex early-nineteenth-century state in America.

While it is true that the coercive power of the state in the American Union was divided between constituent units (or "states") and the federal government—and that the state of the American Union, more generally, was "unsettled" and characterized by *relative* "statelessness"—effective state structures at the center were in place. The federal government both participated in a variety of state activities and established what amounted to the superordination of its sovereignty. The U.S. successfully engaged in a number of wars, and, during the nullification crisis, it affirmed its right to enforce its own laws—suggesting, though not definitively proving, that it possessed the superordination of sovereignty. (The primacy of the federal government is also found in the Supremacy Clause of the Constitution of the U.S.[14]) Furthermore, numerous court cases, the most notable of which is *McCulloch v. Maryland*, established federal law as supreme over state law. From a functional standpoint, it was the federal government that "maintained the currency, funded the national debt, collected the customs, [and] registered patents."[15] Although this state was structurally and functionally distinct from the state found in Europe, it was, nevertheless, a state.

The America State was a stalemated state. It was designed to be weak and political decisions and processes had kept it that way for some time.[16] A variety of formal and informal institutions proved effective in maintaining the relative statelessness of the American state. The balance rule in the Senate, in which the slave and free states were admitted to the Union in pairs, maintained equal representation of slave and free state interests. This informal institution effectively stalemated the American state, allowing one section to veto the policies of the other and effectively preventing the center from passing laws that either section saw as detrimental to its interests. Specifically, this meant that anti-slavery legislation would have virtually no chance of being passed. Even as Northern representation in— and dominance of—the House of Representatives grew (see Figure 2.1), passing a law required the approval of both the free and the slave sections of the Union. In his analysis of the crisis leading up to the Civil War, Barry Weingast describes the maintenance of the "balance rule" as a central component of the second-party system, the breakdown of which facilitated the creation of sectional political parties, thus contributing to the crisis that led to the Civil War.

The second-party system featured the Whig and Democratic parties contesting elections. Unlike the party system that would replace it, in the second-party system, both parties had constituencies in the North and South whose interests they had to represent in order to remain competitive in elections. Thus, the parties were forced to adopt moderate positions on a variety of issues to prevent supporters in one section or the other from defecting to another political party. For example, if Northern Democrats wanted the Democratic Party to continue to win the presidency, they had to continue to adopt a moderate position on slavery, because a radical position on slavery

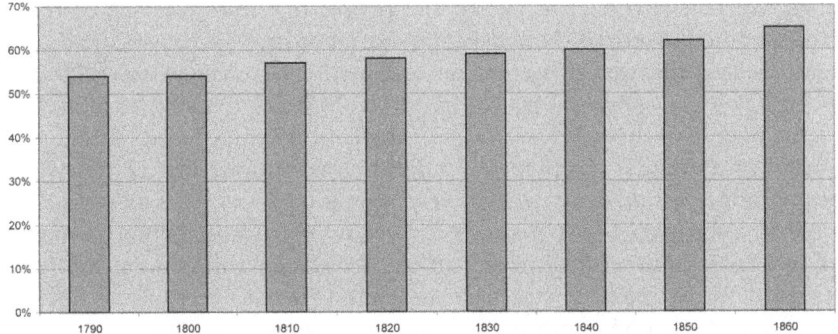

Figure 2.1 Free state representation in the House of Representatives.
Source: Martis and Elmes (1993: 146).

would have alienated the party's Southern constituency. Likewise, a position seen as radically pro-slavery had the potential to alienate the Northern wing of the Democratic Party. Even while Northern anti-slavery was in check, many in the South desired the creation of a political party that had an exclusively Southern constituency in order to more effectively provide them with the policies they sought. Northern members of the Whig and Democratic political coalition knew that a political party platform built rigidly on anti-slavery would have guaranteed the creation of a pro-Southern, pro-slavery party to counterbalance it. Fearing this, the Whig and Democratic parties were at great pains to adopt a largely pro-slavery stance throughout the second-party system. Whigs and Democrats were apparently more concerned about losing the South than losing the North. The perception that the Democratic Party in particular was excessively pro-Southern eventually lead to the creation of the Republican Party in the North.

The state in the U.S. differed from a "real state."[17] It was not a single, coherent, unitary state in which sovereign power was hierarchically organized, peaking at a single point that possessed ultimate sovereignty; rather, this state was the product of a compact between the sovereign and independent separate states that had withdrawn, first, from British authority and, second, from the Union created by the Articles of Confederation. That the Union was conceived of as a compact between constituent units helped to maintain a sense within the constituent units of the American state that they had not surrendered sovereignty to the federal government, but had retained ultimate sovereignty for themselves. In the early days of the republic, adherence to the theory of state sovereignty was prevalent in the both the North and the South. Generally, the belief in the sovereignty of the states was made possible by the extent and import of the powers reserved to these constituent units by the constitution.

According to the central principle of the compact theory of the state, sovereign power did not reside in Congress, the presidency, or the Courts; rather, sovereign power resided in the people of the separate states through their separate state governments and, occasionally, through state conventions. In their sovereign capacity, the people of these states delegated certain specific powers to the federal government in Washington. The central state created through this compact had little intrinsic power. What power it did have was exercised power by virtue of being granted such authority by the people of the separate states of the Union through ordinances passed in conventions that adopted the federal constitution. The Union was not perpetual; it would only be maintained as long as its principles and limits were maintained. Thus, perhaps the most important formal institutions maintaining limited government in the American Union were the powers reserved to the separate states of the Union in their capacity as sovereign parties to the Union compact and the very design of the state.

This government's power was not unlimited; the Constitution of the U.S. granted the federal government a series of enumerated powers. According

The American State and Early Challenges to Central State Authority 15

to the Tenth Amendment, "The powers not delegated to the United States by the Constitution, nor prohibited by it to the States, are reserved to the States respectively, or to the people." For much of the history of the U.S., the federal government was weak and limits on federal authority were respected. This has as much to do with the equilibrium established between the Northern and Southern sections of the Union as it did with the American desire to maintain limited government. In the early years of the republic, the limits placed on central state authority simply could not be exceeded. During this period, Theodore Lowi argued, "The states did almost all the governing." He wrote:

> The states made all the property laws, family laws and estate laws, public health and safety laws, labor laws, occupations and professions laws, credit and exchange laws, banking and insurance laws, the laws of corporations, most of the criminal laws, and most of the other fundamental laws that provide the governmental and legal basis of modern life.[18]

Even military defense was primarily a state function under the militia system.[19] The purpose of the federal government was to facilitate, not regulate, commerce and to protect the territory and citizens of the Union from external predation. Limited to these functions alone, and limited by the equilibrium established between the sections, the federal government did not loom large in the lives of American citizens in the antebellum period. It is hardly an exaggeration to claim that the most salient function of the federal government at this time was assuring the delivery of the mail.[20]

The compact theory of the American state was dominant within the Union, especially in the South, during the antebellum period, but this was not the only theory of the state held by citizens of the U.S. at this time. Some believed the Constitution created a single sovereign people, not a union of several sovereign states. The Union was, from this perspective, an unbreakable whole—not a collection of separate sovereignties. That this Union was approved by the states in their separate, sovereign capacity did not detract from the organic unity of the Union. In the Articles of Confederation, each member-state was listed individually. According to the Constitution, "*We the people of the United States* . . . do ordain and establish this Constitution for the United States of America."[21] This shift in wording was not lost on those who saw the Union as a national, unbreakable whole in which the people, not the states, were sovereign.[22]

There is evidence to support the validity of each position. In his argument in favor of a national interpretation of the Union, Samuel Beer claimed that there is "much blank space" in the Constitution, meaning that a definitive answer to this question cannot be had by examining the Constitution itself.[23] In *Federalist* 62, James Madison argued that the state created by the Constitution had *both* "national and federal character." The "Great

Compromise" between the large states and the small states provided the Union with a House of Representatives that derived its authority from the will of the people and a Senate that gave the states, in their capacity as "political and coequal societies,"[24] equal political representation regardless of size. The institution of the Senate was, Madison further claimed in *Federalist* 62, "at once a Constitutional recognition of the portion of sovereignty remaining in the individual states and an instrument in preserving that residuary sovereignty." Maintaining this residual sovereignty was further enhanced by the fact that the Constitution stipulated that state legislatures, and not a given state's electorate, were to elect U.S. Senators.[25] The election of members of the House, in districts of relatively equal population, suggested that the people, not the constituent states, were sovereign. Despite assertions on both sides, from its inception, the Union had both national and federal attributes.[26] For the most part, it was practical, rather than philosophical, considerations that determined on which side of this debate one sat. The balance of political power in the federal government largely determined adherence to one interpretation or another.

Balance in the Senate, the bisectional nature of the party system in the antebellum period, and the institutional design of the American state were the formal and informal mechanisms employed for arriving at one end: the maintenance of limited government. Although the Constitution could be changed to reflect new realities within the Union, the amending process was arduous. As long as the North was far short of a constitution-amending majority, it could very easily be argued that remaining in the Union posed no danger to the South.

Although many Southerners never saw a danger in remaining in the Union, there were those, especially in the Deep South, who came to believe that remaining in the Union posed a fundamental risk to Southern institutions. The presence of strong, enduring, and sectional political parties had the potential to weaken the Constitutional separation of powers that limited national government. A president and Congress dominated by a single party that was hostile to Southern interests—the Republican Party, for example—could conceivably act in concert, making an end-run around the constitutional separation of powers, and turn their vision of American society into reality. This concern was not particularly prevalent under Democratic administrations, because, at this time, the Democratic Party had a more hands-off philosophy of governance and a constituency that required them to keep certain issues off the agenda. The formal and informal limits on central state authority would be nothing more than paper barriers if the same sectional political party dominated Congress and the Presidency.

The South, in other words, needed balance in the Senate as a specific check on Northern anti-slavery leanings or, at a bare minimum, a president in the White House who had a Southern constituency. Without at least one of these, Southern institutions were not safe in the Union. Under unified Republican rule, it was feared that the federal government would become the consolidated, European-style state that those who desired limited government had always feared. While balance in the Senate and the institutional design of the American state were not directly intertwined, maintaining this balance was perceived by Southerners as an essential part of maintaining limited government. If balance in the Senate were eliminated and the president and Congress controlled by a party with no Southern constituency, it might appear as if the institutional design of the Union had changed, even if no formal alteration in its design had occurred. Thus, Southern apprehensions about the power of the state were magnified by demographic changes within the Union that permitted the North to rule without a Southern coalition partner, which threatened, in essence, to alter the design of the state and turn it over to Northern hands.

EARLY CHALLENGES TO CENTRAL STATE AUTHORITY

Challenges to central state authority predate the Union; they are, indeed, the basis for the formation of the Union itself. Invoking the right of revolution, the colonies separated from the home country. The Southern statesmen that sought to shepherd the South out of the Union regarded themselves as the last of the revolutionary generation, holding tight to the principles that led the colonies out of empire.

The first American Union was created under the Articles of Confederation, a loose confederation of sovereign states. The U.S. under the Articles of Confederation was a true confederation. The central government lacked fundamental authority over the states of the Union. The sovereignty of the separate states under the Articles was not residual, but primary. Article II stated, "Each state retains its sovereignty, freedom, and independence, and every power, jurisdiction, and right, which is not by this Confederation expressly delegated to the United States, in Congress assembled." Article V stated, "In determining questions in the United States in Congress assembled, each State shall have one vote." According to this design, the smallest state of the Confederation enjoyed as much power as the largest state. The separate states were sovereign; the people were not. Under the Constitution of 1787, both population and the sovereign capacity of the state were factors in the distribution of political power; the Articles contained no such provision.

Central government under the Articles was weak and ineffective: The separate states had virtually all of the power, and the center had very little. Under these circumstances, the Founding Fathers met in Philadelphia, charged with revising the ineffectual Articles. Instead, in the summer of 1787, they fashioned a new constitution for the U.S. Under the Articles, it was clear that each state enjoyed essentially unchallenged sovereignty. Under the new Constitution, it was not so clear where sovereignty resided. The principle of state sovereignty established by the Articles was only weakened—not eliminated—by the new constitution. In this new institutional context, state sovereignty continued to be asserted and the central state continued to be challenged.

Following the adoption of the Constitution, the Federalist Party dominated the political institutions of the U.S. They did not enjoy unchallenged authority, however. Looking for a way to blunt the harsh attacks leveled by its opponents, the Federalists passed a series of laws known as the Alien and Sedition Acts in 1798. These laws essentially made it illegal to criticize the government, made it more difficult for foreigners to become citizens, and made it easier for those who were not citizens to be deported. Federalists desired these measures to silence Jeffersonian opponents, many of whom came from France and England. Opponents of these acts saw them as unjust and unconstitutional usurpations of power. Because the norm of judicial review was not yet established, and because the judiciary was packed with Federalists, opponents of the laws had to uncover a different method to challenge the constitutionality of these laws. The Jeffersonians found their method in a corollary of the theory of state sovereignty: state interposition or nullification. The theory of state sovereignty maintained that in the absence of an institution explicitly charged with determining the constitutionality of laws, it was the states that had this right. A state, in other words, had the authority to declare a law passed by Congress unconstitutional.

The best-known challenge to the Alien and Sedition Acts was found in the Kentucky and Virginia Resolutions of 1798 and 1799, prepared by Thomas Jefferson and James Madison. The principles outlined in these resolutions were so widely accepted that they enjoyed almost constitutional authority for a time. The resolutions contained two essential elements: First, the U.S. was held to be a Union of states or sovereignties, brought together through a compact between the states (The federal government was the creature of these states and had no authority apart from the specific powers granted to it in the Constitution); second, because no independent authority was given the power of determining the constitutionality of laws, judgments of whether a law passed by Congress was unconstitutional were within the competency of the separate states of the Union. The Kentucky Resolutions of 16 November 1798 asserted:

> That the government created by this compact was not made the exclusive or final judge of the extent of the powers delegated to itself; since that would have its discretion, and not the Constitution, the measure of its powers; but that as in all other cases of compact among parties having no common Judge, *each party has an equal right to judge for itself, as well of infractions as of the mode and measures of redress.*[27]

According to the 1799 Resolutions, the "rightful remedy" of an infraction of the Constitution was through "nullification . . . of all unauthorized acts done under the color of that instrument."[28] The theory of state interposition was fully consistent with beliefs that were dominant in the early republic, but what state interposition meant in practice was disputed. The lack of clarity on what the practice of state interposition would look like became apparent once South Carolina attempted to nullify federal law.

In the *Federalist Papers*, Madison wrote that the Union was both federal and national in character. That is, both the center and the states shared the attributes of sovereignty. Despite this equivocation, Madison, with Jefferson, made an essential—perhaps critical—contribution to the theory that the separate states were the sovereign units of the Union. The moral authority of the authors of state interposition did not prevent the assertion of state sovereignty with the concomitant power of constitutional interpretation from sitting ill with some. The legislature of Delaware, a slave state, claimed that the resolutions were "a very unjustifiable interference with the General Government."[29] The state of Rhode Island declared that the power of determining the constitutionality of acts of Congress lay within the Supreme Court.[30] Massachusetts denied Virginia's right to determine the constitutionality of laws passed by Congress, even going so far as to claim that the Alien and Sedition Acts were not only constitutional, but also "expedient and necessary."[31] In spite of these rebukes, the compact theory of the Union at the core of state interposition took hold in the North and the South. While the balance of power between the sections was maintained, each section respected the limits on federal power assumed by state sovereignty. Once balance tipped in favor of one section, however, the power-depleted section defensively adopted the theory of state sovereignty.[32]

The election of 1800 was an important moment for the doctrine of state sovereignty. In this election, the centralizing tendencies of the Federalist Party were defeated in favor of the states'-rights-oriented Jeffersonian Republicans. The anti-statist (or, at least, limited-statist) principles of this party formed the basis for the Democratic Party, founded in the late 1820s, initially led by Andrew Jackson and dominant in the Union through the presidential election of 1856. It was in this political context (of jealously guarding states' rights against federal encroachment), which itself was an artifact of the colonial experience, that South Carolinian political attitudes toward the federal state were initially developed.

The War of 1812 interrupted the international trade that was essential to the economic livelihood of the trading states of New England. In response, the New England states called a convention to consider how to have their grievances redressed. In December 1814, representatives from the states of Massachusetts, Connecticut, Rhode Island, New Hampshire, and Vermont met in Hartford, Connecticut. The resolutions passed by the convention did not explicitly refer to secession, but they did state that if no action were taken toward reaching peace with Britain (among other issues), a similar convention would meet in June 1815 "with such powers and instructions as the exigency of a crisis so momentous may require."[33] It seems that the members of the convention were more concerned with the perceived failure of the federal government to defend these states from enemy action than with seceding from the Union. Members of this convention also wanted to limit the power of the federal government to tax its citizens, admit new states into the Union, place embargoes on ships owned by U.S. citizens, and interdict commerce. Ultimately, the convention's efforts were approved by only two states: Massachusetts and Connecticut. Other states, even those represented in the convention, met the convention's efforts with mild remonstrance.

In the early years of the republic, the twin opposing doctrines of states' rights and nationalism were just as likely to be held by Northerners as Southerners. In fact, in the early republic, South Carolina's political elite was strongly nationalistic in orientation.[34] Eventually, Northern areas became more closely associated with the nationalist view, while the South became more associated with states' rights. Late antebellum Northern nationalism, historian David Potter noted, "consisted . . . partly in its control over federal policy, and in the ability to keep it in alignment with sectional interests, while the South's 'sectionalism' was, at least initially, an expression of the lack of such a capacity."[35] As power within the Union shifted from a balance between the sections toward Northern dominance, adherence to states' rights shifted with it. As the North and the old Northwest formed a political coalitions that allowed them to determine (or at least dominate) the political path of the Union, states' rights became the foundational tenet of the weaker section of the Union. Except for a few Southern fire-eaters (secessionist entrepreneurs, radical defenders of Southern rights), adherence to states' rights was not ideological. In the period examined in this project, Southern attachment to states' rights can be explained by the gradual weakening of Southern strength within the Union.[36] The doctrine of states' rights was adopted by Southern leaders as a defensive position. This doctrine provided a coherent and familiar position from which these leaders could challenge Northern and federal encroachment.

CONCLUSION

The divisions that created disunion in 1860 were present at the Union's inception. At the beginning, however, these divisions were not yet the life and death issues that they became. Slavery was not yet a positive good, nor had it created fabulous wealth among the planter class; slavery was not yet threatened by Northern abolitionists and anti-extensionists. In these early years of the Union, states used their considerable institutional resources to push back against central state authority on a variety of issues—not only, or even primarily, slavery. The justification of this push back was found, elaborated, and perfected in a particular interpretation of the Union. Aggrieved states were developing rhetorical strategies that were available to defend any challenge to central state authority. As time passed, the central division within the Union became slavery—whether new territories and states

The American State and Early Challenges to Central State Authority

should be slave or free and, more generally, what limits, if any, should be placed on the institution of slavery. This was, to be sure, not the only division between the states, but it seemed to coincide with many of the other divisions to the point where the Democratic-controlled South seceded to avoid the consequences of living under a Republican-controlled North. In the next chapter we turn to the various crises that constituted the learning process on South Carolina's road to secession.

3 States' Rights in South Carolina
From Nullification to the First Secession Crisis

The previous chapter compared the state as it existed in Europe with the state as it existed in the U.S. and discussed the origins of challenges to central state authority in the U.S. The defining feature of the American state is federalism. A defining feature of federalism is, apparently, territorial-based challenges to central state authority. Secession is the ultimate territorial-based challenge to central state authority. This chapter explores the institutional and structural bases of South Carolinian radicalism and the crises and events through which South Carolina came to exemplify the states' rights tradition in the U.S. The central episodes that are explored in this chapter are the nullification crisis and the first secession crisis.

These episodes are critical to South Carolina's learning curve on the road to secession. Here, South Carolina learned that using the tariff as a stalking horse for slavery would not result in the desired outcome: disunion. While the protectionist tariff certainly represented an overstepping of federal authority, the tariff itself was not salient enough an issue to mobilize support for radical action. Slavery would have to be the issue. Here, too, South Carolina learned the dangers associated with attempting to get the South to act in concert to protect its interests. The South, such as it was, faced an impossible conundrum: it was too divided to secede as a unit on any issue, including slavery, and it was too divided to provide adequate protection of slavery in the face of an increasingly monolithic North. Learning of this conundrum, which South Carolina did in 1852, provided an object lesson of what not to do when a new issue arrived in 1860.

INSTITUTIONAL EXPLANATIONS FOR RADICALISM IN SOUTH CAROLINA

The case and dynamic described in this book hinges on the willingness of one state to take the lead in seceding in order to alter the choice-context for other states, thereby compelling the other states to secede. That one state would be willing to do so cannot be taken for granted or factored out of the equation. South Carolina was uniquely positioned to be that one state. The extent and uniqueness of South Carolina's radicalism is an oft-examined historical puzzle. Not only in 1860, when secession was brought about, but 30 years earlier during the nullification crisis, South Carolina proved itself to be more radical than the other states of the South. What made South Carolina so radical?

Asserting the centrality and importance of slavery in South Carolina might provide an adequate shortcut in accounting for South Carolina's radicalism, but it is not a sufficient explanation. Other slave states, particularly those of the Deep South, were almost as imbued with the institution of slavery as South Carolina. Thus, South Carolina's radicalism cannot be explained by the political, economic, and cultural importance of slavery and slaveholding alone. These elements tell most of the story, but not all of it. In order to provide the fullest account of radicalism in South Carolina, I propose an examination of the formal and informal political institutions within South Carolina. First, the institution of slavery pervaded the state. A threat to slavery was a threat to the existence of the state. Second, institutional factors related to the structure and the power of the state gave slaveholders a larger share of political power than their already considerable numbers would warrant. The planters of the Low Country, long since radicalized, held the levers of power in the state. Finally, two-party competition, which served to moderate other states, including those in the Deep South, was absent in South Carolina. There were other factors, as well, such as the political socialization taking place at South Carolina College and the distinct material influence of cotton and international trade. All of these factors pointed in the same direction: The moderating influences that limited radicalism in other states were absent from South Carolina. The state's political class—mostly large-scale planters—lacked a sentimental attachment to the Union and became convinced that their cotton economy and personal well-being were best protected outside of the influence of the North and of Republicans, who were themselves the functional equivalent of raging abolitionists.

If one were to look for a single factor influencing South Carolina's decisions in the antebellum period, one would (more than likely) examine the influence of slavery and slaveholders in this state. Slavery was the dominant social institution: First, as a proportion of the population, there were more slaves in South Carolina than anywhere else in the South (see Figure 3.1); there were more large-scale planters in South Carolina than in any other state, and, in addition, almost half of South Carolina's free population belonged to slaveholding families (see Figure 3.2).[1] In addition, thanks to South Carolina's traditions and friendly legislative apportionment, slaveholders held a disproportionately large number of seats in the state house (see Tables 3.3 and 3.4). Slavery was the dominant institution in South Carolina. The primary beneficiary of this dominant institution—the planters—controlled the state.

While white male suffrage came to South Carolina comparatively early, offices filled by South Carolina's electorate were limited. South Carolinians

24 Federalism, Secession, and the American State

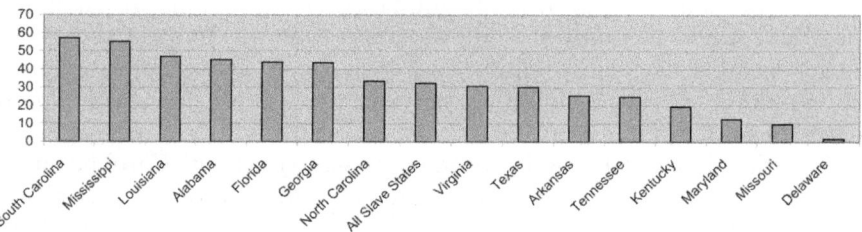

Figure 3.1 Slave population as percentage of total population in slave states in 1860.
Source: United States Civil War Centenniel Commission (1963).

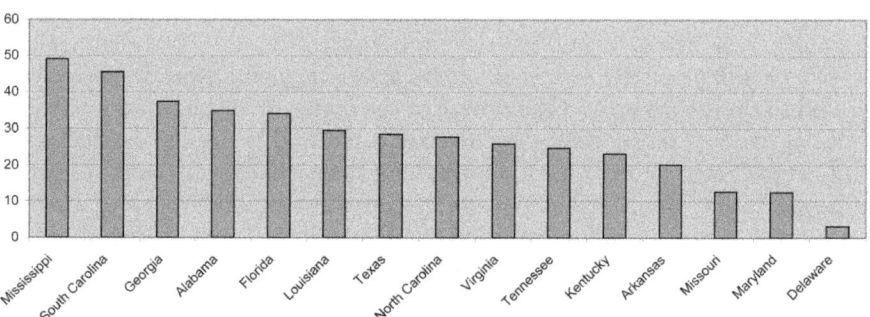

Figure 3.2 Percent of (white) families owning slaves in 1860, by state.
Source: United States Historical Census Data Browser (http://fisher.lib.virginia.edu/cgi-local/censusbin/census/cen.pl?year=860. Accessed January 3, 2001.

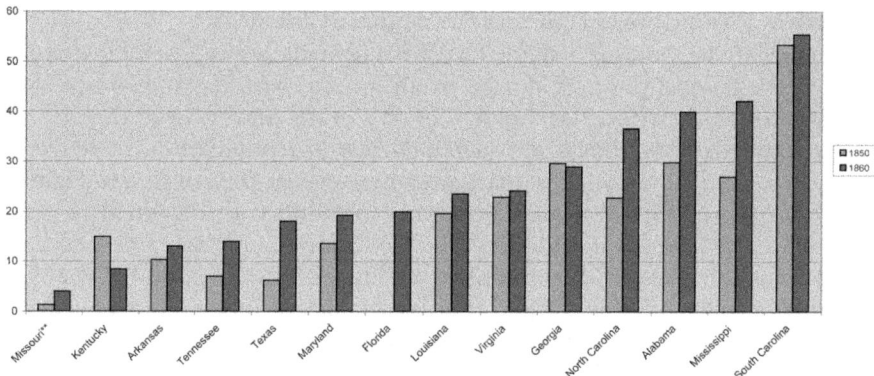

Figure 3.3 Percent of seats held by planters* in southern legislatures, 1850 and 1860. *Planter refers to an individual owning 20 or more slaves. **1860 value for Missouri is approximate.
Source: Wooster (1969) and (1975).

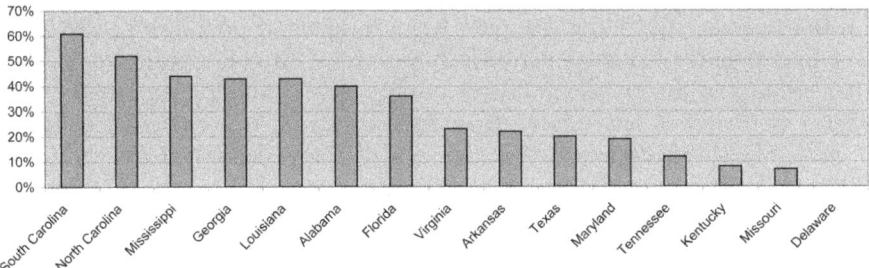

Figure 3.4 Percentage of seats held by planters in secession conventions (or state legislature), 1860–61.
Source: Wooster (1962).

elected members of the State House of Representatives and members of the State Senate, U.S. Congressmen, and little else. Political power in South Carolina, for the most part, was vested in the state legislature: It was the legislature that chose U.S. Senators, governors, presidential electors, and judges.[2] As a member of the South Carolinian political elite James Henry Hammond noted, the Legislature of South Carolina "has all the power. The executive has none. The people have gone beyond electing members of the legislature, a power very negligently exercised from time immemorial."[3] Wooster wrote:

> In no other state of the region did the governor have fewer powers than in South Carolina. In the Palmetto state, the legislature's authority was complete, and the governor was a mere figurehead. Chosen by the legislature for a two-year period, the chief executive in South Carolina could grant pardons and reprieves, remit fines and forfeitures, make recommendations to the assembly, convene the assembly on special occasions, and command the militia; but he had no appointive power, could not veto legislation, and was ineligible for re-election for four years after his term of office.[4]

Davidson claimed, "The Governor of South Carolina, like the king of England, reigned but did not rule."[5] The position of governor in South Carolina was more a gift to the state's most important planter-politicians than a political position in which one was expected to exercise leadership. The weak executive and strong legislative branch was an artifact of the South Carolinian experience under Colonial rule. Like most Americans, South Carolinians had a healthy fear of a strong executive authority and wanted an executive that would be weaker than the legislature.

The Low Country of South Carolina was the first section of the state to be settled. In South Carolina, the legislature controlled the state and the slaveholders of the Low Country dominated the legislature. As the state's population began to spread to the Up Country, political representation did not necessarily follow. Despite the movement of population, the Low Country remained disproportionately powerful in the legislature.[6] Only after regions of the middle and Up Country were "safe" on the question of slavery (which was only after the institution was firmly entrenched—that is, after the slaves constituted a majority of the population) did the Low Country consent to extending to those regions a somewhat more equitable share of the political power of the state.[7] For example, by 1860, areas with majority black populations controlled 40 of 45 seats in the State Senate and 101 of 124 seats of the State House.

Despite the eventual dispersal of political authority to other regions of the state, the Low Country retained its dominance. In 1860, the Low Country contained only 22 percent of the white male population (those eligible to vote) but controlled 48 percent of the Senate and 38 percent of the House. The Up Country contained 78 percent of the white male population, but controlled only 52 percent of the Senate and 62 percent of the House.[8] As one dissatisfied member of the Up Country noted during the nullification crisis, "4,402 voters of one district had no more influence than 53 voters in one of the parishes [a Low Country district]."[9] The Low Country dominated the politics of South Carolina, and Low Country interests were dominated by large-scale slaveholders, hence the wish to protect and maintain slavery. A Low Country unified behind a single political program had proven itself able to dominate a divided Up Country. Thus, many of the successes enjoyed by the pro-slavery forces within South Carolina can be attributed to the power the Low Country exercised over the political path of the state.

By the late antebellum period, South Carolina was the only state in which the electorate did not have the opportunity to vote their preference in presidential elections. In South Carolina, it was not the citizens, but the state legislature, that determined the recipient of the state's presidential electors.[10] The absence of competitive presidential elections in South Carolina all but eliminated the possibility of two-party competition in the state.[11] South Carolina was influential in the Union, and a great part of this influence can be traced to the kind of politics made possible by the absence of two-party competition. Specifically, South Carolina operated under a system of consensus rather than conflict. In states where two-party conflict was common—most of them—there was a dualistic approach to policy formation: Whatever the position taken by one party, the opposite position would be taken by the other party. Parties had an incentive to distinguish themselves from each other in order to appeal to different elements of the electorate. Without this incentive in South Carolinian politics, the state presented a politically unified front that gave it the power, the opportunity, and the domestic support to challenge the center when it felt its rights were at risk. Thus, while other states of the Deep South were almost evenly divided on the question of unilateral versus cooperative secession in the crisis of 1860, South Carolina supported unilateral secession virtually unanimously.

It was not uncommon for South Carolinians to refuse to participate in presidential nominating conventions.[12] Those who were elected to participate in these conventions, especially during times of intense anti-partyism in South Carolina, did so at their own political peril. Political parties, after all, were merely interested factions that rubbed South Carolinian aristocratic disinterestedness the wrong way; furthermore, South Carolinian elites found little difference between the existing political parties.[13] In 1847, Calhoun characterized the leaders of political parties this way: "The leaders on both sides are thoroughly rotten—incorrigibly so—mere spoils men, & hollow hearted hypocrites, without a particle of regard for principles, & perfectly indifferent to country."[14]

The memory of the potential destructiveness of the divisions created during nullification deeply entrenched the desire for unanimity in the state.[15] This desire for unanimity, in turn, helped to establish the unique pattern of politics in this state.[16] Historian Lacey Ford claimed that South Carolina had a unique "penchant for concealing its internal divisions from the eyes of the world."[17] As the radical Charleston *Mercury* noted, while trying to convince the citizens and politicians of the state to secede alone, "Other States are torn and divided, to a greater or less extent, by old party issues. South Carolina alone is not."[18] Thus, the lack of two-party competition allowed South Carolina's radicalism to flourish without being checked by a persistent moderate alternative.

Elections took place, of course, but when they did occur, they tended to be uncontested and won by acclamation. Indeed, more than 66 percent of all elections to the House of Representatives in the state of South Carolina between 1824 and 1860 for which there are reliable results were uncontested.[19] A similar pattern was followed in elections for the state legislature. The state's political leaders assured unanimity in elections by allowing only one name on the ballot.[20] "Elections to the state legislature generally followed earlier no contest patterns except for a few exceptional crisis points," such as nullification and the first secession crisis—but even these produced no permanent party organization.[21] South Carolinians did not want the competition for political office that characterized politics in other states; instead, South Carolinians expected "passive office seeking."[22]

Educational institutions also played a role in developing and maintaining radicalism in South Carolina. Virtually every member of the slaveholding elite was educated at South Carolina College (now the University of South Carolina) in Columbia. As Henry Lesesne wrote, "South Carolina's leaders saw the new college as a way to bring together the sons of the elite from the upcountry and the lowcountry, in order to 'promote the good order and harmony' of the state."[23] In conjunction with the other unique forces in South Carolina tending toward radicalism, South Carolina College provided fertile ground for the development and maintenance of a radical political culture characterized by a high level of consensus on fundamental issues.

Patterns of international trade also worked to increase South Carolinian radicalism. The vast majority of Southern cotton went overseas—to Great Britain, in particular. This provided the South with less attachment to the Union even an opportunity for resentment: by and large, it was Northern companies that shipped the cotton overseas to the textile centers of Great Britain; it was Northern manufacturers that desired tariffs that threatened to suppress the international trade upon which South Carolina thrived. Southern elites chafed at the unwarranted political, economic, and even logistic control the North had over King Cotton. Foreign trade and the centrality of Southern cotton to American foreign trade served to decrease the attachment the Southern planters felt toward the Union. Well beyond this, though, in South Carolina, more than any other state in the Union, these planters were in control of the political institutions of the state.

These institutions—an overwhelmingly dominant legislature dominated overwhelmingly by slaveholders, a lack of two-party politics, a penchant for unanimity, the state's political economy—made South Carolina both uniquely sensitive to threats to slavery and threats to the political power of the slaveholding class and uniquely able to respond to any perceived threat. With these institutions in place, the politics of South Carolina were more radical, and this state was more able to act—and act quickly.

NULLIFICATION

Those who tell the story of nullification in South Carolina often begin with Thomas Cooper, president of South Carolina College, in 1827, suggesting that should federal encroachments persist, South Carolina would be forced "to calculate the value of the Union." The story of nullification could begin earlier—as early, even, as the founding of the American Union as the divisions that ended up tearing the Union apart were built into the Union at its founding. Our focus here, however, is South Carolina. While the antebellum era was rife with state resistance to federal authority,[24] South Carolina was the first to provide a robust invocation of states' rights against the center. Thus, it makes sense to begin in the early 1820s, when South Carolina was attempting to prevent slave rebellion.

Following the hysteria of what could have been had Denmark Vesey's rebellion been successful, South Carolina became convinced that Africans that were not enslaved were at least as much of a danger as those who were. The state passed a law requiring black seamen who ported in Charleston and other South Carolina harbors to be jailed, the costs of which were to be paid by the ship's captain. A federal judge found the law to be unconstitutional. Adhering to the doctrine of state sovereignty, South Carolina continued to enforce the law without challenge.[25]

The success of this early challenge informed South Carolina efforts in its first major conflict with the center: nullification. In this section, I provide a brief outline of the Tariffs of 1828 and 1832, and I examine in detail South Carolina's official and unofficial responses to these tariffs. In addition, I discuss the compromise tariff that helped to diffuse the conflict, the Force Bill, in which the federal government affirmed its right to enforce its laws, and South Carolina's nullification of the Force Bill, which provided the uneasy denouement of the crisis.

The power to levy duties on imported goods has been a contentious issue since the inception of the Union. Under the Articles of Confederation, the separate states often imposed tariffs on goods imported from other states—disrupting interstate trade. Attempting to avoid similar problems, the framers of the Constitution transformed the local economies of the separate states into a single national economy. According to Article I, Section VIII of the U.S. Constitution, Congress has the power to "lay and collect Taxes, Duties, Imposts and Excises, to pay the debt and provide for the common Defense and general welfare of the United States." In the same section, Congress is given the power to "regulate Commerce with foreign Nations." In short, the powers given to Congress include collecting duties to raise revenue and regulating commerce. The question at the base of the debate over the tariff was whether the powers granted to Congress included the ability to impose tariffs to protect nascent domestic industries, or whether the tariff power granted to Congress was only for the purposes of collecting revenue.[26]

Despite its eventual opposition to protection, a tariff bill, passed in 1816 and supported by South Carolina, provided protection to American industry. South Carolina member of Congress John C. Calhoun justified his state's support for this measure by claiming that the primary purpose of the bill was to raise revenue; he claimed the protection it provided was merely incidental.[27] While Northern and industrial forces within the Union became more powerful and Southern influence within the Union began to wane, South Carolina grew increasingly sensitive to Congress overstepping its authority.

The traditional story of nullification centered exclusively on the economic aspect of the Tariff of 1828 and 1830.[28] According to this perspective, South Carolina nullified the protectionist tariffs because it felt that such tariffs interfered with Southern economic prosperity by increasing the cost of goods South Carolina and the South were obliged to purchase while, at the same time, generally suppressing the international market upon which they relied and increasing the likelihood that South Carolina's products would be subject to tariffs in foreign ports. Because as much as 75 percent of Southern cotton went abroad during the antebellum era, the maintenance of international markets was essential to South Carolina.[29] Indeed, cotton was an essential element of the entire American export economy, comprising approximately 60 percent of all U.S. exports.[30] As

Hardy Wickwar wrote, the "raw material producers of the mid-nineteenth century reacted as consumers instead of organizing as producers. They felt that a marginal change in the cost of manufactured goods turned the terms of trade against them. Hence the violent reaction of a considerable party among them against the tariff of 1828."[31] The North, on the other hand, would reap the benefits of protected markets, allowing their goods to compete with foreign products.

Noting that there were actors in South Carolina whose interests were not adversely affected by the tariffs, yet who supported nullification, Freehling and others found it necessary to look beyond pure economic interests to explain nullification.[32] According to this novel interpretation, South Carolinian nullifiers were primarily interested in checking the expanding power of the federal government. Specifically, they wanted to challenge Congress, which, thanks to the demographic transformation the Union was undergoing, was increasingly dominated by Northern political forces (see Figures 3.5 and 3.6). South Carolinian political actors wanted to establish clear limits to federal power in order to protect an institution (slavery) that they saw as being more fundamental to their interests than the maintenance of free trade. According to this interpretation, nullification was not primarily an effort to eliminate tariffs, but instead, was an effort to protect slavery.[33] Economic interests did play a central role in support for nullification, but it was not simply short-term economic interests in lower prices that compelled the nullifiers to act; rather, fear of the economic, political, and social dislocation that would come with anti-slavery agitation in a Northern-dominated Congress that no longer acted within its constitutionally established boundaries drove the actions of the nullifiers. According to this interpretation, the tariff was not the reason for action in South Carolina; it merely provided the occasion for action in South Carolina.

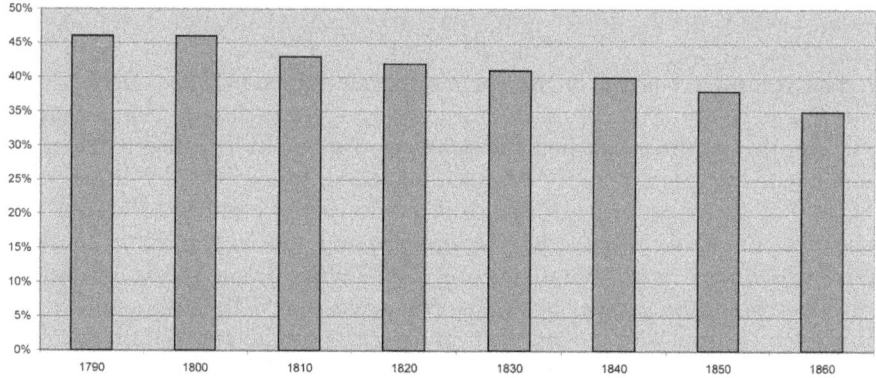

Figure 3.5 Slave State Representation in the House of Representatives.
Source: Martis and Elmes (1993: 146).

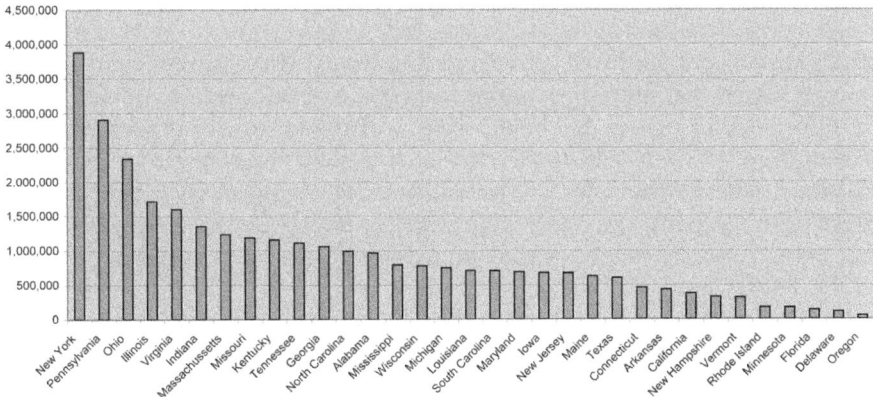

Figure 3.6 Population of states in 1860.
Source: United States Historical Census Data Browser (http://fisher.lib.virginia.edu/cgi-local/censusbin/census/cen.pl?year=860. Accessed January 3, 2001.

Longtime secessionist Robert Barnwell Rhett saw nullification as an opportunity to check the ever-expanding power of the federal government. He thought that the issue was better made on the tariff—an issue upon which the South may have been able to find common ground with forces in the North—than on slavery, an issue for which the South would have had to fight alone. According to biographer Daniel Wallace, Rhett argued that:

> [I]f the South did not check the government on this issue, we would have to face it on the far more difficult, delicate, and dangerous question of slavery; he maintained that this was an easier, safer and less aggravating issue on which to reform the government—for that here there was an identity of interest between the South and the laboring classes and mercantile interests of the North; while on slavery the separation would be broad, and the struggle more sectional and bitter. He foretold that the sectional contest was unavoidable, and that on the heels of our acquiescence in an unconstitutional Tariff, a tenfold more baneful and irreconcilable agitation must ensue on the slavery question. He argued that upon this question the strife would be purely sectional, and must end in the dissolution of the Union, or the ruin of the South.[34]

This statement and this interpretation may seem to compel us to ask the question: Was South Carolina trying to protect states' rights, or was the state trying to protect slavery? In South Carolina, protecting slavery and protecting states' right were the same. If the South was not the dominant force within the federal government (and clearly this was the direction in which things were heading) maintaining the institution of slavery meant maintaining states' rights and providing a strong check on the expanding power of the federal government. From the South Carolinian perspective, it was better to establish limits on the federal government on an issue for which supporters could be found in all sections of the Union than on an issue in which the interests at stake were those of one section alone. South Carolinian elites reasonably hoped that Northerners and Southerners alike would support their anti-tariff efforts, but they were never so deluded that they believed that the North would actively support their pro-slavery efforts. On the contrary, there were many in South Carolina who believed that neither Northerners nor the majority of Southerners could be trusted on the slavery issue.[35]

Ironically, the Tariff of 1828 (called by some the "Tariff of Abominations") was passed as a result of a political game devised by Calhoun and other anti-protectionists. They purposely created an excessively protectionist tariff bill, putting items that were not desired by protectionist forces on the tariff schedule, hoping the bill would win the support of only the most thorough-going protectionists, not of a majority of Congress.[36] The anti-tariff forces made a strategic miscalculation in their assessment of what the moderate protectionists were willing to tolerate. The bill passed in the House and the Senate, thanks to support in the middle and West states and the stalwart protectionists in New England. The bill gathered little more than a sprinkling of votes from the South. As one author noted, "The act of 1828 had thus been passed in a form approved by no one."[37]

Those who supported the tariff bill did so not to collect revenue, but to protect nascent American manufacturing. The willingness of a vast swath of Northerners to support potentially unconstitutional protection piqued the fears of Southerners who were interested in maintaining strict limits on federal power as mandated by their interpretation of the Constitution. After all, the Constitution did give Congress the power to regulate commerce, but it did not give it the power to protect American industry from foreign competition. The willingness of Northern members of Congress to flout the letter of the Constitution disconcerted Southerners who relied on a strict interpretation of the Constitution for the protection of the institution of slavery. If Congress could pass a protective tariff (something that it did not technically have the power to do), then there was nothing that Congress could not do, including passing legislation that was unfavorable to the constitutionally acknowledged institution of slavery.

At least a simple majority of the voting population—and of the legislators of South Carolina—desired action on the Tariff of 1828. However, according to Article XI of the 1790 Constitution of South Carolina, calling a convention of the people of the state required the support of two-thirds of each House in the state legislature.[38] Although nullifiers did not have enough support in the legislature to call a convention, nullification forces were encouraged by Calhoun's revelation that he was an ardent nullifier. Indeed, John C. Calhoun was the author of nullification in South Carolina.

Although Hofstadter's described Calhoun as the "Marx of the master class,"[39] Calhoun was more "the last of the Founding Fathers, the last of a generation of creative constitutional statesman, than an early Marxist."[40] His vision of limited government and of the protection of local interests—both of which were consistent with his support of nullification—affirms this.

Calhoun was, at this time, Andrew Jackson's vice president. His support for nullification put him and Jackson on vastly different sides of a controversial issue, contributing to the already considerable personal antipathy between them.[41] At a 13 April 1830 celebration, Jackson proclaimed in a toast (and in response to nullification talk): "The Union, it must be preserved." To Jackson's toast, Calhoun replied, "The Union—next to our liberty, most dear." This exchange, however brief, summarizes the divergent views between the North and South that would eventually lead to secession and Civil War. For many Northerners, the Union had to be maintained regardless of one's displeasure with any particular policy. For Southerners, the maintenance of the Union was desired only as long as the Union helped to maintain Southern liberties—in this case, slavery. Once the Union became destructive to this end, Southerners increasingly sought to separate themselves from the Union in order better to protect their liberty.

Using ideas outlined by Jefferson and Madison in the Virginia and Kentucky Resolutions, Calhoun's *Exposition and Protest* of 19 December 1828 (published anonymously and distributed by the legislature of South Carolina) outlined what became a foundational set of beliefs in South Carolina. According to this work, every state of the Union maintained its sovereignty, and as a sovereign entity, every state had the right to determine whether acts of Congress were constitutional. For Calhoun, the states were not simply permitted to ascertain the constitutionality of federal laws; they were *required* to do so. The integrity of the Constitution and the Union depended on it. The center could not be expected to offer a fair judgment of whether its decisions were constitutional, because they were its decisions.

For Calhoun, though, the question was not simply philosophical; it was practical. His complaints regarding the Tariff of 1828 center as much on it representing an unconstitutional usurpation of power by the federal government, as on the deleterious effect the tariff would have on the export-oriented economy of cotton-producing states. According to the typical Southern argument, the agricultural regions of the U.S.—especially the cotton-producing exporters of the South—paid for the tariffs with higher prices and depressed international trade, while the Northern section of the Union reaped the benefits provided by protection and received the bulk of the cash collected by these tariffs in the form of internal improvements. Worse than the South paying the cost of protective tariffs and providing the capital to pay for improvements that would primarily benefit the North was the fact that these actions took place despite the presence of constitutional constraints that should have prevented them. South Carolina, having more to fear from congressional encroachment—because it had, by this time, developed a larger stake in the institution of slavery than any other state (even the other slave states of the Deep South), and because the slaveholding class's power was more firmly entrenched in South Carolina than it was elsewhere—was in the best position to attempt to check this usurpation of power.

In 1830, because they did not have the level of support necessary to call a convention to interpose state sovereignty against congressional action, the nullifiers and states' rights men satisfied themselves by developing and defending the theory of state sovereignty and state interposition. During this period, the consequences of the theory of state sovereignty were more fully elaborated and firmly entrenched in the psyche of South Carolina. Calhoun publicly coming out in support of a doctrine that he had supported privately for some time contributed to a transformation in South Carolinian politics. As he stated in his *Fort Hill Address* of July 1831:

> [T]he naked question is whether ours is a federal or a consolidated government; a constitutional or absolute one; a government resting ultimately on the solid basis of the sovereignty of the States, or on the unrestricted will of a majority; a form of government, as in all other unlimited ones, in which injustice, and violence, and force must finally prevail. *Let it never be forgotten that, where the majority rules, the minority is the subject*; and that if we should absurdly attribute to the former, the exclusive right of construing the Constitution, there would be, in fact, between the sovereign and the subject, under such a government, no Constitution; or, at least, nothing deserving the name, or serving the legitimate object of so sacred an instrument.[42]

For Calhoun, clearly, the argument that the Constitution had created a consolidated government did not ring true. From his staunchly states' rights point of view, states were not simply permitted to question and challenge the constitutionality of laws passed by Congress; rather, they were obligated to do so in order to ensure that free government be maintained.

The Tariff Act of 1832 superseded the Tariff of 1828. While many of the "abominations" of 1828 were eliminated, the Tariff of 1832 remained a "distinctly protectionist measure."[43] It placed high duties on cotton, woolens, iron, and other products produced in the U.S. that were seen as being in need of protection. Articles not produced in the U.S. had low duties attached to them—and in some cases, there were no duties at all. The duties on some articles were reduced to a more modest 25 percent, with an average duty of 33 percent on dutiable items.[44] Despite the modifications, the protectionist system was firmly in place in a manner in which proponents of the "American System" hoped would be permanent.[45] South Carolinians feared that protectionism had become "the settled policy of the country."[46]

South Carolina was unwilling to sit idly by as the industrial forces of the Northeast ran roughshod over constitutional limits. Fearing that this usurpation of federal power would lead to a challenge that was more fundamental than the tariff, South Carolina initiated the first significant formal skirmish in the protracted conflict between the adherents of a strict states' rights doctrine in South Carolina and those who wanted to consolidate political power in the hands of the Northern states through the institutions of the federal government. This confrontation provided a first glimpse at the conflict between the sections that would lead to the Civil War.[47] The starting point of South Carolina's efforts to check federal power was winning two-thirds of the seats in the state legislature required for the passage of a bill calling for a state convention.

During times of controversy, distinguishable parties formed and real choice was possible.[48] The legislative election of fall of 1832 served as proof of this general maxim. Unlike later contests in South Carolina, where the fight was generally over a variation of a single theme (e.g., unilateral versus cooperative secession), the contest in 1832 was between fundamentally different schools of thought: On one side were the unionists who supported unconditional adherence to the Union; on the other side were the nullifiers who lacked a sentimental attachment to the Union. In the fall 1832 elections to the state legislature, the nullifiers won an overwhelming victory. Unionists, however, made a significant showing, marring the nullifiers' victory and revealing that there were fundamental divisions within the state about the future of state-federal relations. Although they were far from dominant in this episode, the nullification era was the last occasion in which unionist forces played a central role in South Carolinian politics. In future contests, the conflict would be between unilateral secessionists and cooperative secessionists—those who wanted South Carolina to secede on its own, regardless of the actions of other states, and those who desired secession, but only if it was accomplished simultaneously across numerous states of the South.

The 1832 legislative elections saw an overwhelming victory for the forces of nullification in both the Low Country and the Up Country. In this election, the nullifiers won "80 percent of the seats in the house and 75 percent of those in the senate,"[49] although they won only 59 percent of the popular vote. With overwhelming support in both houses, on 25 October 1832, the state legislature passed a convention bill that called for a convention to meet in November for the consideration of nullification.

Thanks primarily to the clarity of the radical program and divisions among the radicals' opponents, radical forces in South Carolina generally enjoyed an organizational advantage over moderate forces. Although many of those opposed to nullification were also opposed to the tariffs and the expansion of federal power, they lacked a coherent program to defeat the tariff. The same organization that helped the nullifiers to win a strong victory in the elections to the state legislature helped give them a strong victory in the Convention election held 12 and 13 November 1832.

To delegitimize the outcome of the convention, some unionist groups in the state boycotted the convention election; the extent of this boycott is not known, but a number of popular unionists refused to stand for election, seeking to avoid the "odious fame" of participating in the convention itself.[50] Because support for nullification was so strong in the state at this time, and given the strategic concentration of this support in the more radical and better-represented Low Country, the nullifiers would have won overwhelming support in the convention even with full unionist participation.

South Carolinian political actors sought to check political power with a method that had authoritative historical precedent. The course taken by this convention recalled the doctrine outlined in the Virginia and Kentucky Resolutions: state interposition.[51] According to the documents produced by the convention, protectionism is the "striking characteristic in the operation of a simply and consolidated government."[52] Fearing that the policy of protection had become "the settled policy of the country,"[53] the Report of the Committee in the convention stated, "it cannot be denied that the Government of the U. States possesses inherent powers. The States called it into being. The States not only created it, but conferred upon it all its powers, and prescribed its limits by a written charter called the Constitution of the U. States."[54] According to the ordinance of nullification produced by the convention, the tariff acts of 1828 and 1832 "are unauthorized by the Constitution of the United States, and violate the true meaning and intent thereof, and are null, void, and no law, nor binding upon this State, its officers, or citizens."[55]

The right of nullification is not a pre-political, revolutionary right; nor is it an explicitly constitutional right in the sense that the right to free speech is constitutionally granted. Rather, a state possesses the right of nullification on the basis of it being "one of the PARTIES to the compact."[56] The right of nullification, like the right of secession, is a reserved right to be used when the constitutional compact is violated and when the normal means of checking state power are unavailable.

The convention passed an ordinance of nullification in November 1832, but the convention allowed two months to pass before it would go into effect, which permitted the formulation of a compromise.

President Andrew Jackson's response to nullification on 10 December 1832 was unequivocal: "The power to annul a law of the United States, assumed by one State, [was] *uncompatible with the existence of the Union, contradicted expressly by the letter of the Constitution, unauthorized by its spirit, inconsistent with every principle on which it was founded, and destructive of the great object for which it was formed.*" He concluded, "The laws of the United States must be executed."[57] Jackson was willing to compromise on the form the tariff would take, but he would not compromise on the principle. Although he had many de-nationalizing tendencies, Jackson had succinctly articulated the nationalist interpretation of the Union. According to this view, the Union created by the Constitution of the U.S. was singular and unbreakable. The separate states did not have the exclusive right to determine the constitutionality of laws passed by the center. Jackson promised the people of South Carolina that if this pretence were maintained, war would certainly follow.[58]

In spite of the initial pessimism of prominent nullifiers,[59] the House and Senate passed a compromise tariff in February and March 1833. This measure eliminated the despised 50 percent duties, and moved many unprotected items to the free list. Calhoun had hoped for a standard rate of 15 or 20 percent; the compromise established a 20 percent duty on all protected items. On the surface, it seemed that protectionists had given up on the principle of protection. However, they did not give up on the practice of protection until 10 years later. According to the Compromise of 1833, the 20 percent rate would only be reached through a gradual reduction in the tariff ending in 1842. As Freehling noted, "The tariff would be highly protective for almost nine more years; the bulk of the reductions would take place in the last six months."[60] Sixty percent of the reduction, to a 20 percent rate, was to occur between 31 December 1841 and 30 June 1842.

Thus, South Carolina was able to force the center to compromise on its principle (if not its practice), demonstrating that "southern militancy could win victories in Congress."[61] While Congress was seemingly willing to compromise on the principle of protection, it was not willing to compromise on the principle of nullification. Accordingly, along with the compromise tariff, Congress passed a law that was commonly referred to as the Force Bill that gave teeth to Jackson's assertion that "the laws of the United States must be executed." This law empowered Jackson to enforce the collection of duties wherever that power might be challenged. The crisis closed with South Carolina's nullification of the Force Bill.

From the perspectives of the center and the moderate actors in the South, the compromise tariff was a smashing success. Indeed, the existence of moderation in the South was validated by the willingness of the center to pass the compromise tariff. If South Carolina had continued clamoring about the tariff, the state would have very likely been abandoned by those with whom they had the most in common. In any case, the tariff issue had been solved. If South Carolina wanted to continue to push back against federal encroachments, it would have to do so with a different issue.

The nullification controversy was a central moment in the development of South Carolina's theory of state sovereignty. The state asserted its sovereignty through a state convention on a specific question and passed an ordinance nullifying federal law and compelling the federal government to reverse course on its tariff. This episode provided South Carolina with a glimpse of the successes possible by asserting its sovereignty. South Carolina, however, suffered from internal divisions. These divisions would have to be all but eliminated if South Carolina was to continue its efforts.

The nullification episode provided statesman and philosopher Calhoun with an opportunity to develop a political theory of minority protection consistent with both republicanism and democracy. By developing the concept of the concurrent majority (Calhoun's most important contribution to political philosophy), Calhoun sought to establish principles and institutions that protected minority populations from tyrannical majorities by altering the way in which legislation was passed.[62] Under the rule of concurrent majority, simple majorities in both houses of Congress could no longer pass laws. In his *Disquisition on Government*, Calhoun argued that, while the "numerical majority, perhaps, should be one of the elements of a constitutional democracy," to make it the only element of constitutional democracy "is one of the greatest and most fatal of political errors."[63] A republic based on the concurrent majority is not based on the consent of simple majorities. According to the principle of the concurrent majority, government ought to be based upon the consent of a majority of minority interests. That is, local interests, such as those interests dominant within the separate states of the Union, must have some way to resist the sometimes-irresistible influence of majorities. In practice, this meant that each state must have the power to veto legislation detrimental to its interests. This simple alteration in the legislative process would guarantee moderation in government and check the potentially tyrannical power of unadulterated national majorities. Moreover, putting the concurrent majority in practice would force the sections of the Union to compromise with each other in order to get legislation passed. This would have the benefit of developing and deepening the bonds of the larger community.[64] Thus, adopting the principle of the concurrent majority would protect local interests, while also developing the national community.

One specific institutional innovation that Calhoun recommended was the creation of a dual executive, comprised of a president from both sections of the Union.[65] For a law to be passed, each "president" would have to sign it.[66] While the concept of the concurrent majority was not taken seriously anywhere but in South Carolina, the foundational assumption of the concurrent majority—state sovereignty—was widely accepted in the South. It was upon this foundation that Southern states later justified secession from the Union.

While the nullifiers won a victory against the center, at home there were greater questions looming, most of them centering on the deep divisions created during the nullification episode. The South Carolinian desire for unanimity[67] that was so evident during the 1860 secession crisis can probably trace its development to the disastrous effect division had in the state during nullification. At no time in the past, and probably at no time in the future, was South Carolina so deeply divided. The state seemed to be on the brink of civil war.[68] Tempers were so inflamed during this period that a South Carolinian newspaper recounted the story of a citizen of the state defending himself against the "accusation" that he supported and engaged in the enterprise of manufacturing, which had prompted the episode in the first place.[69]

Defending the interests of the state was, obviously, centrally important to this state's political actors. During the nullification episode, differences coalesced around the question of whether this defense could best be made inside or outside the Union. In the future, the unionist element in South Carolina was reduced, and most of the state's political actors would begin to "calculate the value of the Union," determining once and for all that South Carolina was better off outside the Union. Before this improbable outcome could be realized, however, the citizens of the state would have to be brought in line. A large portion of the population supported the radical position, but any permanent change in the relationship between the state and the federal government would require virtual unanimity among the South Carolina citizenry. The radicals, in other words, would have to become the mainstream political group in the state, if they wished to accomplish their revolution.[70]

A second problem looming for South Carolina during this episode was the Southern response to its radical actions. Although the state enjoyed moderate success in this episode, the state was punished for attempting to put Jefferson and Madison's principles into practice. For most of the antebellum period, the North, as well as the South, regarded South Carolina as a pariah. Although the other states of the South despised the tariffs of 1828 and 1832, they did not condone the actions of South Carolina. In late December 1832, the legislature of Georgia declared that it "abhor[red] the doctrine of Nullification as neither a peaceful, nor a constitutional remedy, but, on the contrary, as tending to civil commotion and disunion."[71] The legislature of Alabama claimed that "nullification . . . is unsound in theory and dangerous in practice; that as a remedy, it is unconstitutional and essentially revolutionary, leading in its consequences to anarchy and civil discord, and finally to the dissolution of the Union."[72] The North Carolina legislature maintained that nullification "is revolutionary in character, subversive of the Constitution of the United States and leads to a dissolution of the Union."[73] Similar lack of support prevented South Carolina from seceding in 1852 and made the state act cautiously—and alone—in 1860.

The nullification episode left South Carolina deeply divided and the rest of the South deeply suspicious of South Carolinian leadership. Such an inauspicious beginning to South Carolina's radical debut on the national scene temporarily took away its penchant for leading. But through the steps and missteps of this episode, the political leaders of South Carolina began to ascertain what would be required if true radical action was ever to be taken. If South Carolina were ever to bring its radical program to fruition, it would require two conditions to be in place: First, the political leadership of this state required overwhelming support among its citizens; second, the leadership required a level of support among the other Southern states sufficient to convince South Carolinians that their actions would not result in abandonment—a powerful fear felt by South Carolinians in future confrontations with the Union.

In 1832–33, intrastate divisions prevented South Carolina from pursuing the radical course of action that some desired. Although the radicals were dominant within the state, unionist forces hampered their efforts to pursue a radical path. This confrontation with the Union revealed that there were times when loyalties to the U.S. and to the state were not compatible—loyalty to one, at times, meant a betrayal of the other. This episode decisively eliminated nationalism from the state of South Carolina.[74] Later confrontations with the center separated out unionist forces, leaving the radical position intact without any real opposition and with at least the appearance of unanimous support within the state.

In the aftermath of nullification, a younger generation of South Carolinians that had not been socialized into an unquestioned devotion to the Union was coming to prominence. This generation was willing to adhere to the Union as long as it served the interests of the state. They were not nationalists, and they were only conditionally attached to the Union. This conditional unionism slowly transformed into support for cooperative secession and, eventually, into support for unilateral secession.

THE BLUFFTON MOVEMENT AND THE ORIGIN OF THE FIRST SECESSION CRISIS

Between 1833 and 1846, mobilization for a radical states' rights position was absent or muted. Toward the end of this period of relative quiet, however, prominent secessionist Robert Barnwell Rhett unsuccessfully attempted to jump-start a secession movement. In July 1844, this uncompromising radical and career secessionist initiated the "Bluffton Movement" for unilateral secession. The issue behind which Rhett hoped to mobilize the population centered on the annexation of Texas, which he supported, and the latest tariff bill, which he opposed. In July 1844, he recommended a state convention to consider the question of "secession or nullification."[75] Given his state's—and his own—radical reputation, Rhett knew that the rest of the South would not rush to support him or South Carolina, but he hoped that they would lend their support once South Carolina created a sufficiently important issue. Anticipating an argument that foretold South Carolinian actions in 1860, in 1844, Rhett said:

> It may be next to impossible, as I fear it is, to obtain any cooperation amongst the Southern States, to make the proper issue with the General Government, while it will be very easy to obtain their aid and cooperation (in case it should be needed by the action of the General Government), *after the proper issue is made by the conduct of a single State.*[76]

Thus, Rhett can be credited with early recognition of the necessity of having one state force the issue upon other states in order to force their cooperation.[77] He noted that a single colony made the issue at the start of the American Revolution by throwing tea overboard.[78] He hoped that a single state could initiate the coming "revolution," as well. For Rhett, the only thing needed to defend Southern institutions properly was proper Southern leadership.

Rhett was an ideologue, and he failed to understand that successful action required more than an ideological commitment to secession. It required the right issue, the right strategy, the right sequence, and the right time. In 1844, his calls for secession fell on deaf ears. The quiet that South Carolina had enjoyed for a few years following this was permanently shattered after a member of the House of Representatives from Pennsylvania suggested that slavery should be forbidden in newly acquired American territory.

In August 1846, House Democrat from Pennsylvania David Wilmot attached an amendment to an appropriations bill, created for the purposes of negotiating a treaty with Mexico, which denied slavery any access to territories gained in the war. Using the language of the Northwest Ordinance of 1787 that forbade slavery in the Old Northwest, Wilmot and his Northern allies wanted the following:

> That, as an express and fundamental condition to the acquisition of any territory from the Republic of Mexico by the United States, by virtue of any treaty which may be negotiated between them . . . neither slavery nor involuntary servitude shall ever exist in any part of said territory, except for crime, whereof the party shall first be duly convicted.[79]

The proviso passed the House on a number of occasions, but it never passed the Senate, primarily because balance between the sections provided the South with a veto against this sort of hostile legislation. The Wilmot Proviso was the first volley in a crisis that shook the Union to its core and eventually provided South Carolina with a grievance level sufficient to take this state to the brink of secession. The first secession crisis was a dress rehearsal for things to come.

At the conclusion of the war with Mexico, over 500,000 square miles of territory were added to the Union—the single largest addition of territory to the Union after the Louisiana Purchase. With the territorial expansion of the Union came a new source of instability. The source of the conflict over territories was simply this: would slavery be permitted in the new territories, or would it be excluded? Responses varied more or less according to section. In the North, the common opinion went something like this: because the laws of Mexico already prohibited slavery, the U.S. ought to respect the laws already in place and forbid slavery from expanding into the territorial addition of the Union (this was Wilmot's view of the situation). Wilmot and the North were only asking that "free territory should remain free. . . ." "We demand," Wilmot said, "neutrality of this Government upon the question of slavery."[80] Southerners must have bristled at this particular conception of neutrality. For the South, not allowing slavery to spread into new American territories was not neutral, but radically anti-Southern. Only federal attempts at abolition could constitute a more aggressive attack on slavery.

For its part, the Southern view of what to do with the territories was quite simple: Southern (that is, slave) labor must have the same access to the territories as Northern (that is, free) labor. The South felt that it was owed this—not only because they were equal partners in the Union, but also because they had contributed the vast majority of soldiers to the war that had provided the U.S. with this territorial windfall.[81] According to Southern standards of justice to deny the South access to the territory won with Southern blood was an unacceptable affront to Southern honor.

Political leaders in the South were unwilling to allow the federal government to decide the future of slavery. Many, but not all, political leaders in the North wanted to limit or eliminate the possibility of extending the institution of slavery. Borrowed from Lewis Cass, Stephen Douglas elaborated the principle of popular sovereignty, derisively called "squatter sovereignty," as a compromise between congressional establishment and prohibition of slavery. According to the principle of popular sovereignty, the presence or absence of slavery in a territory was to be determined by the people living in that territory, expressed through the will of the territorial legislature. The territorial legislature, however, derived its power from Congress. Thus, a territorial legislature forbidding slavery in a territory was tantamount to Congress forbidding slavery in a territory. According to the Southern viewpoint, this was another example of Congress overstepping the constitutional bounds of its authority. This argument meant that there was no way to prevent slavery from entering a territory while it was in the territorial stage. Accordingly, Southern political leaders argued that all territories had to be open to slavery. According to the logic of this argument, slavery could be excluded only once the territory took on sovereign status—that is, only once it became a state. Northerners reasoned that once slavery was established in a territory, it probably would not be removed. The South was, in effect, stating "that slavery spread over the territories with the Constitution,"[82] and that all territories were slave territories by default.

Southerners believed they were demanding only that they be given the same freedom to bring their property to a territory as everyone else: Could anyone conceive of an individual being prevented from bringing his livestock to a new territory? Southerners thought the movement of what they believed to be their property ought to be free. Furthermore, they believed that in the absence of a heroic effort to bring actual slave property to these territories (not financially prudent given the risks), these new states would become free states. With the exception of the southern portion of California, many people believed that slavery simply could not thrive in the newly acquired territories.[83]

Among the many ironies of this period was that the one thing slavery required for its survival—positive congressional protection of the institution—was the one thing the most ardent supporters of the institution believed Congress was constitutionally proscribed from providing. Positive protection of slavery was as much out of reach for Congress as the prohibition of slavery. As lifelong-secessionist Robert Barnwell Rhett noted while asserting that the fugitive slave element of the Compromise of 1850 (which was generally regarded as favorable to the South) was unconstitutional, "A law to have its practical effect must move in harmony with the opinions and feelings of the community where it is to operate."[84] The best protection for slavery did not come from Congress or laws, but from the attitudes of the society in which it existed.

During this period, Calhoun, who died 31 March 1850, and the rest of the outraged South focused on the related issues of the organization of the territories with respect to slavery and on the admission of California into the Union. Admitting California as a free state would immediately tip the sectional balance in the Union in favor of the free states, but the status of the other acquired territories was of equal concern. States formed in these territories could either re-establish the balance between slave and free states or further tip that balance in favor of free states. California was eventually admitted to the Union as a free state, but the other territories acquired could be divided into any number of states, leading to a potentially radical imbalance in sectional power. To make matters worse, the newly acquired territories were generally considered to be inhospitable to slavery, meaning that if the South put forth no specific, concerted effort, the territories would be free and would eventually become free states. In addition, the much-maligned Missouri Compromise line placed a northern limit on the extension of slavery, meaning that, even if slavery would spread to the new territories, there were still more territories to the North that would eventually become free states. With these fears in mind, Southern political leaders attempted to formulate a response to Northern and federal encroachments into what they perceived as their rights.

Calhoun's fourth of March speech in the Senate set the stage for Southern reaction to the Compromise of 1850. In it, he argued that the shape of the American state was undergoing fundamental change, and that this change, if taken to its logical conclusion, would end in disunion. Balance in the Senate, which had provided both sections with a veto over unfavorable policy and allowed the South to protect slavery, was about to be thrown off by the introduction of California into the Union. Having both a majority of the states and a majority of the Union's population meant the North would enjoy "the exclusive power of controlling the government."[85] This was not a simple matter of the power of one side waxing while the other side waned, Calhoun argued; rather, this set of changes threatened, in effect, to alter the very "character of the government."[86] If things kept going as they had been, the South would have had no alternative but to secede from the Union. If the Union were to be saved, the North would have to recognize the South as an equal partner in it and give them equal access to the territories. From the

Northern point of view, the federal government had no obligation to make it easier for the South to bring their "property" into the new territories. After all, by supporting the admission of new free states, the people of the North were not violating the letter of the law or of the Constitution.

To respond to rising fears of Northern dominance and federal consolidation, and to determine what method of redress ought to be employed, Southern legislators attending a bipartisan convention in Jackson, Mississippi, in November 1849 vowed to meet in convention in Nashville, Tennessee, in June 1850. Some South Carolinian political leaders hoped this meeting would be the first step toward secession. For most Southerners, though, it was to be a first step in unifying the South so it could press the center and the North to maintain Southern interests.

Unfortunately for the South, this convention was neither a first step toward secession nor an important step in unifying the South behind a common program. Many Southern states sent no delegates to the convention, and most states that did send delegates to the convention sent only a handful. Only South Carolina sent a full delegation to the convention; Virginia, Georgia, Mississippi, and Texas elected a partial slate of delegates; Florida, Alabama, Arkansas, and Tennessee sent irregularly selected delegates; Delaware, Maryland, Kentucky, Missouri, North Carolina, and Louisiana sent no delegation. As constituted, it could hardly be called a Southern Convention, and it certainly was not a legitimate realm in which binding decisions could be made. The convention did not unify the South behind some common response to Northern usurpation. It only demonstrated the extent to which serious divisions within the South prevented any collective action from being pursued. The North learned that the South was rife with internal divisions and did not have to be taken seriously.

While the South revealed, in essence, that there was no "South," in Washington, politicians were working out the Compromise of 1850, which, supporters hoped, would settle the territorial issue once and for all. The compromise was constituted by five separate elements: first, California was to be admitted as a free state; second, the boundary dispute between Texas and the federal government was solved with Texas agreeing to cede territory in return for the federal government assuming Texan debt; third, a very strong fugitive slave law was passed; fourth, the existence of slavery in the District of Columbia was affirmed, but the slave trade in it was ended; and fifth, the territories of New Mexico and Utah were established without restrictions on slavery. Henry Clay's original effort was to include each separate compromise element in a single omnibus bill, using the theory that each section would be more likely to grant concessions if the other side were forced to grant concessions simultaneously. Clay's efforts failed, but thanks to the tireless efforts of Senator Steven Douglas from Illinois, each element of the compromise was passed separately.

From the Southern perspective, the admission of California into the Union as a free state was the most problematic element of the Compromise

States' Rights in South Carolina   45

of 1850. Most states were admitted to the Union only after having gone through a territorial phase. California did not go through this phase. Furthermore, it was admitted without providing for a paired admission of a slave state. Paired admission was established at the time of the Missouri Compromise. With the admission of California, and without preparations for a slave state to be admitted to balance it, the balance between the free and slave states was permanently altered in favor of the free states, with 16 free states and 15 slave states. Northern numbers had long dominated the House of Representatives, and after the admission of California, even the Senate, long the bulwark against Northern anti-slavery leanings, was in the hands of "free-soilers" (see Table 3.1). Still, as long as political parties had constituents in both sections, Northern dominance of governing institutions would not translate into the implementation of anti-slavery policies. The only factor mitigating the South's minority status was the Southern-dominated bisectional coalition called the Democratic Party. As long as the Democratic Party remained powerful, and the South powerful within it, Southern institutions were safe.

Table 3.1   Free State and Slave State Additions to the Union

Free	*Slave*
Connecticut	Delaware
Massachusetts	Georgia
New Hampshire	Maryland
New Jersey	North Carolina
New York	South Carolina
Pennsylvania	Virginia
Rhode Island	Kentucky (1792)
Vermont (1791)	Tennessee (1796)
Ohio (1803)	Louisiana (1812)
Indiana (1816)	Mississippi (1817)
Illinois (1818)	Alabama (1819)
Maine (1820)	Missouri (1821)
Michigan (1837)	Arkansas (1836)
Iowa (1846)	Florida (1845)
Wisconsin (1848)	Texas (1845)
California (1850)	
Minnesota (1858)	
Oregon (1859)	

Source: Martis and Elmes (1993: 142).

Efforts to re-establish balance in the Senate failed spectacularly and served as a wedge issue to divide Northern and Southern politicians. Southern politicians attempted to force the admission of Kansas as a slave state with the Lecompton Constitution both against Northern wishes and against the wishes of the majority of Kansas's population, merely confirming Northern fears of a Southern slaveholders' conspiracy. With the admission of Minnesota in 1858 and Oregon in 1859, Southern hopes of restoring balance to the Senate were shattered: Organizing a single slave state proved difficult enough. Organizing three more slave states was an insurmountable barrier to Southern safety in the Union. For the South, this meant permanent minority status in both the House and the Senate, which, in turn, meant that policies unfavorable to the South could be passed at will. If the addition of free states into the Union continued unabated, the North would eventually have the super-majority required to pass a constitutional amendment abolishing slavery.

Although the compromise actually succeeded in slightly alleviating the conflict between the North and South, the manner in which it was passed suggested that the compromise was nothing more than an "armistice" between the two sections.[87] Separate sectional majorities passed each element of the compromise. That is, all or most Southerners voted for the elements most favorable to the South, while all or most Northerners voted for the elements most favorable to the North. Potter noted, "In the Senate, four Senators voted for the compromise measure every time, and eight others did so four times while abstaining on a fifth measure; in the House 28 members gave support five times and 35 did so four out of five."[88] Furthermore, the "final settlement" enjoyed sectional interpretation. Stephen Douglas, for example, claimed that the compromise meant slavery could be forbidden in a territory, while Robert Toombs of Georgia claimed that the "right of people of any state to hold slaves in common territories" had been affirmed.[89] Both positions, obviously, could not be simultaneously true.

While "compromise" was being established at the center, some Southerners were entreating South Carolina to secede alone. Virginian professor and secessionist Nathaniel Beverley Tucker wrote to James Henry Hammond, "Secession must begin somewhere, or absolute subjugation must ensue. . . . If she [South Carolina] alone can act with unanimity then she alone can save herself and us."[90] Despite Tucker's confidence in South Carolina's leadership, most Southerners were fearful of the effect this state's leadership would have.

The Nashville Convention had agreed to reconvene in November 1850. With moderate forces boycotting the convention, the radicals controlled the convention that reconvened. Although it would be unable to convince the South to secede from the Union, the convention did manage to assert the existence of the right of secession.[91] Because cooperative action was impossible, South Carolinians began to consider unilateral action. In the meantime, however, events in Georgia, the Deep South state with the most national importance, prevented the possibility of radical action for the next decade. These events would serve to make the unilateral secession of South Carolina almost suicidal.

Given that California was admitted into the Union as a free state under irregular circumstances (not having gone through a territorial phase), the state of Georgia, like most other Southern states, felt obliged to call a state convention. Concerned that calling the convention was first step toward secession, Up Country unionist Benjamin Franklin Perry asked in his diary: "How much of California will she have after secession?"[92] Georgia's state convention met in December 1850, more than three months after the passage of the final compromise measure. This lag time gave whatever resentment there was surrounding the passage of the compromise measures an opportunity to subside. In part because of this lag time, Georgia unionists won a massive victory in the convention election. The convention that eventually met produced the "Georgia Platform," a conservative document that, Holt notes, "ended the threat of secession throughout the South for 10 years."[93]

Echoing the sentiment of Calhoun's 1830 toast ("The Union—next to our liberty, most dear"), the platform stated that the Union "is secondary in importance . . . to the rights and principles it was designed to perpetuate." While this was not a radical document, conditions were attached to Georgia's continued adherence to the Union. According to the fourth resolution of the Georgia Platform,

> The State of Georgia, in the judgment of this Convention will and ought to resist, even (as a last resort) to a disruption of the Union, any future Act of Congress abolishing Slavery in the District of Columbia, without the consent and the petition of the slaveholders thereof, or any Act abolishing Slavery in places purchased by the United States for the erection of forts, magazines, arsenals, dock-yards, navy-yards, and other like purposes; or in any Act suppressing the slave-trade between slave-holding States; or in any refusal to admit as a State any Territory applying because of the existence of slavery therein; or in any act prohibiting the introduction of slaves into the Territories of Utah and New Mexico; or in any Act repealing or materially modifying the laws now in force for the recovery of fugitive slaves.

In conditionally supporting the compromise, Georgia alone guaranteed that the Southern states of the Union would not secede from the Union. But, if the words of the Platform are taken to be true, it put the Georgia on a hair trigger for secession, because any future threat to slavery essentially committed the state to disunion.

Despite the threats and posturing—which had by now become customary in the face of perceived Northern encroachments on their rights—the document was still conservative: Georgia promised to "abide by" the elements of the Compromise of 1850 "as a *permanent adjustment of the sectional controversy.*"[94] If Georgia was going to abide by the Compromise of 1850, there was little else for the rest of the South to do, except fall in line behind this state.

SOUTH CAROLINA'S ATTEMPT AT COOPERATIVE SECESSION

South Carolina, once again adopting its role as hotspur, was not deterred from taking action against Northern and federal threats to its survival. On 20 December 1850, less than one week after Georgia adopted the Georgia Platform, the legislature of South Carolina passed a bill calling for a state convention and a Southern convention to determine the state's course of action. By calling for a Southern convention and a state convention to follow, South Carolina was attempting to encourage cooperative (rather than unilateral) secession. South Carolina's plan was to initiate a Southern-wide convention, which would meet in January of 1852, in order to determine the exact path the separate states of the South would take. After the convention met, and a path was decided upon, state conventions throughout the South would meet in February of 1852 to put the decision of the Southern Convention into effect. South Carolina, however, was out of touch: Southerners did not wish to hold another convention, and they certainly did not wish to secede from the Union at this time. Nonetheless, South Carolina pressed its plan for radical action.

The forces in favor of unilateral secession in South Carolina put their superior mobilizing machine to work and trounced the cooperationists in the February 1851 elections for the state convention that was to be held following the Southern Congress. While no official results of this election remain, it was widely reported that the unilateral secessionists won 127 of the 169 Convention seats.[95] The *Southern Patriot,* newspaper for the Up Country district of Greenville, claimed that no more than 50 or 60 of the delegates were "even qualifiedly against secession."[96] Recent historiography of this election suggests this outcome was a result of low or depressed voter turnout: In some historically conservative (cooperationist) districts, the polls did not even open.[97]

Although it was clear that other Southern states had no intention of participating in another Southern convention, South Carolina went through the motions of electing delegates to the Southern Congress. Confident that a conservative reaction had finally taken hold in South Carolina, and fearful that the radical majority in the state convention would choose to unilaterally withdraw the state from the Union, South Carolinian cooperationists successfully turned the election for the Southern Congress into a referendum on the state convention's actions.[98] With the tide of public opinion finally flowing in their direction, the cooperationists mobilized voters and defeated the unilateral secessionists on 13 and 14 October 1851, by a vote of approximately 25,062 to 17,617.[99] Despite the overrepresentation of the more radical sections of the generally more radical Low Country, supporters of unilateral secession were "grievously cast down."[100]

Even in defeat, members of the state convention (elected primarily from the radical ranks in the February election) recognized that, although the recent defeat at the polls meant they could not secede, the convention had to accomplish something—lest South Carolina once again damage its reputation by engaging in "bravado and submission."[101] While formally free to secede, if the convention had followed a radical path, the movement for a Southern Confederacy would have been ruined. Georgia, after all, had rejected secession, and this rejection was supported by the other states of the South. If the convention did nothing, Northern actors would be more certain that Southern threats, even those emanating from South Carolina, did not need to be taken seriously. Ultimately, the form of resistance adopted departed little from the resolutions passed at the reconvening of the Nashville Convention and the Georgia Platform. Members of the convention affirmed the right to secede, but they rejected it for the time being. There were, however, other plans of resistance in the works.

Sometimes-cooperationist, sometimes-radical James Henry Hammond devised a plan of resistance according to which South Carolina was to withdraw its participation in all federal politics. According to "The Plan," as it came to be called by his apprentice A.P. Aldrich, South Carolina would cease sending Senators and Congressman to Washington, cease participation in presidential elections, and officially deprive all those who took federal offices of citizenship of the state.[102] The Plan offered *de facto* secession from the Union that would, for the time being, avoid all the problems associated with *de jure* secession; The Plan, however, smacked too much of South Carolina's repudiated radicalism, and it was not adopted by the convention.

There were, in effect, two groups in South Carolina at this time. With the unionist forces all but decimated, there were the unilateral secessionists, like Robert Barnwell Rhett, who wanted secession regardless of the cost. On the other hand there were the cooperationists who desired secession, but only if it was accomplished in conjunction with other states of the South and linked to the creation of a Southern confederacy. A.P. Aldrich fit comfortably into the latter category. During this crisis, the cooperationists were the dominant force within the state.

Although the preference structure of the political elite in South Carolina was largely unchanged between the 1852 and 1860, the outcome of these two crises is vastly different. The difference in outcomes is linked to the differing levels of grievance. The perception of a lower grievance level in 1852, compared to 1860, meant that, in 1852, South Carolina could not be certain that it would have a sufficient level of internal unity and a sufficient level of support abroad in the South. In 1860, these concerns were largely absent because of the strength of the grievance experienced and the speed with which action was coordinated. The speed with which coordination was accomplished was largely a function of lessons learned during the nullification crisis and the first secession crisis.

Support for unilateral secession—even if it would mean that South Carolina would exist as an independent republic—was demonstrated in a series of articles that first appeared in the Edgefield *Advertiser,* penned by an individual calling himself Rutledge.[103] These articles provide an excellent glimpse into the thinking and strategies of those seeking the immediate and unilateral secession of South Carolina. According to this perspective, every evil that befell South Carolina, from anti-slavery to the redistribution of Southern wealth to the North, would be remedied if South Carolina seceded from the Union. Rutledge wrote, "The sole danger is while we are in the Union."[104] If South Carolina seceded, the problems confronting it would be removed. This was true, Rutledge suggested, whether the rest of the South joined South Carolina or not. Any effort to force South Carolina back in the Union would result in the dissolution of the Union, and any effort to cut off South Carolina's foreign trade would unite "half of Europe" in waging war against the U.S.[105] The benefits derived from international trade were South Carolina's "Ace in the Hole." Similar arguments were provided by other South Carolinian planter-politicians: Lewis Malone Ayer, member of the South Carolina legislature, and member of the secession convention elected in 1860, argued in favor of unilateral secession in 1851. In a speech given in Barnwell district, he argued that by seceding unilaterally, South Carolina would

> gain peace, quiet, happiness, independence, and the glorious privilege of living entirely under laws of our own choice. We gain $5,000,000 of revenue now annually imposed on us by our enemies for the benefit of their section. We gain entire exemption from the impudent, offensive and dangerous intermeddling of Northern Abolitionists with our domestic affairs.[106]

This perspective did not win the day in South Carolina's secession convention of 1852. Although the state had come to be dominated by those who supported the creation of a Southern Confederacy, conventional wisdom held that unilateral secession in 1852 would prevent, rather than facilitate, this objective. Armistead Burt, member of the House of Representatives for South Carolina, wrote, "As God is the judge of my sincerity, I believe this Union and slavery cannot stand together," but he nonetheless opposed unilateral secession unless the cooperation of other Southern states was absolutely guaranteed.[107]

The convention itself was a fascinating example of the strategic action employed by those whose ultimate desire was the creation of a Southern Confederacy, but who were willing to wait for more favorable circumstances. Robert Barnwell Rhett would never oppose secession—even if it meant that South Carolina would be separated from the rest of the South, as well as the North. (Disgusted with President Davis's leadership during the course of the war, Rhett may have even wished to have South Carolina secede from the Confederacy.[108]) Although they held the majority of the convention's seats, Rhett and the unilateral secessionists did not hold sway in that body. Regardless of the argument in favor of secession, those able to bring it about saw the existence of South Carolina as an independent republic as an unmitigated disaster.

Hammond protégé A.P. Aldrich desired the eventual creation of a Southern Confederacy, but he opposed secession in 1852 because he was certain that unilateral action by South Carolina at that time would have devastated the movement for a Southern Confederacy. During the first secession crisis, in other words, Aldrich believed he had to oppose secession in order to realize its eventual success. Eight years hence, Aldrich played a central role in silencing opposition and assuring South Carolina's unilateral secession.[109] South Carolinian member of the House of Representatives W.W. Boyce played a similar role in opposing secession in 1852. The purpose of secession, he wrote, had to be to protect slavery. If South Carolina followed a course of action that put the institution of slavery at risk, he wrote, "We accomplish nothing."[110]

Under these circumstances, the 1852 Convention was another Southern non-starter: James Henry Hammond, disgusted with belated efforts to consider his plan of non-intercourse with the North, recommended to Aldrich that the first order of business in the convention ought to be to adjourn *sine die*.[111] It met, but accomplished little. Knowing they were defeated both abroad and at home, the radicals did not force the convention to take action that would further isolate South Carolina. A course of resistance amenable to all parties was impossible to find. With 19 votes in the negative, the state convention of 1852 could only muster the following declaration:

> South Carolina, in the exercise of her sovereign will, as an independent State, acceded to the Federal Union, known as the United States of America; and that in the exercise of the same sovereign will, it is her right, without let, hindrance, or molestation from any power whatsoever, *to secede from the said Federal Union* . . .
>
> That the frequent violations of the Constitution of the United States by the Federal Government, and its encroachments upon the reserved rights of the Sovereign States of the Union, especially in relation to slavery, amply justify this state, so far as any duty or obligation to her confederates is involved, in dissolving at once all political connection with her co-States; and that she forbears the exercise of this manifest right of self-government from considerations of expediency only.[112]

This was nothing short of another humiliating defeat for Southern radicals. By this time, few doubted the existence of the right to secession. In effect, South Carolina barely went beyond what the resolutions of the Nashville Convention and Georgia's convention offered in late 1850.

This episode highlights the centrality of timing in the movement for secession.[113] The beginning of the first secession crisis can be traced to the conclusion of the war with Mexico and the introduction of the Wilmot Proviso, which occurred in 1846. As part of the Compromise of 1850, California was admitted to the Union and the slave trade was made illegal in the District of Columbia. More than three months passed between the passage of the compromise measures and the passage of a convention bill in South Carolina. In the meantime, the people of Georgia assembled in Convention and provided an alibi for conservative citizens of the South. The Georgia Platform immediately closed whatever window of opportunity for cooperative secession had been open, successfully providing political cover for anyone in the South who did not wish to secede or who was not yet ready to do so. If South Carolina wanted to secede, the state would have to go it alone.

The political preferences of the planter-politicians remained little-changed from 1850–52 until secession was accomplished in December of 1860. Most wanted secession, but they were unwilling to go it alone. Those who had the power to make such a move would not support secession unless they were certain they had the support of their own population and at least a minimum of support from the other states of the South. Short of this, any forward action was seen as being suicidal. The lesson learned from this episode sounds something like this: "Too early, you break your neck; too late, you lose your time."[114] In other words, finding the right time is critical: if you go too early, you risk being singled out; if you wait too long, you might not go at all.

The creation of a Southern Confederacy depended upon the ability of secessionist entrepreneurs to find an issue upon which secession could be mobilized. It also depended upon the willingness of a single state to take prompt action before any conservative reaction inside or outside the state could take hold. Upon examining the fall and winter of 1860, it becomes evident that this important lesson was taken to heart by those seeking to create a Southern Confederacy. Preparations for secession had begun long before the issue upon which secession was justified occurred. Once that issue did occur, South Carolina did little more than respond to it (the election of Lincoln), as it promised it would.

One necessary condition of secession is grievance. The central element preventing secession in 1850–52 was the lack of such a grievance. The South lost California, even though more Southern than Northern blood was shed winning that land.[115] The admission of California as a free state tipped the balance in the Senate in favor of free states. However, the Compromise of 1850 gave slaveholders the opportunity to take their institution to other territories gained from the war with Mexico. Though impracticable, the extension of slavery was theoretically possible, giving the South at least a glimmer of hope that the institution remained safe within the Union. There was, in other words, no real grievance behind which support for secession could be mobilized.

In 1852, the grievance experienced by the South was too distant and too uncertain to activate the other conditions in the Union that tended toward secession. That is, it did not matter that the institutional design of the Union gave the separate states a high level of institutional capacity at the state level (thus lowering the cost of secession), or that the federal government's minimal function meant that secession could be undertaken with minimal disruption; nor did it matter that the borders of South Carolina were long-established, or that there was a (challenged) political leadership in place that supported secession. The Compromise of 1850, especially after the passage of the Georgia Platform, did not present an immediate, palpable menace to slavery. To achieve sufficient mobilization to accomplish any radical action, it was clear that there would have had to be an immediate, palpable threat to slavery. There was not, in other words, a sufficiently strong grievance leading to a sufficiently strong fear among citizens of the South to provide fodder for mobilization for secession in 1850–52. The next time South Carolina confronted the Union encroachments on its rights, circumstances would be vastly different.

CONCLUSION

South Carolina went a long way toward establishing its radical credentials between 1828 and 1852. No other state in the South was willing to press for Southern rights to the same extent. Some of the reasons for this thoroughgoing radicalism are outlined above. Yet, we must wonder what, if anything, South Carolina had accomplished in its years of pushing for states' rights: Protective tariffs were still passed; Northern challenges to slavery were growing with each year; abolitionism, while still on the fringes of Northern society, was enjoying ever-increasing support; South Carolinian nullification was repudiated by both the North and the South; secession, either cooperative or unilateral, was proscribed for the foreseeable future. Had South Carolina made any lasting contribution to the Southern fight within the Union? Despite the state's obvious failures, South Carolina helped to keep states' rights and state sovereignty on the national agenda, making the South sensitive to perceived wrongs committed against it. From the moment Thomas Cooper suggested that his state might be compelled to "calculate the value of the Union," South Carolina's political elite gradually convinced its population that secession might be necessary at some time in the future.

In 1852, South Carolinian elites recognized that the time for secession had not yet arrived. Accordingly, Robert Barnwell Rhett, the rest of the fire-eaters, and South Carolina in general faded into the woodwork for the next few years. Rhett resigned his Senate seat in disgust, believing that he was not the best person to represent his state. Democrats regained the White House in 1852 and won it again in 1856. During the latter election, a new party opposed to the extension of slavery contested the Presidency and came dangerously close to winning with a Northern, sectional vote. In spite of this obvious danger, it seemed that Southern power was once again on the rise. The Kansas-Nebraska Act repealed the Missouri Compromise line, opening territory above this line to slavery. The Supreme Court's Dred Scott decision affirmed the actions taken by Congress, and even went so far as to imply that there were very few places that slavery could actually be excluded. Between 1852 and 1858, the future of the Union (with South Carolina in it) did not seem in doubt. Southern safety within it seemed more certain than it had toward the end of 1850, for example. Up County unionist B.F. Perry put it this way in 1857: "[B]efore our enemies can reach us, they must first break down the supreme court—change the Senate & seize the Executive & by an open appeal to revolution, restore the Missouri line, repeal the fugitive slave law & change in fact the who government."[116] For Perry, and others confident in the future of the Union, the enemies of the South had insurmountable obstacles in their way. As one South Carolinian noted after the end of the first secession crisis, "We must either be in a political fury, or else be asleep."[117] For the time being, South Carolina slept.

In this chapter, I have examined the historical background of the secession crisis of 1860, concentrating in particular on the numerous occasions in which constituent states challenged central state authority. One unique feature of the American political landscape is that challenges to central state authority were originally common in both Northern and Southern states. Given the extent and nature of the demographic and political changes within the Union, challenges to central state authority eventually became associated with the South—and, in particular, with South Carolina. The foundation of this challenge was the sovereignty of the separate states of the Union, a theory to which South Carolina had long since adhered.

A positive feedback loop developed: The more powers the separate states exercised, the more tenable the theory of state sovereignty. The more tenable the theory of state sovereignty, the more incursions against that sovereignty by the center chafed. As an extension of state sovereignty, South Carolina and, to a lesser extent, the rest of the Deep South gradually developed a theory of states' rights that provided them with a means of defending themselves against encroachments on their rights. The South Carolinian defense of states' rights, in particular, eventually came to include the right to secede from the Union. If the Union was a compact between sovereignties, and the separate states were sovereign, then each party to the compact had the right to withdraw from it if its terms were violated. From the South Carolinian point of view, secession was the "ultimate states' right."[118] As demographic changes within the Union were translated into Northern political dominance, the theory of states' rights that had a long tradition in both sections of the Union became associated with the South alone. South Carolina's commitment to states' rights and secession was, essentially, a defensive position adopted by a weakened political coalition partner that was consistent with one of the dominant interpretations of the Union.

Not surprisingly, South Carolina was at the forefront of the movement for Southern rights and, eventually, the movement for secession. The nullification controversy was the first extended crisis between South Carolina and the center, and it was there that the idea of state sovereignty came to take its central role in the maintenance of Southern Rights. If the states were indeed sovereign, each state was competent to determine the constitutionality of laws passed in the center. While President Jackson maintained that the federal government's laws would be enforced, South Carolina enjoyed a victory in forcing the center to back away from the principle of protection. This victory, however, was bittersweet: South Carolina was convinced that it could not count on sympathetic Northerners or fellow Southerners to provide a strong check on federal government encroachments on states' rights (or a check on the overextension of federal authority). Although it was attempting to protect Southern Rights, South Carolina's leadership, came to be regarded with suspicion in the South. Northerners, not surprisingly, regarded Southern Carolinian efforts with suspicion as well.

South Carolina's effort to nullify federal tariffs was supposed to be an easier confrontation than one that openly centered on the much thornier issue of slavery. Opposition to protection and tariffs was supposed to provide the state with coalition partners who were, like South Carolina, committed to maintaining strict restrictions on federal power. The coalition partners they sought in this fight could not be counted on if their purpose was to defend slavery. Though they succeeded in getting tariffs reduced, South Carolina's effort to establish a coalition that was willing to check the expansion of federal authority failed. In their next confrontation with the Union, South Carolina did not misrepresent the source of their concern. In the first secession crisis, the issue over which South Carolina fought was the power the federal government had over the institution of slavery. By openly challenging federal authority over the institution of slavery, South Carolina abandoned any efforts at finding sympathy among Northern voters who had come to view slavery as an immoral institution. South Carolina was ultimately hoping for strong support among its fellow Southerners; in this, they were partly successful, but they continued to be looked upon with suspicion. No state was willing to go as far as South Carolina in protecting slavery.

After the passage of the Georgia Platform, the possibility of employing a strategy of either simultaneous or sequential secession was eliminated. Despite this, South Carolina went through the motions of holding its convention. In the convention, political elites who were committed to the eventual creation of a Southern Confederacy were forced to defeat unilateral secession for the time being. All the convention could muster was an assertion of the existence of a right to secede at a time when few in the state doubted that it existed anyway; South Carolina waited so long to act that other more conservative and more influential states ended up committing themselves (and a large portion of the South) to the Union until a new issue arose.

The lessons learned by South Carolina were hard ones: The North could not be trusted to oppose the consolidationist tendencies of the federal government; although it vehemently opposed Northern anti-slavery, even the South could not be trusted to press for Southern rights strongly enough to successfully protect them. The only state willing to go as far as necessary to protect Southern rights (South Carolina) was looked upon askance.

After the secession convention had affirmed the right to secede and eschewed actual secession out of "expediency" only, the radical face of South Carolina withdrew from the national stage. (South Carolinian politicians even played a role in national political parties, with James L. Orr serving as Speaker of the House during the 35th Congress.) Once it became clear that a Republican might actually win the presidency, South Carolinians and other Southern secessionists began to work toward making a Republican victory *the* issue that would precipitate and justify secession in South Carolina and the South. As the next chapter demonstrates, political actors in South Carolina were finally successful in achieving their radical ends.

4 South Carolina Secedes

The previous chapters provided the general historical context of secession by concentrating on cases in which South Carolina was poised for confrontation with the federal government, only to back down. In this chapter, I provide a narrative of the immediate events surrounding secession, beginning with John Brown's raid and ending with the decision to secede on 20 December 1860. At the heart of this narrative is a discussion of the manner in which the changing strategies of South Carolina's leadership (from cooperative to unilateral secession) successfully brought about secession. This change in strategy brought about secession in South Carolina and lead to the sequential exit of most of the remaining Southern states. Secession did not occur simultaneously (or cooperatively)—as many had hoped. Instead, it occurred sequentially, with the most radical state leading other less radical states. The recognition of the importance of this using this strategy helped South Carolina to pursue a path that that radically altered the strategic context of choice in other states. The secession of South Carolina made secession nearly inevitable in the states of the Deep South. South Carolina's secession also set up an inevitable confrontation with the federal government—one that eventually forced the hand of most of the Upper South states.

BEGINNINGS OF SECESSION

"Can the Union and Slavery exist together?"[1] This was the question that Southerners asked themselves as they contemplated the Union and their place within it. Despite mild threats to the institution of slavery, there had been a consensus that maintaining the Union was the best way to maintain slavery. Conflict between the sections became more severe, and as changes within the Union made Northern political dominance more thorough, however, Southern opinion on the compatibility of the Union and slavery shifted. No longer was maintaining the Union regarded as the best way to maintain and protect slavery. The Union had come to constitute a fundamental threat to slavery. William Henry Trescott, Under-Secretary of State

Table 4.1 Popular Vote in the 1856 Presidential Election, by State

Free States	Buchanan	Fremont	Fillmore	Total Vote	% for Fremont
California	53,342	20,704	36,195	110,255	19%
Connecticut	35,028	42,717	2,615	80,360	53%
Illinois	105,528	96,275	37,531	239,334	40%
Indiana	118,670	94,375	22,356	235,401	40%
Iowa	37,568	45,073	9,669	92,310	49%
Maine	39,140	67,279	3,270	109,689	61%
Massachussetts	39,244	108,172	19,626	170,048	64%
Michigan	52,136	71,762	1,660	125,558	57%
New Hampshire	31,891	37,473	410	69,774	54%
New Jersey	46,943	28,338	24,115	99,396	29%
New York	195,878	276,004	124,604	596,486	46%
Ohio	170,874	187,497	28,121	386,640	48%
Pennsylvania	230,772	147,963	82,202	460,937	32%
Rhode Island	6,680	11,467	1,675	19,822	58%
Vermont	10,569	39,561	545	50,675	78%
Wisconsin	52,843	67,090	580	120,513	56%
Total	1,227,106	1,341,750	395,174	2,967,198	45%

Slave States	Buchanan	Fremont	Fillmore	Total Vote	% for Buchanan
Alabama	46,739	0	28,552	75,291	62%
Arkansas	21,910	0	10,732	32,642	67%
Delaware	8,004	310	6,275	14,589	55%
Florida	6,358	0	4,833	11,191	57%
Georgia	56,581	0	42,439	99,020	57%
Kentucky	74,642	0	67,416	142,058	53%
Louisiana	22,164	0	20,709	42,873	52%
Maryland	39,123	285	47,452	86,860	45%
Mississippi	35,456	0	24,191	59,647	59%
Missouri	57,964	0	48,522	106,486	54%
North Carolina	48,243	0	36,720	84,963	57%
South Carolina			No popular vote		
Tennessee	69,704	0	63,878	133,582	52%
Texas	31,995	0	16,010	48,005	67%
Virginia	90,083	0	60,150	150,223	60%
Total	608,966	595	477,879	1,087,430	56%

Source: Austin (1986: 136–137).

in the Buchanan administration, answered the above question, his own, with the following assessment: "I do not believe they can. Slavery our institution of it at least—is scarcely half a century old. It is just beginning its career and to develop naturally will require freer people than is allowed by the bondages of the Federal Constitution."[2] This formulation is telling: the Constitution, once the protector of liberties, became the very thing holding the South in bondage.

Thanks to an electoral realignment over the issue of slavery that decimated the Whig Party, the second-party system in the U.S. ceased to exist.[3] In the North, the Republican Party rose from the ashes of the Whig Party and, by the late 1850s, began to make great electoral strides toward promoting an activist federal government and opposition to the extension of slavery. The Republican Party made its first significant showing in the presidential election of 1856, in which Democratic candidate James Buchanan narrowly defeated the Republican candidate, Southern-born and educated John Frémont (see Table 4.1). Recognizing the effect a Republican victory would have on the willingness of Southerners to pursue a radical course of action, some Southerners actually hoped that Frémont would be victorious in the 1856 election so that the issue between the sections would come to a head sooner.[4] Gaining strength, the Republicans faired well in the congressional elections of 1858. While the Democratic Party continued to hold sway in the Senate (with more than 55 percent of the seats), Republicans held a plurality of seats in the House (occupying 116 of 238 seats). Ongoing Democratic dominance of other national political institutions mitigated some of the effects of the 1858 congressional election, but these mitigating forces were shattered along with the Democratic Party in 1860.

RHETT'S FOURTH OF JULY SPEECH

Some claim that longtime radical Robert Barnwell Rhett initiated the movement for secession on 4 July 1859, with a speech given in Grahamville, South Carolina.[5] In this speech, Rhett noted that the condition that brought the Union into existence (fear of domination by foreign power) was no longer present, meaning that the rationale for the Union's continued existence was absent. Affirming the principle of state sovereignty, Rhett suggested there was a parallel in the relationship between the separate states of the Union and the relationship between the U.S. and the rest of the world. He said the purpose of the Union was for the American people to "be so united as to be *one people*, in relation to foreign nations for self-protection—and yet, in relation to one another, be separate, distinct and independent States."[6] This meant that Southerners and Northerners were to see each other as members of separate sovereignties, not as members of the same nation. The only people who should look upon Americans as a single people or members of the same nation were those who viewed the U.S. from beyond its borders. According to Rhett, Americans shared the same foreign policy and the same currency, but ought to share nothing more. Through its depredations, the North had violated the solemn compact between the states and between two very different peoples. Rhett claimed that:

> The sectional majority from the North grows stronger and more resolute every day. They have the power of controlling the legislation of Congress. They failed in controlling the executive, also, in the late Presidential election, but by a few votes. They expect, confidently, to succeed at the next Presidential election. Having mastered these two great departments of the government, they openly declare their determination to command the third—the Judiciary of the United States—and to sweep away every obstacle to their sectional domination and the consolidation of the government.[7]

Northerners refused to look upon the borders between the states in the same manner in which they looked upon the borders between the U.S. and a foreign country. The goal of the North "is to rule the South."[8]

The issue upon which a successful movement for secession could be mobilized had always eluded those who sought it. Between 1828 and 1832, there was talk of mobilizing secession on the tariff question, although nullifiers denied that secession was their goal. In 1844, Rhett initiated a failed movement for secession over the tariff issue in the Bluffton Movement. In 1850–52, South Carolinians attempted to mobilize support for secession around a cluster of issues relating to slavery and the territories won from Mexico. Tariffs and distant territorial issues were never able to provide sufficient fodder for successful secessionist mobilization; they were a grievance, but as long as these issues remained distant and abstract, they would never create a level of fear sufficient to mobilize secession.

Rhett was an early convert to secession and the creation of a Southern republic. For him, the solution to the problems facing the South had always been clear. Indeed, this solution was written, albeit implicitly, into the structure of the Constitution itself: secession. Rhett needed to convince the populace of the rectitude of this solution, and he needed to provide the South with an issue behind which secession could be mobilized. He recommended that his state "meet the contest in the next Presidential election." Despite his own commitment to secession, Rhett knew that secession was not inevitable, because the outcome of the upcoming election was not inevitable: "If our rights are victorious in the next Presidential election, we may consider it as a kind augury of a more auspicious future. If they are overthrown, let this election be the last contest between the North and the South; and the long, weary night of our dishonor and humiliation be dispersed at last, by the glorious day-spring of a Southern confederacy."[9] Given the Union's (meaning the North's) "fatal tendency toward despotism," he wanted South Carolina to "dissolve her connection with the North, and . . . establish . . . a Southern confederacy."[10] Many years before Rhett determined that the state "meet the contest in the next presidential election," James Henry Hammond prophesied in a letter to Georgian scholar and friend William Brown Hodgson: "[T]he Executive is the rock on which our Institution will split when they split."[11]

South Carolinians had established themselves as those who would cry foul at all affronts, real or imagined, early and often. Sadly, Northerners had become so accustomed to South Carolinian "bravado and submission"[12] that they ignored it at a time when listening to it had become essential. When South Carolinians claimed that the election of a Republican president would precipitate a crisis, most Northerners assumed that South Carolinians were merely up to their old tricks, and they were confident that this potential crisis would pass, just as had all the rest. After all, Northerners reasoned, how could anyone in the South justify seceding in response to the constitutional election of a president? But for the South, particularly South Carolinians, the election of 1860 satisfied only the thinnest form of constitutionality: it was not constitutional in substance. This made all the difference, and it made this otherwise constitutional election justification for South Carolina's action. What came next helped to convince the South that the North was committed to violent anti-slavery.

JOHN BROWN'S RAID

John Brown first became known as an abolitionist radical in an attack on a pro-slavery faction in Kansas. It was thanks to this event, and others like it, that the territory came to be known as "Bleeding Kansas." Brown's most famous escapade, though, was his raid on Harper's Ferry, Virginia (now in West Virginia), during which he attempted to incite a slave rebellion that he hoped would spread throughout Virginia and the South, ultimately leading to slave freedom. On 16 October 1859, John Brown and his followers captured the government arsenal at Harper's Ferry. After the successful first phase of the plan, Brown and his followers waited for word to spread and for the slave uprising to follow. Word spread, but the rebellion failed to materialize. Potter noted, "white abolitionists believed that the Negroes were all on the brink of a massive insurrection, yet they seldom consulted any Negro for corroboration and they conducted their own abolitionist activities."[13] Without a widespread uprising, the plan was doomed to failure because Brown did not have enough men to hold off troops that would inevitably come to capture them. A mere day and a half after the beginning of the raid, Robert E. Lee and his troops captured Brown and his supporters. Later the same year, Brown was tried and hanged.[14] From the Southern point of view, the most concerning element of the John Brown episode was the Northern reaction to Brown's hanging. His death was met in many Northern towns with ringing church bells, marking the death of a martyr. Moderate Northern anti-slavery seemed bent upon destroying the South.

Brown's mission had failed, but not before it had increased tensions between the sections and convinced many Southerners that the North was committed not just to anti-slavery, but to a violent form of abolition that included literal war upon the slaveholder. The larger implications of this incident presented a common threat to the South, but, tellingly, did not unify the South behind a common program for its protection. Even in the face of John Brown's attack on Southern institutions, the South did not have the requisite unity to develop and implement a program for its protection. Ironically, it was the presence, persistence, and extent of this very disunity that helped to convince political leaders in South Carolina of the need for unilateral secession.

Additional concerns were wrought by Brown's selection of Harper's Ferry as the starting point for the slave rebellion. Brown did not select the Deep South—where slavery was firmly entrenched, where the population had a unique vigilance regarding threats to the institution, and where any such plotting would surely become known and quashed, as it had in the past;[15] instead, he focused his efforts on the most vulnerable slaveholding area in the U.S.: the Upper South. In particular, his efforts were centered upon a portion of the Upper South that did not have a large slave population—a portion of the Upper South where he thought the population might be sympathetic to his plan. In the mountains of Virginia, the institution of slavery was not as firmly rooted as it was in South Carolina or in the tobacco growing areas of Virginia. The Deep South had a higher proportion of slaves in its population; in some areas, slaves constituted more than 90 percent of the population. This demographic fact made the slave-owners in these areas constantly vigilant for conspiracies. In the Upper South, there were fewer slaves and fewer vigilance committees looking for potential slave rebellions. Brown reasoned—incorrectly as it turns out—that this made the Upper South ripe for abolitionist activity.

Despite the obvious failure of Brown's mission, it was, on larger canvas, a resounding success. Brown's failed efforts forced the South to question two of its most fundamental beliefs—beliefs that many knew to be erroneous: one, that the slave actually enjoyed being a slave; and, two, that the Upper South was safe for slavery. This threatened belief set meant that even the smallest challenge to slavery would have to be met with the nineteenth century equivalent of "massive retaliation." Thus, mere Northern anti-slavery would have to have to be treated like the most venomous abolitionism. Many Southerners, especially South Carolinians, would not or could not distinguish between Brown's radical, abolitionist views and the moderate anti-slavery felt by the typical Northerner—or the Republican Party. This inability or unwillingness to distinguish between these vastly different forms of anti-slavery meant that there was potential for a violent reaction against *any* form of anti-slavery, no matter how innocuous.[16]

In the Southern world-view, a threat to slavery was a threat to survival. Freedom for slaves meant mortal danger for the whites who remained in their midst. According to one author, "Carolinians had come to believe that the most immediate response by the slaves to emancipation would be a violent, murderous uprising."[17] Any form of anti-slavery, therefore, put Southerners on the defensive, but Southern divisions over what could or should be done in response to the potential anti-slavery leanings in the North meant that a single comprehensive program for Southern protection could not be developed. It was under these circumstances that South Carolina made one last effort to bring about true cooperative secession.

MAKING VIRGINIA "TAKE THE LEAD"?[18]

South Carolina saw the aftermath of John Brown's raid as an opportunity to unite the whole South behind some measures for their common defense. The raid was fresh in the minds of South Carolinians when the state's legislative session began in the fall of 1859. Fearing further Northern encroachments, Christopher G. Memminger, a member of the South Carolina House of Representatives from 1836–51 and 1854–59, and an opponent of both nullification in 1832 and unilateral secession during the 1850–52 secession crisis, tabled a number of resolutions pertaining to South Carolina's relationship to the federal Union and the rest of the South.[19] While "still deferring to her Southern sisters," Memminger recommended that the "slave-holding States should immediately meet together to concert measures for united action."[20] He also recommended that the resolutions be communicated to the state of Virginia so that South Carolina and Virginia could "unite with them in measures of defense."[21] For the immediate defense of South Carolina, he recommended that "one hundred thousand dollars be appropriated for military contingencies."[22] His resolutions were passed unanimously, and Memminger was selected as South Carolina's commissioner to the State of Virginia to communicate the substance of these resolutions to it.

Memminger selected Virginia as the starting point for two reasons: First, Brown's raid occurred within the territory of Virginia, and South Carolinians hoped that Virginia's experience with radical abolitionism might prompt it to support a Southern Convention; second, Virginia was a large state with a large population, and developing substantial industrial capacity. Many individuals inside and outside of South Carolina thought that Virginia's support was essential to any united or coordinated effort defending the South against Northern aggressions.

Forces opposed to secession condemned Memminger's efforts as nothing more than an attempt to force secession. Memminger, however, like most South Carolinian moderates, sought only to develop a plan that would assure the safety of Southern institutions. It mattered little if this safety was had in the Union or out of it. Memminger wrote:

The legislature of our State seems to have been persuaded that if we could get the Southern States to meet in Congress, considerable progress would be made towards a Union of the South. All of us are persuaded that in this Union there is no security—and either there must be new terms established or a Southern Confederacy is our only hope of safety.[23]

Southern hopes often centered on creating a union of interests among the Southern states in order to press Southern interests within the Union more effectively. Conservatives initially pinned their hopes on a Union with new terms—a Union in which slavery would be assured of its safety. Absent new terms in the existing Union, the creation of a Southern Confederacy was essential for Southern safety. "My own opinion and I think the opinion of our State," Memminger wrote to South Carolina member of the U.S. House of Representatives William Porcher Miles, "is that the Union cannot be preserved; and that a sectional Government such as we now have is not worthy of preservation. New terms, fresh constitutional guarantees might make another Union desirable. But in this, we will soon be deprived of every defense against the Northern section."[24]

Memminger delivered his speech to the Virginia legislature on 19 January 1860. By this time, Memminger knew that Virginia would not only not take the lead, but it would not even support a Southern Conference at this time.[25] Not even John Brown's raid and the support for it seen in the North convinced Virginia to take steps for its defense. South Carolinians who had been poised to act for so long must have wondered just what would convince Virginia to act.

There is considerable historiographical debate about the motive behind Memminger's mission to Virginia. Even though Memminger was widely regarded as a conservative, some have claimed that his mission was undertaken to mobilize support for secession among the conservatives of Old Dominion.[26] (Who better to convince conservatives of the need for action than a fellow conservative?) Whatever the true motive, the failure of the mission accomplished just as much as, if not more than, what a successful mission might have accomplished. The failure of this mission proved that, even in the face of egregious crimes against the South, the conservative states of the Upper South could not be counted on to join the other states of the South to defend Southern interests.

Even in failure, South Carolina's interests were served, because the very attempt to facilitate cooperation had the added benefit of allowing the state to credibly claim that it had abandoned its more extreme tendencies. The mission's failure also helped South Carolina to ascertain what steps would need to be taken to provide needed protection to Southern interests. The persistently unreliable states of the Upper South would not take any action in defense of Southern interests; nor would they work to help create a united South. Even in the aftermath of the egregious crime committed against it, Virginia was "rapidly cooling down" on the idea of united action for Southern interests.[27] Recognizing the position Virginia was about to take on South Carolina's requests, Memminger lamented that he saw no men who would "take the position of leaders in a Revolution."[28] But this was hardly a tragedy, because central to South Carolina's future strategy, including the decision to secede unilaterally, was being able to know exactly how Virginia would respond to such threats. In fact, pursuing a Southern conference probably would have thrown cold water on the movement for a Southern Confederacy as it had in the Nashville Convention of 1850. Delay was dangerous. Wait too long, you lose your nerve.

With the implicit and explicit support of the Deep South, South Carolinians realized they would have to act alone in providing safety for the South. Despite the support of important citizens of the Deep South, South Carolina knew that the Deep South would be nearly as skittish as the Upper South in initiating action. The primary difference between the Deep South and the Upper South was that, while the Deep South would not lead, it might be counted on (unlike the Upper South) to follow hot on the heels of South Carolinian action. Recognizing this was central to the strategic thought of South Carolinian political actors. As historiographer Schulz wrote, "For the secessionists of South Carolina, the course of Alabama and Mississippi was far more important than that of Virginia."[29] If South Carolina determined (and followed) a course of action that would pull these states out of the Union, reticent Virginia would be forced to make a decision that it appeared unable to make voluntarily.

Memminger, a true cooperationist in early 1860, gradually began to recognize the necessity of unilateral secession. At the conclusion of his mission, while still in Virginia, Memminger wrote to South Carolinian member of the U.S. House of Representatives and recent convert to separate state secession William Porcher Miles that he was "brought to the opinion that we farther South will have to be compelled to act, and to drag after us these divided states."[30] He wrote that he knew "of no remedy but secession and that of course must be at home."[31] Although his previous commitments were to cooperative secession, Memminger was now committed to unilateral secession, a position that had formerly been adopted by only the most radical citizens of South Carolina.

Miles reluctantly agreed with Memminger's contention that the other states of the South would have to be dragged along. He wrote of his disappointment that the movement to defend Southern interests was to be placed in the hands of South Carolina once again:

> I am deeply pained and mortified to hear that Virginia is so utterly apathetic. You are right in your views. We further South must act and "drag her along." I was, as you know, opposed to separate secession of our state in '51—but in the event of the election of a Black Republican President I would be inclined to advise South Carolina to go out of the Union at once and end the present government. It is very certain that

the withdrawal of any single state must break up the Union. However I would much prefer to see Alabama or Mississippi lead off. Our state would certainly follow.[32]

Fearing that the political leaders of South Carolina were "behind the people," Miles concluded this letter with a request for Memminger to indicate what "practical action" should be undertaken in order to press forward in the movement for Southern safety. In South Carolina, politicians were supposed to lead, not follow. He hoped that some "practical action" would put South Carolina's politicians ahead of the people—or at least equal with them.

The disappointment experienced in Virginia was an effective mobilizer of unilateral secession. Memminger, who was originally moderate, was pushed into a Rhett-like position in support of unilateral action. Without John Brown, and the failed mission to Virginia, support for unilateral action may have remained outside of the political mainstream. Thanks to these events, support for unilateral action was no longer the provenance of the state's original extremists; moderates had begun to see the necessity of unilateral secession. In one of the many ironies of this episode, the deep entrenchment of Upper South moderation was fortuitous for supporters of unilateral secession. That this moderation was confirmed long before the November election presented the issue upon which secession would be ultimately justified further aided the cause of unilateral secession. If Upper South reticence had not been confirmed early, there was a risk that Deep South states that were ready to act would have waited too long to accomplish secession—"too late, you lose your time." Upper South moderation and Deep South reluctance to lead guaranteed that South Carolina would make the first move toward protecting Southern interests. Given this state's predilection for radicalism, this meant that the movement to defend Southern interests would most likely proceed according to a strategy consistent with South Carolina's interpretation of the Union—a strategy involving secession. Thus, an Upper South that would not act and a Deep South that would not lead foisted the obligation of leading upon South Carolina.

ALABAMA MAKES A MOVE . . . AND AN ISSUE

Despite the fact that South Carolina moved toward secession early and often, it was not South Carolina that made the first formal move toward secession, but Alabama. Recognizing the probability that a Republican would be elected president, and that such an election would pose a threat to the institution of slavery, in early 1860, the Alabama legislature passed a law requiring the state to call a convention within 40 days of the election in order to consider actions necessary for the safety of Southern institutions. Accordingly, the convention was charged to "consider, determine, and do whatever in the opinion of said convention the rights, interests, and honor of the State of Alabama require to be done for their protection."[33]

The forward movement of Alabama provided some relief for South Carolinians fearful of taking the mantle of leadership in the movement for a Southern Confederacy. However, when the time came for action, Alabama's forward movement was tempered by Alabama Governor A.B. Moore's unwillingness to initiate the movement for secession. Moore defended his position by referring to a technical question: Did the election of the president take place when the popular vote was cast, or when the Electoral College exercised its constitutional duty and selected the next president of the U.S.? On 5 December 1860, Governor Moore claimed that "the election of Lincoln could not constitutionally take place until a majority of electors had voted for him."[34] It is entirely conceivable that Governor Moore was hopeful that the electors could somehow be convinced to support someone other than Lincoln. Regardless, from this view, the constitutional election of Lincoln would not take place until mid-December, more than a month after the popular election took place. This put the brakes on what originally looked like a promising first move, and the fear that this might lead to a delay in the movement for secession helped to further strengthen South Carolinian resolve in the waning days of 1860. Recalling the impact of delay on the movement of 1850–52, South Carolina was determined not to allow calls for delay to put the current movement at risk.

THE DEMOCRATIC CONVENTION(S) OF 1860

Long before the presidential nomination process had reached its current level of democratization, party conventions were central to the selection of a presidential candidate. In 1860, the party convention held real power and had real functions. It was fortuitous for secessionist entrepreneurs that the Democratic nominating convention of 1860 was held in Charleston, South Carolina. This gave the radical forces, from both within and without, a suitably radical backdrop to press their views. Thanks especially to the machinations of secessionist William Yancey and the rest of the Alabama delegation, the Charleston Convention was a dress rehearsal for secession.[35]

In the Charleston Convention of April 1860, there were two related issues that increased the already considerable tension between the sections. First, there was the question of a candidate. Northern Democrats would accept no one but Stephen Douglas, whereas Southern Democrats had long since soured on Douglas—thanks to his support for the doctrine of popular sovereignty and his opposition to the Lecompton Constitution, which would have paved the way for admitting Kansas as a slave state. With Northern Democrats unwilling to accept anyone other than Douglas, and the Southern Democrats unwilling to accept Douglas under any circumstances, the stage was set for a showdown.[36]

The second issue was the platform the convention would adopt. The proximate cause of the withdrawal of Southern delegates was the convention's adoption of a platform that did not conform to the wishes of the Southern members of the Democratic Party. Central to the dispute, of course, was slavery. In general, Northern Democrats wanted a reaffirmation of the Cincinnati Platform of 1856, in which the doctrine of popular sovereignty was affirmed—though they were willing to compromise on this by agreeing to defer to the Supreme Court on the question of Congress's and territorial governments' authority over slavery.[37]

Believing that selection of a platform would be less controversial than selecting a candidate, convention delegates took up the question of platform first. A platform was thought to be easier to adopt because it merely required a simple majority of the convention attendees for adoption, rather than the two-thirds of the entire convention required to nominate a candidate. While the Southern delegation lacked the numbers to dominate the whole convention, the platform was developed in committee, where each state had a single vote, allowing the Southern delegation (with the support of California and Oregon) to hold sway over the committee's work. The "majority platform" created by this committee contained the provisions demanded by the Alabama delegation as the condition for their remaining in the convention. These provisions were known as the Alabama Platform.

The Alabama delegation and other Southerners sought the positive protection of slavery in the commonly held territories. They demanded a reaffirmation of the specific principles outlined in the Dred Scott decision that made it difficult to prevent the spread of slavery. Provisions outlined in the Alabama Platform mandated positive protection of slavery in a manner that would establish slavery in all territories of the U.S. What the South demanded in the platform of the regular Democratic Party, but could not have, was stated clearly in the platform eventually adopted by the Southern Democratic Party:

> Resolved, That the Platform adopted by the Democratic Party at Cincinnati be affirmed, with the following explanatory Resolutions: 1. That the Government of a Territory organized by an act of Congress, is provisional and temporary; and during its existence, all citizens of the United States have an equal right to settle with their property in the Territory, without their rights, either of person or property, being destroyed or impaired by Congressional or Territorial legislation.[38]

In Charleston, the Southern delegates maintained that neither the citizens of a territory nor Congress had the power to prevent the institution of slavery from being established. The North—even Northern Democrats who were decidedly moderate on the question of slavery—was unwilling to oppose popular sovereignty and support the extension of slavery into a territory if it were against the wishes of a majority of the territory's population.

Northern supporters of popular sovereignty believed a territory's population ought to be able to prevent slavery from being established just as it could allow slavery to be established. From the Southern perspective, Douglas' doctrine of popular sovereignty and the "compromise" proposed by Northern Democrats was just another way to exclude slavery from the territories: it was, in other words, the Wilmot Proviso in practice. Although the Supreme Court had already appeared to resolve this specific controversy in the Dred Scott decision, the platform adopted by the Democratic Party in 1860 returned the question of a territorial government's power to forbid or establish slavery to the Supreme Court. The Democratic Party Platform adopted in April 1860 resolved:

> That it is in accordance with the true interpretation of the Cincinnati Platform, that, during the existence of the Territorial Governments, the measure of restriction, whatever it may be, imposed by the Federal Constitution on the power of the Territorial Legislature over the subject of the domestic relations, as the same has been, or shall hereafter be, finally determined by the Supreme Court of the United States, shall be respected by all good citizens, and enforced with promptness and fidelity by every branch of the General Government.[39]

Unsatisfied with the effort at compromise, and having been instructed by their state to withdraw from the convention if its demands were not met, fire-breather William Yancey and the Alabama delegation withdrew from the convention as the results of the vote on the platform was announced. Following the Alabama delegates out of the convention were delegates from Mississippi, Louisiana, South Carolina, Florida, Georgia, Arkansas, and Delaware.[40]

The convention leadership decided that two-thirds of the *entire* original convention was required to nominate a candidate. Thus, the withdrawal of delegates did not make the nomination of a candidate any easier. Under these circumstances, the successful nomination of Douglas would require virtual unanimity among the remaining delegates. While Douglas had the support of a majority of the remaining delegates, he did not have support of two-thirds of the entire original convention. Thus, no nomination was made in Charleston. Those remaining in attendance decided that the convention would reconvene in Baltimore on 18 June 1860, in an effort to secure a nomination. In the meantime, those who withdrew from the convention agreed to meet in Richmond, Virginia on 11 June 1860. Closing the door on the possibility of party reunion, South Carolina and Florida permitted their states' delegations to attend the Richmond convention only.[41]

As the regular convention reconvened in Baltimore, controversy arose over who would be authorized to be seated in the convention. Delegates from Louisiana and Alabama were commissioned by their states to participate in both the regular Democratic convention in Baltimore and the

Southern Democratic convention in Richmond, but members of the Baltimore Convention refused to allow them to participate in the regular convention. This refusal precipitated the withdrawal of delegates from 20 states. The rump convention (composed of the delegates who did not withdraw) was finally able to nominate Douglas on the Democratic ticket, while the withdrawn and refused delegates from the Baltimore Convention met and nominated John Breckenridge, James Buchanan's vice president from Kentucky, as a candidate for president on the Southern Democratic ticket. Awaiting the result of the Baltimore Convention, the Richmond convention affirmed Breckenridge's nomination.

This split in the Democratic Party established and illuminated the battle lines between North and South and helped to aggravate the already tense relationship between the sections. The split in the Democratic Party, however, was neither a necessary nor a sufficient condition of the election of Lincoln. Abraham Lincoln and the Republican Party enjoyed a strategic concentration of support in enough states to win a majority in the Electoral College in 1860, even though he polled less than 40 percent of the vote nationally. Former Whigs in the North who were "resistant to supporting any Democrat"[42] played a central role in Republican victory. Seymour Martin Lipset credited the victory of the Republican Party in the North to the fact that "all northern anti-Democratic votes were gathered together under one party for the first time since the Whig victory of 1848."[43] That is, this victory did not suggest a sea change in Northern opinion; rather, circumstances simply happened to be fortuitous for the Republican Party.

GOVERNOR GIST PLUMBED THE DEPTH OF SOUTHERN SENTIMENT

The movement for secession began in earnest in the fall of 1860, when South Carolina's governor, William Gist, wrote a series of letters to Deep South and Upper South governors—asking them what they would do in the event of a Lincoln victory and informing them of the path South Carolina would take if the Republican was to win. On 5 October 1860, Gist wrote letters to the governors of North Carolina, Louisiana, Mississippi, Georgia, Alabama, and Florida. Gist's brother, appropriately named States Rights Gist, delivered them.

These letters were both an effort to mobilize support for secession and an effort to plumb the depths of radicalism in the other states. Unfortunately, many of the letters are either not possessed by public archives or were destroyed; but given the wording of the responses he received, each letter seems to have been identical. I refer here to the letter Governor Gist sent to Governor Moore of Louisiana in order to provide an illustration of the sentiments they contained. Gist wrote:

It is the desire of South Carolina that some other State should take the lead, or at least move simultaneously with her. She will unquestionably call a convention as soon as it is ascertained that a majority of the electors will support Lincoln. If a single State secedes, she will follow her. If no other State takes the lead, South Carolina will secede (in my opinion) alone, if she has any assurance that she will soon be followed by another or other States; otherwise it is doubtful.[44]

This letter provides a perfect enunciation of the preference structure of most political elites in South Carolina. Their first hope was that another state would take the lead. If this was not possible, they hoped that another state (or group of states) would act in concert with South Carolina. Third, as a last resort, if South Carolina had assurances that another state would soon follow, South Carolina would secede alone. This signaled the state's willingness to take a calculated risk; the state could, after all, never be certain of the reaction other states would have to its secession. This represented a new strategy on the part of South Carolina. That the state was willing to accept this risk virtually assured the establishment of a Southern Confederacy. According to Governor Gist, South Carolina needed nothing more than the assurance that one state would follow in order to bring about the state's secession.

The responses that poured in during the following weeks ranged from somewhat encouraging to devastatingly discouraging. Governors John Ellis of North Carolina, Thomas Moore of Louisiana, and Joseph E. Brown of Georgia wrote that secession would not and should not follow the election of Lincoln. Governors John J. Pettus of Mississippi, A.B. Moore of Alabama, and M.S. Perry of Florida wrote that while they would not secede alone, they would be influenced by the actions of one or more other states. Given the importance of these letters to the eventual realization of secession, I would like to quote the responses from each governor at length.

From John W. Ellis of North Carolina:

Upon the whole I am decidedly of the opinion that a majority of our people would not consider the occurrence of the event referred to [the election of Lincoln] as sufficient grounds for dissolving the union of the States. For which reason I do not suppose that our legislature, which will meet on the 19th prox., will take any steps in that direction—such, for instance, as the calling of a convention.[45]

Governor Ellis did, however, state that he "could not in any event assent to, or give my aid to, a political enforcement of the monstrous doctrine of coercion."[46] Thus, even absent a guarantee that this state would immediately follow South Carolina out of the Union, there was some cause for optimism about the eventual consequences of South Carolina's secession.

Thomas O. Moore of Louisiana wrote:

> I shall not call a convention in this state, if Lincoln is elected, because I have no power or authority to do so . . .
>
> Even if that deplorable event shall be the result of the coming election, I shall not advise the secession of my State, and I will ass[ume] I do not think the people of Louisiana will ultimately decide in favor of that course. I will recommend that Louisiana meet her sister slaveholding States in council to consult as to the proper course to be pursued, and endeavor to effect a complete harmony of action. I fear that this harmony of action, so desirable in so grave an emergency, cannot be effected. Some of the cotton States will pursue a more radical policy than will be palatable to the Border States, but this only increases the necessity of convening the consultative body of which I have spoken. I believe in the right of secession for just cause, of which the sovereignty itself must be the judge. If, therefore, the general government shall attempt to coerce a state, and forcibly attempt [to prevent] the exercise of this right, I should certainly sustain the State in such a contest . . .
>
> The recommendation of such a body assembled [a southern convention] in such a crisis must necessarily carry great weight, and if subsequently ratified and adopted by each state by proper authority, will present the south in united and harmonious action.[47]

John J. Pettus of Mississippi wrote:

> Our friends in this state are willing to do anything they may have the power to do to prevent the State from passing under the black Republican Yoke. Our people know this and seem to approve such sentiment, yet I do not believe Mississippi can move alone.
>
> I will call our legislature in extra session as soon as it is known that the black Republicans have carried its election. I expect Mississippi will ask a council of southern States, and if that council advises secession, Mississippi will go with them. If any state moves, I think Mississippi will go with her.[48]

Joseph E. Brown of Georgia wrote, "Should the question be submitted to the people of Georgia, whether they would go out of the Union on Lincoln's election without regard to the action of other States, my opinion is they would determine to wait for an overt act."[49] Brown did, however, indicate that the "action of other States may greatly influence the action of the people of this State."[50]

A.B. Moore of Alabama wrote:

> My opinion is that the election of Lincoln alone is not sufficient cause for a dissolution of the Union; but that fact when taken in connection

with the avowed objects and intentions of the party whose candidate he is, and the overt acts already committed by that party in nullifying the fugitive slave law, and the enactment of personal liberty bills in many of the non-slave holding States, with other acts of like kind, is sufficient cause for dissolving every tie which binds the southern States to the Union.

It is my opinion that Alabama will not secede alone but if two or more States will cooperate with her she will secede with them; or if South Carolina or any other southern State should go out alone and the Federal Government should attempt to use force against her, Alabama will immediately rally to her rescue.

Should Lincoln be elected I shall certainly call a convention under the provisions of the resolutions of the last general assembly of the State. The convention cannot be convened earlier than the first Monday in February next . . . I regret that earlier action can not be had, as it may be a matter of much importance that all the States that may determine to withdraw from the Union should act before the expiration of Mr. Buchanan's terms of service.[51]

M.S. Perry of Florida wrote:

We are in the midst of grave events, and I have industriously sought to learn the public mind in this State in the event of the election of Lincoln, and am proud to say Florida is ready to wheel into line with the gallant Palmetto State or any other cotton State or States in any course which she or they may in their judgment think proper to adopt, looking to the maintenance of the rights, interests, honor, and safety of the south. Florida may be unwilling to subject herself to the charge of temerity or immodesty by leading off, but will most assuredly cooperate with or follow the lead of any cotton state which may secede. Whatever doubts I may have entertained upon this subject have been entirely dissipated by the recent elections in this state.

Florida will most unquestionably call a convention as soon as it is ascertained that a majority of the electors favor the election of Lincoln, to meet most likely upon a day to be suggested by some other state.[52]

Three of the six governors' responses were not encouraging for radical South Carolina, but three others were at least moderately encouraging, with Florida's governor promising that his state would "follow the lead of any cotton state which may secede" and the governor of Mississippi claiming that "If any state moves, I think Mississippi will go with her." While Gist may not have received the full support of perhaps the most important state of the Deep South, Georgia, he did get enough assurance to convince himself and his state that if they led the secession movement, their actions would be followed in sequence by at least one or two other states, which would set in motion a chain of events that would lead (Gist hoped) to the secession of all (or at least most) of the other states of the South. Furthermore, Brown of Georgia indicated that "the action of other States may greatly influence the action of the people" of Georgia. This statement appeared to leave open the possibility that the unilateral secession of South Carolina could prompt the secession of even Georgia.

Despite the encouraging news received from some of the states, Gist received no assurance that his first preference, that another state take the lead, would be realized; however, he did receive enough promises of a sequential exit, upon which a forward movement could be based.[53] South Carolinians became resigned to the fact that their state would lead, but they also knew that, even if no state followed South Carolina, their state would be protected by the non-seceding Southern states in the event that the federal government would attempt to coerce South Carolina. For a South Carolinian attempting to map out a strategy of secession, the promise to resist coercion was almost as important as the promise to secede.

The conditions outlined by Rutledge in 1851 were still largely present; that is, many were convinced that, even if no state immediately followed South Carolina out of the Union, any attempt at coercing South Carolina would effectively dissolve the Union between the states. The failure to promise to initiate secession or cooperatively secede, coupled with the promise to resist coercion, convinced South Carolinian political elites that the best—and perhaps the only—possibility of creating a Southern Confederacy lay in its actions alone.

THE *MERCURY* PLAN

The Charleston *Mercury* newspaper was owned and controlled by the radical Rhetts. The *Mercury* was, in many respects, a leader of opinion in South Carolina—at least among South Carolinian radicals. During the first secession crisis, the *Mercury* advocated the unilateral secession of South Carolina from the Union. Prior to the presidential election of 1860 and the convening of South Carolina's legislature in special session, the *Mercury* proposed a plan of action for both the legislature and the state. The main purpose of this plan was to convince the legislature to call an early convention. The papers proposed 22 and 23 November 1860, as the dates of election and 15 December 1860, as the date for the convention to meet.[54] Such an early convention would mean unilateral secession, and unilateral secession would mean the eventual creation of a Southern Confederacy.

The *Mercury* argued that the "issue before the country is the extinction of slavery." The state had to act and act alone, but the paper believed that "Co-operation will follow the action of any State." South Carolina had to act quickly, the *Mercury* argued, because the "course of our Legislature will either greatly stimulate and strengthen, or unnerve the resistance elements of the whole South." Moreover, the paper attempted to convince

Table 4.2 Popular Vote in the 1860 Presidential Election, by State

Free States	Lincoln	Douglas	Breckinridge	Bell	Total Vote	winner %	Electors
California	39,173	38,516	34,334	6,817	118,840	33	4
Connecticut	43,972	15,522	14,641	3,291	77,426	56.8	6
Illinois	172,161	160,215	2,404	4,913	339,693	50.7	11
Indiana	139,033	115,509	12,295	5,306	272,143	51.1	13
Iowa	70,409	55,111	1,048	1,748	128,316	54.9	4
Maine	62,811	26,693	6,368	2,046	97,918	64.1	8
Massachusetts	106,353	34,372	5,939	22,331	168,995	62.9	13
Michigan	88,480	65,057	805	405	154,747	57.2	6
Minnesota	22,069	11,920	748	62	34,799	63.4	4
New Hampshire	37,519	25,881	2,112	441	65,953	56.9	5
New Jersey*	58,324	30,000	30,000	2,801	121,125	48.2	7
New York	353,804	203,329	50,000	50,000	657,133	53.8	35
Ohio	231,610	187,232	11,405	12,194	442,441	52.3	23
Oregon	5,270	3,951	5,006	183	14,410	36.6	3
Pennsylvania	268,030	78,871	100,000	12,776	459,677	58.3	27
Rhode Island	12,244	4,000	1,000	2,707	19,951	61.4	4
Vermont	33,808	6,849	218	1,969	42,844	78.9	5
Wisconsin	86,110	65,021	888	161	152,180	56.6	5
Total	1,831,180	1,128,049	279,211	130,151	3,368,591	54.4	183
Slave States							
Alabama	no ticket	13,651	48,831	27,875	90,357	54	9
Arkansas	no ticket	5,227	28,732	20,094	54,053	53.2	4
Delaware	3,815	1,023	7,337	3,864	16,039	45.7	3
Florida	no ticket	367	8,543	5,437	14,347	59.5	3
Georgia	no ticket	11,590	51,889	42,886	106,365	48.8	10
Kentucky	1,364	25,651	53,143	66,058	146,216	45.2	12
Louisiana	no ticket	7,625	22,681	20,204	50,510	44.9	6
Maryland	2,294	5,966	42,482	41,760	92,502	45.9	8
Mississippi	no ticket	3,283	40,797	25,040	69,120	59	7
Missouri	17,028	58,801	31,317	58,372	165,518	35.5	9
North Carolina	no ticket	2,701	48,539	44,990	96,230	50.4	10
South Carolina			No popular vote				8
Tennessee	no ticket	11,350	64,209	69,274	144,833	47.8	12
Texas	no ticket	no ticket	47,548	15,438	62,986	75.5	4
Virginia	1,929	16,290	74,323	74,681	167,223	44.7	15
Total	26,430	163,525	570,871	515,973	1,276,799		120

152/303 to win
Source: Richard McPherson. 1865. The Political History of the United States of America *during the Great Rebellion. Philp & Solomons: Washington, D.C., page 1.*
*New Jersey gave 3 electors to Douglas and 4 to Lincoln.

South Carolinians that the institutional impediments to cooperative secession made unilateral secession not only necessary, but also consistent with the South Carolinian interpretation of the Union: "These States are separate sovereignties, each must act separately." In other words, South Carolinians should not be unnerved by the need to secede unilaterally.

In its endeavor to convince its reading public to support its plan, the *Mercury* offered six arguments in favor of early unilateral secession. First, the agricultural products of the South were about to go on the market; seceding at this moment would give South Carolina a great deal of leverage over both the North and the rest of the world. Second, immediate action would reduce the economic consequences of insecurity. Third, acting quickly would provide an important demonstration effect for the rest of the South once they had determined what path to follow in this crisis. Fourth, South Carolina ought to act quickly, because the Republicans would take office in four short months. Fifth, the actions the South would take had to be presented to Congress and the president as soon as possible. Sixth, seceding would precipitate a conflict with the center that would go a long way towards compelling the other states of the South to secede. The author of the *Mercury* editorial wrote that, for these reasons, "prompt action" by South Carolina would "tend to unite the Southern members of Congress" and "unite and stimulate state action in the states we represent." The *Mercury* and its patrons had advocated separate state secession at least since the first secession crisis; in November 1860, with the support and guidance of former moderates, the *Mercury* plan was about to become reality.[55]

THE ELECTION OF LINCOLN

On 6 November 1860, Abraham Lincoln won 1,866,452 votes, compared to Douglas's 1,375,157 votes, Breckenridge's 847,953 votes, and Bell's 590,631 votes (see Table 4.1). Lincoln was elected president with less than 40 percent of the 4,680,193 votes cast, and virtually every vote cast for Lincoln came from the free states. Strategic concentration of Republican support virtually guaranteed the Republican Party victory in 1860. Lincoln won a simple majority in states that gave him 169 of 303 presidential electors. Including the states in which he received a plurality augmented his Electoral College total to 180 votes, bringing him a comfortable—albeit sectional—victory. Lincoln needed neither the split in the Democratic Party nor a single vote in any slave state (in 10 of the 15 slave states he was not even on the ballot) to snatch victory from the Democrats.

While it is unlikely that the split at the Charleston convention was initiated for the purpose of denying Lincoln an Electoral College majority, a small shift in votes in a small number of states could have done just that. If Lincoln had lost New York, which would have been possible with a shift of only 3.7 percent of the voting population, or if the Democratic fusion ticket had defeated Lincoln in Pennsylvania and California (as the regular Democratic ticket had in the 1856 election) the election would have been thrown into the House of Representatives. In the House, each state delegation had a single vote, which would have given the South a greater influence than its population warranted. Rhett, for one, had hoped that the election would fall into the hands of the House, so that "more justice" could guide the selection of the president than if it were allowed to be a simple majoritarian exercise.[56]

The Democratic Party had dominated the national politics of the U.S. during the antebellum period of 1829 to 1861. During this time, this party occupied the White House for 24 of 32 years and enjoyed unified government for 18 of those years. During the same period, the Whig Party held the White House for only eight years and had unified government for only two. Prior to the presidential election of 1860, it is no exaggeration to claim that the Democratic Party was the single dominant political party in the national realm. (The Republicans matched this dominance during the Civil War and reconstruction, enjoying unified Republican government from 1861 until 1875.) This election was the end of the Democratic Party's dominance in the Union and finally provided proponents of secession with an issue behind which support for it could be mobilized.

According to the classical tradition in political economy, the primary purpose of the state is to protect property and maintain the contracts that permit the free use and accumulation of property and other wealth.[57] Yet, definitions of property are not set in stone. Different states have legalized and forbade different sorts of property. The Southern economy was based on a contested definition of property and a unique household economy that sold primary goods on the international market. The continued economic viability of Southern institutions and the Southern economy required political protection for the institution of slavery. Achieving this level of protection, however, only appeared to be possible in a Union dominated—not divided—by the institution. Without overwhelming public support for, and political protection of, their property, the South would be unable to thrive economically. The South feared that a shift in the dominant forces within the central state—from a dominant party that was itself dominated by the South to a new party dominated by Northern interests—would mean that Southern property and, in turn, Southern well-being (or even Southern survival) would be threatened.

Despite Southern fears, the Republican Party of 1860 was not radically anti-slavery. It did not demand the immediate abolition of slavery, nor did it threaten the existence of slavery in states where it presently existed. Yet, none of these overtly anti-slavery elements had to be present in order to create the perception that this party posed a fundamental threat to Southern interests; the Republican Party was a threat simply by virtue of its fundamental principles. Examining the Republican Party platform from the 1860 election can provide some illumination of the political preferences of those who called themselves Republicans.

One of the first principles outlined in the 1860 platform was the approval of an idea expressed in the Declaration of Independence: that "all men are created equal; that they are endowed by their Creator with certain inalienable rights; that among these are life liberty and the pursuit of happiness...." Moreover, the platform asserted that these principles were "essential to the preservation of our Republican institutions."[58] Southerners were uneasy about the principles outlined in the Declaration of Independence because of the tension between the Declaration's assertion of fundamental equality and the inequality that lay at the base of the institution of slavery. For Republicans, "all men" included men of all races; for Southerners, the Declaration was meant only for white men. The Southern insistence that slavery was a "positive good" meant that the Declaration had to be racialized, despite the fact that this document was significantly silent on race.

For Republicans opposed to the extension of slavery, even Douglas' popular sovereignty conceded too much to the slave power. The Republican platform declared, "the normal condition of all the territory of the United States is that of freedom... and we deny the authority of Congress, of a territorial legislature, or of any individuals, to give legal existence to Slavery in any Territory of the United States."[59] Even their recognition that "the maintenance inviolate of the rights of the States, and especially the right of each state to order and control its own domestic institutions according to its own judgment exclusively" did not assuage Southern fears. Slavery's long-term survival depended not only on the continued existence of slavery in the current slave states, but also upon spreading to the common territories in order to maintain the Union's delicate political balance. Even if the Republican Party maintained that it did not wish to abolish slavery, preventing it from taking root in the territories would have eventually accomplished that very goal. Innocuous as the platform was on the surface, a Republican Party victory was as much a threat to the South as were John Brown and immediate abolition.

Southerners occupied the presidency for 17 of the 32 years between 1829 and 1861.[60] Even when a Northerner was president, the South could be confident that the bisectional nature of the dominant political parties in the Union would prevent any administration from taking action contrary to its interests. Under these circumstances, Southerners knew that congressional encroachments on Southern rights and institutions would be met with a presidential veto. Southern strength in Congress—even if it was waning—meant a president's veto could not be overridden.

Although Congress was the dominant institution of the federal government during the antebellum era, the formal powers of the presidency provided the South with a sense of safety for their institutions. Southern confidence in the institution was augmented when the president himself was a slaveholder.[61] The election of Lincoln was a double tragedy for the South: He had no Southern constituency to influence and moderate his policies, and the policies he did advocate—though not necessarily abolitionist—were conceived of as a direct threat to Southern interests. With Lincoln in the White House, the South had lost its final veto point to an individual (and a party) fundamentally opposed to the extension of slavery.

Did the election of Lincoln mean the immediate abolition of slavery? Scholarship on what effect, if any, Lincoln's election would have on the institution of slavery is divided. Some thought Lincoln's election posed an immediate threat to slavery.[62] Fogel and Engerman argued that "Hard-headed business" drove the decision to secede, because the threat of abolitionism was real and would significantly damage Southern economic prosperity.[63] According to others, Lincoln's election posed no significant danger to the institution of slavery. Those looking for an excuse to secede simply used the election to justify the actions that they already wanted to take.[64] But for many in the South, there was simply no difference between the anti-extension Republican Party and the most radical abolitionist. The only difference, if any, was timing: What the radical abolitionist would do immediately, a Republican Administration would accomplish gradually. The fears, of course, were real, but Lincoln had neither the authority nor the stated desire to abolish slavery where it existed. The Republican Party did not enjoy a majority in the House or the Senate, which, made anti-slavery policies difficult, if not impossible, for Lincoln to implement.

Notwithstanding these impediments to the vigorous pursuit of anti-slavery politics, the election of 1860 was not without dangers to Southern institutions. Although the immediate abolition of slavery was quite unlikely, Lincoln had the authority to take actions that would weaken the institution and could facilitate its eventual demise. Over the long term, a commitment to anti-extension was the best way to accomplish this, but there were also a number of short-term actions that could significantly weaken the institution of slavery.

Southern fears focused on the possibility that, through the distribution of party patronage positions, Lincoln would preside over the creation of an indigenous Republican Party in the South.[65] An indigenous Republican Party that appealed to non-slave-owning Southerners would be capable of challenging slave-owning elites for control of the political institutions of the state. Thus, even if Lincoln's election did not pose an immediate threat to the institution of slavery, the long-term consequences of a Republican administration were devastating to its long-term viability.

Southerners were particularly concerned about the appointments of local postmasters general. While he was alive, John C. Calhoun had been so concerned about the dangers posed by the content of the mail that he advocated state rather than federal control of the post office.[66] A Republican appointed postmaster general might open Southern mails to Northern abolitionist writing.[67] Many Southerners feared that allowing abolitionist tracts (pamphlets, etc.) to make their way through the mail and into the hands of non-slaveholding citizens of the slave states—or into the hands of the slaves themselves—would seriously weaken support for the institution.

Thus, the mere dispersal of patronage positions might pose a grave danger to the South.

As evidenced by the conflict over territories during the first secession crisis, the hypothetical threat to slavery posed by Lincoln's election would not, most likely, help mobilize support for secession. The hypothetical threat had to have some real urgency to mobilize support for radical action. In order to succeed in their mission to establish a Southern Confederacy, Southern secessionist entrepreneurs had to collapse the time frame of this threat to slavery. If the threat was not seen as an immediate one, the grievance felt might not be strong enough to mobilize secession. Their argument went something like this: Southern secessionist entrepreneurs believed that Republican Party policies—most importantly, the refusal to allow slavery access to the territories—would ultimately result in the eventual abolition of slavery. More free states and a proportionate decline in the number of slave states meant that the forces against slavery would eventually have the numbers required to pass a constitutional amendment abolishing slavery. What this threat lacked in immediacy, it made up for with certainty.

Thanks to the threat—both real and perceived—posed by the election of a Republican president, Southern secessionist entrepreneurs were able to reduce the range of options available to the South to protect themselves; the middle ground was eliminated. For South Carolina and the other radicalized states of the South, the issue after the election of Lincoln was a matter of deciding between consenting to the destruction of the South's defining institution (slavery) or taking action that would protect it. The South, in other words, was confronted with choosing resistance or submission.[68] Under these circumstances, South Carolina and the rest of the seceding South were forced by fear to secede from the Union of states.

AN EARLY CONVENTION BILL PASSED

As early as the presidential election of 1832, every state in the Union but South Carolina gave the electorate the power to select members of the Electoral College. Living up to its long-standing aristocratic and anti-democratic tradition, South Carolina's legislature chose the state's presidential electors. Well apart from everything else, this meant that the state's legislature would be in session to select electors once it was known that Lincoln had been elected president. This gave the most radical state of the South a unique opportunity to take decisive action long before any other state. Even before the legislature was able to consider any action for the defense of the state, federal Judge A.G. Magrath and federal District Attorney James Connor resigned their federal offices after receiving word of the election, indicating support among the establishment—federal employees—for the creation of a Southern Confederacy.[69]

Because leaders of the secession movement throughout the South saw South Carolina as the lynchpin state in the movement for secession, professional secessionists from other Southern states converged on South Carolina to give the state the assurances it needed to guarantee the success of the movement. Edmund Ruffin, a Virginia planter and a lifelong secessionist, arrived in Columbia, South Carolina on 7 November 1860. Knowing Virginian conservatism, Ruffin could not make the claim that his native state would secede from the Union immediately after South Carolina, but he did manage to bolster the argument of those who had long advocated the unilateral secession of South Carolina by claiming that the attempted coercion of South Carolina by the federal government would bring other states to South Carolina's defense—in turn defeating coercion and dissolving the Union.[70]

Although he played a significant role in precipitating secession in South Carolina, Ruffin's role was largely informal. He watched the legislature debate and pass the convention bill, but he did not address the legislature. His articles in the *Mercury* and the conversations he had with South Carolinian politicians helped to convince these South Carolinians of the rectitude of their actions. Although he left South Carolina during the convention campaign, Ruffin returned to the state in time to watch it secede. Five years later, when the Confederacy was on the verge of collapse, Ruffin committed suicide rather than live under Yankee rule again.

In the South Carolina legislature, there was a strong cooperationist presence that initially hobbled efforts for an earlier secession convention. George A. Trenholm, House member from Charleston, attempted to adjourn the special session of the legislature immediately after the presidential electors were selected and a special commissioner to Georgia whose purpose would be to facilitate simultaneous action by Georgia and South Carolina had been chosen.[71] Supporters of an early convention feared that closing the special session of the legislature without first providing for a convention would delay the movement—perhaps fatally. Trenholm's resolution was put aside in favor of a debate between those who preferred an earlier convention date and those who preferred a later one.

That South Carolina planned to call a state convention upon learning of Lincoln's election was not surprising. The debate then was not over whether to call a convention, but when to call it. The date the convention would be held appeared to be crucial to the success of the movement. Supporters of an early convention wanted it to be held as soon as possible, zeroing in on a mid-December date. Supporters of a late convention thought a January convention was more appropriate, allowing other Deep South states to have the opportunity to consider a course of action before South Carolina put them in a position to act. Likely, supporters of the late convention hoped that another state would initiate unilateral secession, or that a number of states would secede from the Union cooperatively.

Many saw a danger in seceding too early. For them, the prospect of seceding before it was certain that other states would join them was simply revisiting (and going well beyond) the mistakes of the past: The late conventioneers feared that an early convention date would guarantee that South Carolina would lead the charge out of the Union, potentially subjecting the state to ignominy, humiliation, abandonment, and unopposed coercion.

The dilemma confronting South Carolina was simply this: If the state seceded unilaterally, and if no other state joined them, South Carolina would once again be humiliated and abandoned; however, if the state waited too long to act, a conservative reaction might set in and the dream of a Southern Confederacy might never be realized. South Carolinians recognized that, first, no other state was as uniquely positioned to act early, and, second, that waiting for other states to act first would ultimately be as fatal to the movement as it had been in 1850–52. If the late conventioneers had had their way, some feared the movement for a Southern Confederacy would be killed by the contemporary equivalent of the Georgia Platform or by a general cooling of the population's passions.

Initially, it appeared that the late conventioneers had the upper hand in the state legislature. This is not to suggest that they had more support than the early conventioneers, but that the early conventioneers did not want to provoke what could be a divisive and potentially fatal fight over timing. Calls for an early convention were still quite strong. M.W. Gary, member of the state House of Representatives from Edgefield, argued against waiting for the other states of the Deep South and for an early convention, stating, "It is too late to wait for counsel with your neighbors when the destiny of our property and families are in peril. It is too late to wait for concert of action, when the blow of dishonor has been stricken."[72] Gary worried, like many others, that the purpose of delaying the convention "was calculated to throw coldness upon the immediate action of this State."[73]

After little debate, in the interest of unanimity, the early conventioneers relented, and the convention bill, calling for a January rather than a December convention, passed the Senate by a vote of 44 to one. South Carolina's desire to achieve virtual unanimity obviously played a part in the decision to support the late convention. According to professional secessionist Edmund Ruffin, all but eight of the 44 who voted for the January convention bill desired an earlier convention, "But to conciliate & secure these 8 votes, & for harmony, this later time was agreed upon."[74] As matters stood on 9 November 1860, South Carolina was preparing for a January convention.

As the South Carolina legislature was in the process of passing the late convention bill, a number of events occurred more or less simultaneously to force the legislature to reconsider the earlier date. While debates over convention timing were raging, a large contingent of Georgians arrived in Charleston to celebrate the completion of the Charleston-Savannah Railroad, the first direct rail linkage between the two Southern cities. On the night of 9 November 1860, a secession rally, evidently attended by both the Georgia contingent and citizens of Charleston, took place in which the South Carolina legislature was urged to call for a convention "at the earliest possible moment."[75] The Charleston *Mercury*, which was, up to this point, very critical of actions taken by the legislature, claimed that the public was extremely dissatisfied with the legislature's caution.[76] At the same time, the state of Georgia signaled its intention to call its own convention, a move generally regarded as the first necessary step toward secession. Perhaps the most important influential news received was that Senator Robert Toombs of Georgia had resigned his seat in the U.S. Senate.[77] This resignation helped to convince South Carolina that circumstances were progressing rapidly and that the state should move quickly, lest caution destroy the movement. At this point, U.S. Senator from South Carolina James Chesnut abandoned equivocation, proclaimed his support of secession, and promised to drink all of the "blood that might be shed as a result of secession."[78]

In reality, Toombs had not resigned from the Senate; the information received in South Carolina was, at best, premature. What Toombs did in early November was express his intention to the legislature of Georgia not to serve in the Senate after Lincoln became president. A telegraph sent to South Carolinian Lawrence Keitt officially encouraged Keitt and the state of South Carolina "to act at once,"[79] and before it was known that the rumor was false, "all hesitancy was ended."[80] Those desiring an early convention were energized and pressed forward.

All that remained for South Carolina's legislature to do was to change the dates for the convention; before it could do this, however, it had to convince those who were afraid of being abandoned by the states of the South that South Carolina's unilateral secession would be followed sequentially by secession in the other states of the South. Memories of abandonment in 1832 and 1852 were fresh in the minds of the South Carolinian leadership. Furthermore, members of many Up Country districts wanted to make sure that their constituents were informed and prepared for action. They believed that an early convention would not give district leaders the opportunity to convince the conservative citizens of the Up Country that unilateral secession was necessary and that it would be followed by secession in other states. They thought that if the state waited for a later convention, actual unanimity could be achieved. On the other hand, those who desired immediate, unilateral secession believed that delay, even of only a few weeks, was fatal to the movement and to the creation of a Southern Confederacy. For them, it did not matter if all of the Up Country was with them. This perspective was revealed in a speech given in the state House of Representatives by John Cunningham of Charleston; in this speech, Cunningham argued that it was "better to lose York District [of the South Carolina Up Country] through haste than Alabama through delay." He asked, "When they invoke us to lead, is there a cooperationist on the floor that will ask us to wait until cooperation is tendered, or will he not tender it by taking the lead?"[81]

Cunningham and the other unilateral secessionists transformed unilateral secession into cooperation. With this, the Up Country cooperationists were challenged to accomplish cooperation by agreeing to secede unilaterally. This argument was obviously successful, because on Saturday, 10 November 1860, the South Carolina House altered the convention bill passed by the state Senate, changing the date the convention would meet to 17 December 1860, and changing the date of the election to December 6. Later that same day, the South Carolina Senate approved the changes made in the House and passed the altered convention bill unanimously—though some, like Senator McAliley from the Up Country District of Chester, abstained from voting after the third reading of the bill, probably out of disapproval of it.[82] Even Trenholm, who had initially wanted to adjourn the legislature so a convention bill could not be passed, had come to support unilateral secession. As he put it, the time had come to "Acquiesce in the common sentiment of 'Immediate Secession.'"[83] With the passage of this bill, South Carolina moved closer to unilateral secession, though there were still those whose concerted action could put the movement at risk.[84]

"HAMMOND'S DEFECTION"[85] AND THE PARADOXICAL POSITION OF THE SOUTH

Given the devastation that division within the state might subject the movement to, the legislature of South Carolina took every effort to increase the legitimacy of the decisions it had made and was about to make. Part of this entailed getting prominent South Carolinians to support unilateral secession. If South Carolina's elites were behind secession, the tradition of deference to elites among the population would compel them to follow. Few South Carolinians were more prominent than U.S. Senator James Henry Hammond. Believing that Lincoln was about to be elected president, in late October, 1860, a number of members of South Carolina's legislature wrote Senator Hammond and asked him to provide them with his perspective on Lincoln's election and the advisability of secession. For these members, it was especially important to have Hammond's support, because they believed he was one of the few people in the state who could initiate an effective cooperative movement for secession that could stall plans for unilateral secession. Hammond's support was that much more important, because, despite his former radicalism, he had taken to making conservative speeches around South Carolina since 1858, including his Beech Island and Barnwell Court House speeches of 1858.[86] Hammond was the perfect candidate to take the mantle of leadership in the state, because his recent conservative speeches gave him the credibility to lead the current movement for secession. After all, if the movement could convince newly conservative Hammond of the rectitude of unilateral secession, there was no one in the state it could not convince.

For a long time, James Henry Hammond was an advocate of disunion if other states would follow;[87] now, Hammond was, perhaps, the only elite in South Carolina whose preferences shifted away from secession. It is probably no coincidence that Hammond's view on secession changed once he acquired a long-coveted seat in the U.S. Senate. Despite this, Hammond's transformation seemed to have had at least as much to do with his position in the Senate as it did with his developing opinion that the career of antislavery was waning, and, more importantly, his ongoing concern that the South was not unified enough to take any collective action, let alone secede. In his last, and potentially most important, antebellum work, Hammond wrote that he was convinced that if this election could be endured, the South would be able to remain in the Union and control it as it had in the past. Hammond argued that the South, at the very least, ought to see what a Union under Northern control would look like, given that the North had long endured a Union under Southern control.

The statement Hammond produced for the legislature was not the confirmation of radical opinions desired by the members of the South Carolina legislature, however. He wrote, "it would probably require for four years more the oppression of a sectional administration and the disaster of a second defeat, to bring the South up to the point of secession."[88] Despite his earlier position, especially in his voluminous correspondence with Virginian professor and secessionist Nathaniel Beverley Tucker, Hammond now indicated that secession should only be undertaken cooperatively. Divisions in the South over how to confront Northern aggressions did not bode well for the success of secession in the South. Hammond wrote, "Such disunion among ourselves augurs ill for dissolving our union."[89] Moreover, the perception that South Carolina was radical, and that the state was scheming to dictate the path of the rest of the South, had not abated. Because of this, South Carolina risked abandonment once again. If South Carolina were determined to secede, he reasoned, the state should at least let Alabama lead matters off. Hammond claimed that he did not regard "circumstances in the Union as desperate now and [he] would not . . . advise rash and desperate remedies."[90]

According to Hammond, the South was stuck in a "catch-22." He argued that the South should not secede because it was not unified, but if it were unified, it would not need to secede, because it could then rule the Union as it once had. Hammond did offer some good news: The trials and tribulations facing the South, thanks to abolitionism in the North, were coming to an end, because the career of abolitionism was at an end. Hammond believed the South had only to endure one Republican administration—by the end of which abolitionism would exhaust itself—and the Union would be able to go on as it had, with enlightened and disinterested Southern statesmen at its helm. All he had to do to end the talk of disunion was convince his fellow citizens of the possibility of continued Southern safety in the Union.

Hammond, however, lacked the courage of his convictions: He was unwilling to make an appearance at the legislature to present his letter; former political allies suppressed his conservative letter, and he did nothing to make his views known in an alternative medium; in addition, rather than keeping his position in the U.S. Senate, where he could provide a moderate Southern voice from a state where moderation was desperately needed, he resigned once it was known that the other Senator from South Carolina, James Chesnut, had resigned his post in preparation for secession.

Hammond's decision to refuse to make a public appearance at the state legislature and to resign his Senate seat can probably be attributed to the self-destructiveness that he sometimes nurtured and sometimes conquered. In a letter to his brother, in which he explained his decision to resign his Senate seat, Hammond likened his action to the Japanese tradition of disemboweling oneself in order to avenge an insult[91]—begging the question of which insult Hammond was referring to: the election of Lincoln or the willingness of the legislature of South Carolina to silence his views? Regardless of his motivations, Hammond's unwillingness to provide a moderate voice in South Carolina has been called one of the greatest tragedies in the history of the pre-Civil War era.[92] Despite this late shift away from secessionism, Hammond "never entirely lost hope" that the confederacy could thrive.[93]

The story of Hammond's movement away from supporting secession cannot be told but in conjunction with the attitudinal shift of Hammond's protégé A.P. Aldrich. Aldrich's attitude toward secession shifted almost imperceptibly between 1852 and 1860. In 1852, he opposed the unilateral secession of South Carolina because he believed that it would not accomplish cooperation. In 1860, the situation had transformed enough that he now supported unilateral secession because he thought it would precipitate secession in other states. In perhaps the single most important letter written during the course of the secession movement, on 25 November 1860, Aldrich wrote Hammond to explain why his conservative letter to the state legislature had to be suppressed, and why secession had to be started by the few in South Carolina rather than the many in the South as a whole.

Aldrich wrote to Hammond that he had showed the letter to four of his fellow politicians, including Governor Gist. Gist recommended against publishing or revealing the contents of the letter in any way. Aldrich himself was convinced that "the publication would have been serious injury to [Hammond], and might have had the effect of organizing an ineffectual opposition to the secession movement."[94] Aldrich was convinced that Hammond was simply out of touch with the wishes of the state and was unaware that South Carolina's unilateral secession would be met by secession in other states, making the long-sought cooperation a reality. Aldrich wrote, "If you had been in possession of the telegraphic news that we had, I felt certain that you would not have desired its publication." Indeed, Aldrich claimed that if Hammond had all of the information that Aldrich had, "[He] would not have spoken as [he] did."⁹⁵ Aldrich believed that by concealing the letter, he acted as Hammond's "true friend."⁹⁶ Like most of South Carolina's elites, Aldrich was convinced that "the right path of South Carolina is to go right ahead in the direction in which she is now moving."⁹⁷ That direction, of course, was toward unilateral secession, which meant forcing secession on other states by accomplishing secession in South Carolina. In the quintessential statement of South Carolinian aristocracy and paternalism, Aldrich asserted, "I do not think the common people understand it; but whoever waited for the common people when a great move was to be made. We must make the move and force them to follow. This is the way of all revolutions and all great achievements, and he who waits until the mind of every body is made up, will wait forever and never do any thing."⁹⁸ This certainly describes South Carolina's previous experiences. Thus, Aldrich argued, South Carolina had to secede unilaterally and force everyone else to follow.

Hammond may have been out of step with his state, but Aldrich did not want Hammond to simply fade away; rather, Aldrich saw Hammond as the proper leader of the movement. Aldrich wrote, "men as [Senator] Chesnut, [member of Congress] Keitt, [member of Congress] Bohnam are not the men for the times, you are the man, all the States and all the South looks to you." Aldrich continued, "Here is Rhett, discoursing to midnight crowds some good things, with many undigested ideas, but he is no prophet, and people will not believe him to be a prophet. You have the ear of the state, and the sense to tell them what is right, and what is wrong, why not speak and throw off the lethargy which has kept you back so long."⁹⁹ Hammond was not persuaded to lead the movement or to make his opposition to the present movement known. Thus, the movement proceeded in South Carolina with virtually no opposition.

A COUNTER-REVOLUTION? GIST'S THREAT

Even though the passage of the early convention bill clearly indicated the intention of South Carolina's political leader to withdraw their state from the Union unilaterally, the possibility that a conservative movement would arise and sabotage unilateral secession still existed. After all, the convention still had to vote for secession, and it could be influenced by a change in opinion in the state. As South Carolina's experience in 1852 illustrated, even a slate of delegates committed to secession might not vote to secede. Between the beginning of November and the meeting of the convention, a movement sprung up, apparently on the initiative of Buchanan's Treasury Secretary Howell Cobb from Georgia, to encourage South Carolina to postpone its passage of an ordinance of secession until 4 March 1861, in conjunction with secession ordinances from Georgia, Alabama, and Mississippi.¹⁰⁰ Upon hearing of this movement from South Carolina

Congressmen Milledge Luke Bonham, Governor Gist threatened to force secession by precipitating a conflict with the federal government over the forts in Charleston Harbor. Gist wrote to Bonham that he told a prominent player in the delay movement, "If the convention postponed the ordinance until the last of February, I would go to Charleston [to] make a speech & advise the taking of the forts at once & I will do it." Any action that was intended to slow the movement was futile, according to Gist: "Tell those from other states in favor of delay; that attempt to delay action would only precipitate it in this state & force us to do what we would prefer not doing before the ordinance is passed." Finally, Gist described his plan to prevent South Carolina from re-entering the Union:

> My plan is to pass the ordinance of secession [and] send a commissioner or commissioners to the President to inform him of the fact, direct the Legislature to take the necessary steps to carry out the movement & adjourn *sine die*, without providing for any other meeting of the convention. The door will then be locked & the key lost and it will take two thirds of both branches of the Legislature to find it; if they want to go in again.

Although secession would be difficult to accomplish, coaxing South Carolina back into the Union in a new convention would be impossible, because of the level of support required to call a convention. Gist was willing to do almost anything to assure unilateral secession, including precipitating a conflict with the federal government over the forts. The resolve of South Carolinians like Gist and Bonham convinced those who wanted concerted action that South Carolina would leave the Union regardless of what other states were doing.

116-DAY WINDOW OF OPPORTUNITY: BUCHANAN'S GUARANTEE

On 6 November 1860, Abraham Lincoln was only very likely to be the next president. The Electoral College would not meet until December. Further, Lincoln would not officially take office until 4 March 1861. This gave secessionist leaders 116 days to act before Lincoln took office. The Charleston *Mercury* insisted, "Before that time all that South Carolina or the other Southern States intend to do, should be done."[101] Any action that took place before Lincoln took office would not be based on any "positive action" by the Republican president-elect, but would rather be based upon the imagined fears of a Republican Presidency. Thus, the South had a clear window of opportunity. Any effort at compromise was pointless. What, after all, could there be to compromise on hadn't even officially been elected and would not take office for months? (Efforts at compromise did actually fail thanks to the intransigence of Deep South secessionists and Northern supporters of the Republican Party.)

The peculiarities of the American political system were designed to lead to stable transitions of power, but they worked to the advantage of the secessionists in 1860 and 1861. Between November 1860 and March 1861, the South could exaggerate fears of Republican rule and take action without its being proven that their fears were exaggerated. Aiding Southern machinations was the fact that President James Buchanan and many cabinet-level officials were seen as sympathetic to the Southern cause. Even though there was a crisis in the making that could potentially pit South Carolina against the federal government, Buchanan's Secretary of War, John B. Floyd of Virginia, assisted South Carolina in its efforts to arm the state for the coming conflict by transferring arms from a federal armory to the state's armory.[102]

Further aiding South Carolina's case were the principles outlined in President James Buchanan's last State of the Union address given on 3 December 1860. In this address, Buchanan stated that he was unwilling to condone secession justified by the constitutional election of a president. He stated that "the election of any one of our fellow-citizens to the office of President does not of itself afford just cause for dissolving the Union."[103] Further, he claimed that there was no right to secession. Still, Buchanan found nothing in the Constitution to permit the coercion of a state that seceded from the Union. He argued, "no such power has been delegated to Congress or to any other department of the federal government."[104] For Buchanan, neither secession nor coercion were constitutional. Thus, while Buchanan was president, the Southern secessionists knew they could act without fear of coercion.

According to Buchanan, the North was to blame for everything going wrong in the Union: "The long continued intemperate interference of the northern people with the question of slavery in the southern States has at length produced its natural effects."[105] He continued:

> They [Northerners], and they alone, can do it [settle the slavery question forever]. All that is necessary to accomplish the object, and all for which the slave States have ever contended, is to be let alone and permitted to manage their domestic institutions in their own way. As sovereign States, they and they alone are responsible before God and the world for the slavery existing among them. For this the people of the North are not more responsible, and have no right to interfere, than with similar institutions in Russia or Brazil.[106]

This demonstrated the extent to which the compact theory of the Union and state sovereignty pervaded the Union. The U.S. had a national economy, a common defense, and a common currency, but when it came to the domestic institutions of the separate states, one state had no more right to interfere with the institutions of another as the U.S. had a right to interfere with the domestic politics of foreign countries. Despite their differences on the advisability and constitutionality of secession, when Buchanan stated that the North had no right to interfere with the domestic institutions of the Southern states, he was echoing an assertion made by Rhett in his Fourth of July speech. These statements and others like it illustrate the extent to which the compact theory of the Union pervaded the Union. South Carolina helped develop this and used it to its advantage when the time was appropriate.

Buchanan's unwillingness to coerce a seceded state provided South Carolina with a guaranteed window of opportunity within which secession could be accomplished with impunity. Taking advantage of the opportunity offered by Buchanan's promise meant, however, that action had to be taken before the Republican administration took over. Knowing the dangers of coercion and the fickleness of the population, South Carolina hurried rather than sauntered out of the Union. The states that followed South Carolina were emboldened both by South Carolina's action and Buchanan's promise of non-coercion.

THE CONVENTION CAMPAIGN IN SOUTH CAROLINA

The campaign for the convention went as expected: The immediate secessionists dominated the campaign, and the unionists and cooperationists barely let out a peep. One observer of events in a parish of South Carolina in 1860 noted, "men there simply 'could not vote for the union.'"[107] Given the radical tradition in the parishes of South Carolina, and given the extent to which slaveholding interests dominated politics there, it is doubtful that citizens of the parish would vote for the Union if they could. The consistency and clarity of the program that unilateral secessionists espoused contributed to their victory. Potter wrote:

> [T]he [separate state] secessionists were all somewhat united on one clear program; but the cooperationists represented a spectrum of positions ranging from genuine secessionism, firmly linked to the belief that action through a southern convention was the best policy, to strong Unionism masquerading as cooperative secessionism for tactical reasons.[108]

Not only did unilateral secessionists have the organizational advantage, but they also enjoyed the advantage of having a clear program behind which support could be mobilized. Opponents of unilateral secession lacked both organizational power and a clear program. They were almost completely ineffectual in mounting a campaign.

There were, perhaps, two prominent unionists in all of South Carolina at the end of 1860. Up Country politician Benjamin Franklin Perry allowed himself to be placed on the unionist ticket in Greenville in an effort to stem the tide of secession, but this ticket was announced only three days before the election. Even with Perry on it, the unionist ticket performed miserably in comparison to the secessionist ticket, which was elected.[109] Unlike the convention elections of 1832 and 1851, in which there were divisions within the state, in November 1860 unilateral secessionism dominated the state.

Perry demonstrated his fealty to his state by giving his ultimate loyalty to it, rather than to the Union. Life-long unionist James Louis Petigru never supported secession and was a unionist until the day he died. As Petigru himself sadly noted, once it appeared that secession could not be stopped, "We shall be envied by posterity for the privilege that we have enjoyed living under the benign rule of the United States."[110] After secession, Mary Chesnut, antebellum diarist and wife of U.S. Senator James Chesnut, wryly noted, "Mr. Petigru alone in South Carolina has not seceded."[111] Petigru himself famously remarked that "South Carolina is too small for a republic, but too large for an insane asylum."[112] Generally, once secession was accomplished, the few unconverted unionists remaining in the state supported the convention's actions.[113]

THE CONVENTION ELECTION IN CHARLESTON

Results for the convention election are not readily available (nor are they especially significant given South Carolina's political proclivities), but an examination of one of the districts for which there are results will help outline the forces at work in the convention campaign and election. In the Charleston District, there were 22 seats available in the state convention, equal to the city's total representation in the South Carolina House and Senate. There were 47 men in the race for those seats. (It was not uncommon for more men to run than seats available in Charleston. That there was competition for seats should not be attributed to divisions over the path to follow. Instead, this can be attributed to the desire among prominent men of the state to participate in the historic convention. Edgefield was more typical of South Carolina: There were seven seats available, and there were seven men who ran for them.[114])

The Charleston *Mercury* helped to set the terms of the contest for the convention. In an article penned by "Secession," each candidate was asked to respond to the following statements in the affirmative:

1. That the Convention, when assembled, should withdraw South Carolina from the Confederacy of the United States, as soon as the ordinance of secession can be framed and adopted.
2. That after South Carolina withdraws from the Confederacy of the United States, she would never be reunited with any of the non-slaveholding States of the Union in any form of government whatever.[115]

Charleston District elected three types of candidates: in the first category were 17 who responded to both statements in the affirmative; in the second group there were three who answered the questions, "but not according to the *Mercury's* ideas, explicitly"[116] (John Townsend, Robert Gourdin and J. H. Honour); finally, two were elected who would not or did answer the questions at all (Christopher G. Memminger and State Senator Edward McCrady). Despite their unwillingness to toe the *Mercury* line, both Memminger and McCrady supported unilateral secession. Unlike the Charleston of 1851 that supported cooperation, and the Charleston of 1832 that was divided almost evenly between nullification and union in the 1832 legislative elections, the Charleston of 1860 was completely behind secession.

The individual who received the most votes in Charleston was A.G. Magrath, a federal district court judge for Charleston who resigned upon hearing of Lincoln's election. He had been a conditional supporter of the Union who threw his support behind immediate, unilateral secession once it became clear, through the election of Lincoln, that the North meant harm to the South. Magrath's resignation did a great deal to bolster the resolve of the members of the South Carolina legislature. In the same race in which this former conservative was at the top of the polls, Southern firebrand Robert Barnwell Rhett had enough votes to be elected to the convention, but ended up running in seventh place. C.G. Memminger was in eighth place. The shift from supporting cooperative secession to supporting unilateral secession that these formerly conservative Charlestonians (Memminger and McGrath, not Rhett) experienced the central transformation in South Carolina that guaranteed secession in 1860.[117]

Much like the Charleston *Mercury*, the 1860 Association of South Carolina, formerly known as "the Society of Earnest Men,"[118] was instrumental in bringing about secession in South Carolina. The Association was constituted by "the conservative lawyers, the Cooperationists who opposed secession in 1852."[119] Members of the 1860 Association sought to take the secession movement out of the hands of South Carolina's radicals and put it in the hands of a trusted group of citizens who would be more effective at producing unanimity in the population than the radicals ever could be.[120]

The main output of the 1860 Association was a series of pamphlets that argued for the sovereignty of the separate states of the Union, formulated responses to the possibility of federal coercion, and communicated the necessity of the South governing itself. In addition to the pamphlets they distributed within South Carolina and to other states in the South, this group corresponded personally with other Southerners in an effort to bring them up to the South Carolina standard of secessionist sentiment.

It is impossible to determine the exact influence exerted by the 1860 Association and the other organizations within South Carolinian civil society. Still, the group did well in the convention elections: This group's electoral ticket performed especially well, with 13 of the 14 people on it winning seats in the convention.[121] Furthermore, the arguments used in their pamphlets were the same arguments used in the political realm to justify South Carolinian actions. For example, the first 1860 Association pamphlet was a reprint of a speech given by South Carolinian planter and politician John Townsend on June 7, 1860. In this speech, Townsend argued that the South ought not "to wait in this Union a single day after it shall be ascertained that a Black Republican President has been elected; but that we should proceed forthwith to organize a government for ourselves, and withdraw from the fatal connection."[122]

THE STRATEGY OF UNILATERAL SECESSION

The antebellum South Carolinian political ideology was dominated by republicanism.[123] In South Carolina, this meant that political loyalty was owed to the state more than the federal government, and it was consistent with those who sought the "eternal separation" of South Carolina from the Union.[124] From the moment Thomas Cooper first recommended that the South "calculate the value of the Union," a number of actors in South Carolina sought the unilateral secession of the state without any promise of cooperation from other states. The foundational tenets of the small republicans flew in the face of the received wisdom of the American republic. According to their perspective, freedom was not more easily enjoyed in a large republic, as Madison famously argued in *Federalist* 10, but in a small republic. The "vice of faction" that Madison thought would be controlled in the large republic was, according to the small republicans, actually its primary danger. The danger that Madison and other advocates of the Constitution claimed a large republic would obviate—a majority faction able to establish tyranny over a minority of the population—was the danger that the South confronted.[125] Only in the confines of a small republic—such as South Carolina or, at worst, a more homogenous South—could the vice of faction be controlled and freedom be guaranteed.

Unlike Rhett, Rutledge, and the rest of the small republicans, a majority in South Carolina (and an even larger majority in the Deep South) appeared to have desired secession for some time, but they were only willing to support it in the context of simultaneous action in the slaveholding states of the Union; that is, they desired cooperative secession or no secession at all. Supporters of simultaneous action felt cooperative secession would have two possible effects: the South would either find safety within the Union, or it would find safety outside of it. If Southern states could move simultaneously, they could successfully indicate to the North that they were unified in their demands. This unity might prompt the North to agree to the creation of a new constitutional compact that would provide more certain protection for the institution of slavery; if new constitutional assurances were not forthcoming, the united South could create its own confederacy, which would, almost by definition, assure the safety of Southern institutions. Thus, regardless of the outcome, be it new terms within the Union or the creation of a Southern Confederacy, cooperative action would assure Southern safety.

The primary drawback of this scenario was that simultaneous action required prior Southern unity: it put the protection of Southern interests into the hands of the whole South, not just the Deep South. Making action dependent upon the prior approval of the whole South would accomplish little more than a repetition of the mistakes of the past at a most inopportune time.

The South occupied a uniquely paradoxical position: If all of the South were unified behind slavery, seeking to protect it at all costs, there would be no need for secession. With a unified South, cooperative secession would be possible, but it would also be unnecessary. Without unity, cooperative secession was impossible and slavery was in danger. There was no unity in the South. There was, for that matter, no South. South Carolina found itself freed from the conservative and moderating influences of its fellow slave states. Free of this moderating influence, South Carolina was able to pursue its preferred strategy. Because there was no unity in the South, the only way Southern institutions could be protected was through the secession of a single state, and the only state in a position to take this risk and secede alone was South Carolina. By the time South Carolina seceded, there was a slight reduction in the risk level associated with unilateral secession, because the state had received assurances that its actions would be followed by similar actions in similarly situated states. While it sounds counter-intuitive, secession and the creation of a Southern confederacy was a function of division in the Southern states over how best to protect slavery.

Freed from the moderating influences of the rest of the South, South Carolina needed to choose a path that would facilitate action in states that were inclined to secede, but that would not secede alone—while also forcing the states of the South that were not inclined to secede to take sides in the inevitable conflict between the seceding state(s) and the host state. Promises to resist coercion enunciated in the letters from the Southern governors to South Carolina's Governor Gist were essential to the eventual success of this strategy. South Carolinian leaders assumed that at least the promises to resist coercion contained in these letters were true, and so South Carolinian leaders acted accordingly.

The strategic brilliance of the South Carolinian strategy was that establishing an enlarged Southern Confederacy did not require the precipitation of conflict between the North and an independent South Carolina. If conflict were precipitated, the South would rally to support the seceded state(s). If there were no conflict or coercion, South Carolinian elites believed the other states of the South would elect to secede anyway, because, in the absence of coercion, there would be nothing to lose and everything to gain by seceding. It was this fundamental belief that determined South Carolina's actions in 1860. The unilateral secession of South Carolina made sense from a strategic and tactical standpoint.

South Carolina's actions were driven by the grievances I have elaborated upon, but the specific path it followed was dictated by the strategic thought of South Carolinian secessionist entrepreneurs. Given South Carolina's unique preference structure, regardless of the courses of action followed by the center and the other Southern states, secession remained the best path to follow. As South Carolinian Congressman William Boyce pointed out, if South Carolina seceded alone, "only two courses remain to our enemies. First they must let us alone; secondly, they must attempt to coerce us . . . [S]uppose they attempt to coerce us; then the Southern states are compelled to make common cause with us."[126] The absence of coercion by the central state was an equally positive scenario, because it meant the central state conceded secession, opening the door for a wider confederacy.

THE CONVENTION MEETS: SECESSION IS ACCOMPLISHED

While the legislature of South Carolina cleared the way for unilateral secession by voting for an early convention, it was the convention that actually had to carry it out. Shortly before the secession convention assembled, John Elmore, commissioner from Alabama, and C.E. Hooker, commissioner from Mississippi, arrived in South Carolina with instructions to advise South Carolina to secede without waiting for action from other states.[127] Both commissioners addressed the convention on the first day of its meeting, publicly promising its members that their home states would secede as soon as their conventions were held.[128] Thanks to the actions of these individuals, members of the South Carolina convention felt confident that the actions of their state would be duplicated in other states of the South.

Soon after the convention convened in Columbia on 17 December 1860, a smallpox scare compelled its members to move it to Charleston for the formal declaration of secession. On 20 December 1860, South Carolina repealed the 1788 ordinance that ratified the Constitution, and, by doing so, seceded from the U.S. In typical South Carolinian fashion, the secession ordinance was passed unanimously, and the citizens of the state were not given the opportunity to approve the actions of the convention in referendum. Using the distinction discussed by James Madison in *Federalist* 10, South Carolina was a republic—not a democracy; that is, the population of South Carolina, including slaves and women (who together constituted the vast majority of the state's population) were represented, but they did not rule directly.

South Carolina's promise to defend Southern rights and institutions to the last extremity, first made in 1828, then in 1832, and again in 1852, was finally kept. What South Carolinians now needed to do was to defend their actions to themselves, the South, the U.S., and the world. They hoped that such a defense would drive the other Southern states out of the Union and prevent the federal government from attempting to coerce them. (Despite the strategic benefits of coercion, South Carolinians undoubtedly preferred that a Southern Confederacy be created without the use of federal force.)

South Carolina's official justification for its actions was contained in two documents produced by different forces within the convention. One document, titled the "Declaration of the Immediate Causes which Induce and Justify the Secession of South Carolina from the Federal Union" and written in a committee headed by C.G. Memminger, outlined the immediate causes of secession. The justification for secession outlined in this document presented a familiar argument. It stated:

> On the 4th of March next, this party will take possession of the Government. It has announced that the South shall be excluded from the common territory, that the judicial tribunals shall be made sectional, and that a war must be waged against slavery until it shall cease throughout the United States.[129]

According to the "Declaration of Immediate Causes," secession was caused and justified by Northern agitation against slavery. The compact theory of the Union made secession a legitimate response to the threats confronting South Carolina and the rest of the South.

The other document, titled "The Address of the People of South Carolina, Assembled in Convention, to the People of the Slaveholding States of the United States," and written in a committee headed by Robert Barnwell Rhett, presented a more complicated case. Secession, it claimed, was not a result of Northern agitation against slavery, but a result of the incompatibility of Northern and Southern cultures within the same government. Rhett had long believed that the American experiment that combined these two ultimately incompatible peoples was a failure. From this point of view, action did not have to be taken against the evil of Northern anti-slavery, as Memminger argued, but in order to prevent what Rhett called "the overthrow of the Constitution of the United States."[130] According to this document, anti-slavery sentiment in the North was nothing more than evidence of the Northern intention to accomplish its own revolution and overthrow the Constitution. The history of tariffs and discriminatory redistribution provided even better evidence of Northern and Southern incompatibility. As the Address noted, it was "by gradual and steady encroachments on the part of the people of the North, and acquiescence on the part of the South, the limitations in the Constitution have been swept away; and the Government of the United States has become consolidated, with a claim of limitless powers in its operations." Later, the address stated, "The agitations on the subject of slavery are the natural results of the consolidation of the Government."[131] It was not anti-slavery sentiment *per se*, but Northern consolidation that threatened—and had always threatened—the South. The remedy this document justified was nothing more controversial than invoking the rights implied by a compact theory of the Union.

From Rhett's point of view, the North and the South had always been incompatible partners in a political union, but the maintenance of a political balance between the two sections prevented one section from imposing its policy preferences upon the other. This balance between the sections had only recently been destroyed. Still, the fundamental incompatibility between the sections posed a mortal threat to the South. For Rhett, the original and enduring incompatibility between the sections provided the groundwork for secession.

Thus, while South Carolinians appeared to have eliminated most of the divisions within the state and silenced opposition where it still existed, the documents produced by the convention betrayed an ongoing division in the state; in each, secession was invoked as a right that existed by virtue of the institutional design of the state, but the proximate cause of the invocation of the right was different. For Rhett, the general incompatibility between the North and South, coming to a head in the election of Lincoln, justified secession. For Memminger, secession was justified entirely by the immediate threat to slavery the election posed. Regardless of the difference in justification, secession was the proper course of action for the state.

In 1855, South Carolinian politician, journalist, and eventual member of the 1860 secession convention L.W. Spratt claimed, in an article written for the Charleston *Standard*, "There are no such thing as masses at the South."[132] Spratt was asserting what supporters of slavery had long been convinced of: slavery was not only a positive good for the enslaved blacks—the paternalism of the institution, according to this argument, rescued blacks from their own savage nature—but it played the role of reducing formerly inevitable conflicts between white haves and have-nots. Even if a white Southerner was poor, worked with his hands, and did not own slaves, he remained a member of the privileged class in South Carolina by virtue of the color of his skin. He was white, and he was not a slave. Although confident that poor whites were content with their position, Southern elites seemed as interested in keeping abolitionist pamphlets and books out of the hands of poor whites as they were in keeping them out of the hands of slaves. There may have been no masses in the South (as understood by Southern elites), but these elites knew that the maintenance of slavery depended upon the continued support of non-slaveholders, and the presence of class-consciousness would have put this support at risk. (Hinton Helper's *The Impending Crisis of the South* was an attempt to create this class-consciousness.[133]) In South Carolina, in which about half of the white population belonged to slaveholding families, elites appeared to be successful in maintaining support for the institution of slavery among non-slaveholders.

The political leaders of South Carolina sought secession primarily in order to protect the institution of slavery. People like the radical Rhett may have had an ideological opposition to remaining in the Union. The North and the South were different peoples, after all, but Rhett had always been in the minority on the question of irreconcilable differences between the North and South and how these differences should be resolved. Without quite adopting Rhett's standard, Southern elites were concerned with their ongoing ability to maintain their slaves as property and were distressed at what seemed like the increasing likelihood that abolition would be brought about, with disastrous effect to Southern society, culture and economy.

Memminger's cooperationist views were always looked upon more favorably than Rhett's radical views. Given the clear link between secession and providing protection for the institution of slavery, and given that the benefits of secession appear to accrue to slaveholders alone, what is it that explains the willingness of non-slaveholders to support secession? Why, in other words, would the "poor and envious neighbors of the 'slaveholding lord' [vote] as he desired"?[134]

EXPLAINING NON-SLAVEHOLDERS' SUPPORT FOR SECESSION (AND SLAVERY)

Stephanie McCurry suggested that both the large-scale planter and the self-farming yeoman had a stake in maintaining Southern society as it was then constituted, because the prerogatives of mastership did not end at the boundaries established by race. Concurring with McCurry on this point, William Freehling claimed, "Although poor white males did not own blacks they loved to dominate their wives."[135] Likewise, South Carolina historian Walter Edgar wrote, "A Yeoman farmer might not be a slaveholder, but he could understand this role as head of his household."[136] Paternalistic domination of the female and children was qualitatively similar to paternalistic domination of the black slave, both of which occurred within the inviolate space of the household. In other words, the culture of master and slave did not stop at the relationship between black slaves and (usually) white owners.

The qualitative similarity between the master-slave relationship and the man-wife/child relationship can best be appreciated when one considers that South Carolina was the only state in the Union in which divorce was outlawed.[137] The wife, like the slave, was not a contractual part of the household, one that could depart freely, but an organic part of the household, one whose membership in it was determined by what white, male South Carolinians regarded as the natural order of things. Like the slave, the wife or the child could not choose to leave. When a slave was sold, organic membership was transferred from one household to another. That wives could not be sold did not alter the qualitative similarity between the institutions of slavery and marriage (in the South). Despite the fact that the life of the slave was more appalling, and that the relationship between the master and slave was outlined in law, the end result was the same: Both the slave and the wife or child were in a permanent position of dependence upon the master of the house. The yeoman farmer, the laborer, and the planter-politician all had a common interest in maintaining their qualitatively similar positions within their households.

Northern ideas of freedom centered on free labor and a household consisting of contractual agreements between equals. These ideas posed a challenge to *anyone* who had a stake in South Carolinian (or Southern) society. The people who had the most to lose (white, male adults) were the only individuals permitted to cast ballots concerning the future of South Carolina's relationship with the federal government. Not surprisingly, these voters decided to support a course of action that would guarantee their place of primacy in their households.

South Carolinian non-slaveholders were also concerned about the prospect of slave insurrection, which some argued was a sure consequence of abolition.[138] According to this common line of thinking, once freed, the slaves would proceed to rise up against everyone who had either owned them, or who had done nothing to prevent the institution of slavery from being maintained. Despite the professed confidence that slaves were content to be slaves, everyone in the South had similar fears regarding the consequences of abolition. Nowhere were these concerns more acute than in South Carolina, where a greater proportion of the population than anywhere else was enslaved.

Southerners were not unconcerned about the political implications of abolition. South Carolina was one of the few states in the Union in which slaves were the majority of the population; if slaves were freed, they would hold the balance of political power in the state. (This, of course, assumed that blacks would be given the right to vote, but if abolition were to be accomplished, what would prevent slaves from receiving political rights as well?) With their numerical advantage, political equality would put poor whites on a lower footing than freed slaves. Abolition, combined with the electoral franchise, would put free white males in the dreaded positions of dependence, a condition that South Carolinians endeavored to avoid.[139]

On 4 March 1858, James Henry Hammond, U.S. Senator from South Carolina, famously argued that every society needed "mud-sills" to do the menial labor, allowing others to enjoy true independence.[140] As long as slavery existed, even those who did not own slaves were free from menial, dirty, and dangerous work. The whites of the South were formally free in the same way as whites in the North, but Southern formal freedom was enhanced by the recognition that poor free whites were, by definition, raised above those who did menial, degrading labor. Southern whites of all economic levels were freer than Northern whites were. Furthermore, South Carolina's poor whites were not in economic competition with the slaves; however, if freed, the slaves would be able to compete for and hold some of the same jobs that the poor whites held. Thus, slave freedom was a direct economic threat to the mass of poor, free whites. Given the sheer size of the slave population in South Carolina and the Deep South, the possibility of this competition was terrifying.

Maintaining the institution of slavery also held out hope to non-slaveholders that they, too, could one day free themselves and their families from menial labor by purchasing one or more slaves and joining the slave-owning class. The abolition of slavery would also eliminate the possibility of a poor white becoming a member of what was generally understood to be the ruling class of the South.[141] Indeed, calls to reopen the foreign slave trade—a wedge issue used on occasion by the pro-slavery movement—were often couched in populist language aimed at the common (white) man, giving him the opportunity to own slaves.[142] (Some even hoped that reopening the slave trade would eventually eliminate non-slaveholding in the South, which would further enhance Southern security.[143]) In addition, non-slaveholders often benefited from the slaveholders various kindnesses, such as access to the slaveholders' cotton gin, providing them with another direct "economic stake in the regime."[144]

Finally, poor whites had reason to fear the abolition of slavery for the very real reason that the wealthier class of South Carolinians could choose to leave South Carolina for a state in which blacks would not hold the balance of political power.[145] Poorer South Carolinians did not have the means to leave the state and would have to remain even if political power were to be held by the majority of the populace—the freed slaves.

No single factor completely explains why poor, white, non-slaveholding South Carolinians supported the slaveholding class's experiment with secession, but taken together, these motives provide an illustration of why the South Carolina's non-slaveholders supported the actions that were taken for the specific purpose of defending slavery (an institution in which they had no immediate interest). While abolition would not have eliminated some of what they considered to be their property (as it would have for the slaveholders), it would have immediately threatened their way of life and their future prospects in a variety of ways. Indeed, it seems that the poorest of South Carolina's citizens would have had the most to lose were slavery to have been abolished. The wealthiest South Carolinians possessed land, homes, capital, and other possessions (apart from their slaves), while the poorest possessed only the advantage of white skin. In the absence of that single advantage, there was little else to distinguish the poor, white, male South Carolinian from the slave population. Being white would no longer be synonymous with holding political power by virtue of the electoral franchise; being a poor white would be no different from being a freed slave, with the exception being that freed slaves would hold the political power of the state in their hands.

Let us also not forget that despite its slavery and paternalism, South Carolina was a democracy, of sorts, in which a certain privileged majority ruled. A majority of this white and male majority were part of families that owned slaves. While it makes sense to consider why South Carolina's non-slaveholders would support secession, their support was simply desirable, not necessary.

CONCLUSION

The crisis of 1860 situated secessionist entrepreneurs in a radically different context than past crises. Long before the decision to secede was made, and long before the event that would justify secession had occurred, secessionist entrepreneurs had successfully established the issue that would justify secession: the perception of a real and immediate threat to slavery. For once, South Carolina's forward position in the crisis was an asset rather than a liability. But exactly how was 1860 different from 1852 (when many in South Carolina desired secession) and 1832–33 (when South Carolina asserted the sovereignty of the state, only to retreat from the brink—thanks, in part, to the willingness of the center to compromise)?

During the nullification controversy of 1832–33, two forces—one within the state and one outside the state—had hobbled South Carolina's forward action. Within the state, unionist forces (while not enjoying a majority of support) had enough support to make sustained radical action difficult. South Carolina found itself on the verge of its own civil war over the issue. For some, nullification meant secession at a time when secession was not in favor. Unionist leaders had been brought up on a love for the Union that transcended any particular law or policy—even anti-slavery. For South Carolina's unionists (reversing Hammond's famous phrase) the Union was a principle, not a policy.[146] That is, the Union was something to be maintained even when conceding it posed some risk—not something to be discarded once its utility had expired. One could not, from this point of view, calculate the value of the Union; its value was incalculable.

The second force that had mitigated the action South Carolina desired to take during the nullification controversy was the lack of support for radical action in the rest of the South. While other Southern actors may not have endorsed the protectionist tariffs of 1828 and 1832, they were not willing to go to the extremes that South Carolina was. These states did not condone South Carolina's actions, and their declamations against South Carolina were as severe as those of Northern states. Radical action was also mitigated by the actions of the center—specifically, Congress's willingness to compromise on the tariff issue. This compromise had eliminated the ostensible point of conflict between South Carolina and the federal government. If South Carolina had wanted to continue the fight, it would have had to do so over the highly contentious issue of slavery—not over the less contentious tariff. Finally, unlike James Buchanan, Andrew Jackson had determined that the laws of the U.S. would be enforced no matter what the local circumstances. Were this state to have continued its agitation, it would have had to do so without support from other Southern states, with declining support at home, without an issue upon which to mobilize support, and against the wishes of a determined executive. This episode taught South Carolina a number of lessons: First, its leadership would always be suspect in the North and the South; second, action could only be undertaken in the presence of a more serious issue, and if sustained radical action was desired, the issue must be perceived as irresolvable; and finally, a strong unionist presence in the state would make any action difficult.

In 1852, the situation confronting South Carolina was vastly different, but the outcome was remarkably similar to the state's experience in 1832–33. Unlike the nullification controversy, the first secession crisis did not feature considerable unionist strength. (Unionist forces were not absent from the state, but these forces were largely subsumed within and neutralized by the cooperationist camp.) This weakening of the unionist position meant the differences of opinion in the state during the first secession crisis were less extensive than they were during nullification. By 1852, many in the state had arrived at the conclusion that secession must occur at some point, but they were also convinced that 1852 was not the appropriate time. Thus, the state was not divided on the question of the ultimate necessity of secession; rather, division was present over the necessary preconditions of secession. The unilateral secessionists won a significant victory in the first referendum on secession, thanks in large part to the movement afoot to prevent slavery from having access to the territories and thanks to the unorthodox admission of California as a free state. As time went on, however, a conservative reaction set in, allowing cooler heads to prevail in South Carolina. Cooperationists won the second referendum on secession in 1851. If South Carolina were going to act, it would have had to do so before conservative reaction had had a chance to set in. Preventing cooler heads from prevailing would go a long way toward taking the wind out of the cooperationist's sails. Ultimately, South Carolina realized that its leadership was both necessary and despised. Selecting the proper issue upon which to mobilize action and proper timing would prove to be central to the success of the movement.

In these earlier episodes, Northern dominance in national institutions was far less established than it was about to be. Southerners even disagreed on the depth of the conflict between the sections; for some, there were no incommensurable divisions between the sections. In 1860, Northern dominance within the political institutions of the Union was reaching its apex, and the issue that would ultimately be used to justify Southern action had been established long in advance. Sincere cooperationists gradually became convinced that unilateral secession was the best way, if not the only way, to accomplish the dream of cooperative secession. Learning the importance of timing from the first secession crisis, the political actors of South Carolina guaranteed that any action would be taken immediately, which would allow no time for a conservative reaction to set in. Having gone to Virginia and failed to accomplish true cooperation among the states of the South, South Carolina decided not to risk the collapse of the movement by waiting for another state to take the lead. Thus, this state seceded unilaterally.

THE CASE IN PERSPECTIVE

The institutional design of the American state meant that, in the presence of a sufficiently strong grievance, secession would be more likely than in a state designed according to an alternative set of principles. The federal design of the American state contributed to secession in at least three ways: First, it meant that a high level of state capacity would exist at the local level; second, a high level of state capacity in the states meant the center was comparatively weak (The center did not have many functions that were considered crucial or irreplaceable by the separate states); finally, the federal design of the Union contributed to the development, establishment, and entrenchment of a discourse of states' rights in the U.S. that eventually dominated the Southern perspective on the Union. The South defensively adopted a strong states' rights stance in the face of perceived Northern and federal encroachments on Southern rights. The South was not the only region in the U.S. to adopt the principles of states' rights and state sovereignty, but it was the only region that turned the theory of state sovereignty into reality, if only for a short time; the design of the state, therefore, played a fundamental role in the success of the movement for secession in the South. Establishing and eventually invoking the right of secession was consistent with the perception of state sovereignty and states' rights.

Secession would not have been possible without a sufficiently strong grievance experienced by the political elite of the South. A variety of interrelated changes, culminating in Northern political dominance, meant that Southern institutions were no longer safe within the Union. For a group of Southern political elites, the election of Lincoln was established as the issue that would justify Southern withdrawal from the Union. With Lincoln's election, Southern secessionists established a sufficiently strong grievance against which support for secession could be mobilized. Finally, once the decision to secede was made by South Carolina, the centrality of timing and sequencing strategies came into play. South Carolina knew that there was a high level of support for secession in the Deep South, but they also knew that, regardless of the level of support among the Deep South states, none of these states would ever initiate the movement, and, as history had shown, simultaneous secession was nothing more than an unrealizable dream—the hope of which had actually crushed an earlier movement for secession. Thus, with the knowledge that cooperation was impossible and with assurances from the Deep South that they would follow South Carolina's lead (or at least defend the state against coercion), South Carolina seceded from the Union unilaterally.

It took more than South Carolina's willingness to lead to compel the states of the Upper South to secede from the Union, however. The action of South Carolina and the states of the Deep South set the stage for a confrontation between the newly formed Confederate States of America and the United States of America. It was this confrontation, and the imperative to take sides that followed from it, that compelled the states of the Upper South to join South Carolina and the Deep South in getting out of the Union. First among the states of the Deep South, and then among the states of the Upper South, South Carolina's actions played a central role in altering the strategic context for choice.

With South Carolina's secession established as a *fait accompli*, the rest of the South was confronted with a fundamentally changed decision context. Would it follow South Carolina out of the Union? Would it remain in the Union to fight for Southern rights without radical hotspur South Carolina? Would it allow South Carolina or any other seceding Southern state to be coerced back into the Union? The strategic genius of South Carolina's movement was that the South would no longer need to debate the advisability or process of secession.[147] Secession was now a fact. The remaining South now had to confront this fact, not debate its advisability. Cooperation no longer meant going through a complicated and cumbersome Southern convention to determine an agreed-upon course of action, which would then be brought back to the separate states for action. Cooperation now meant joining South Carolina out of the Union. How the rest of the South responded to this new circumstance is the subject of the next chapter.

5 The Path of Secession in the Three Souths

The inauguration of Abraham Lincoln was scheduled to take place on 4 March 1861. This transfer of power from the until-recently Southern-dominated Democratic Party to the Northern-dominated Republican Party meant different things for the various states of the Union. Endogenous forces within the states of the South made the difference between seceding and not seceding. The more thoroughly slaveholding interests dominated a state, the more likely that state would secede from the Union (see Tables 3.4, 3.5, 3.6, and 3.7). Where slaveholding interests were less dominant and where slavery was less established, secession was either more difficult to accomplish, accomplished for different reasons, or not accomplished at all.

Given the rise of sectionalism in the Union in 1860, it is not surprising that Lincoln's election was subject to sectional interpretation. For the North, Lincoln's election signified Northern victory over Southern parties and politicians. For once, the more populous North could rule without being balanced or hobbled in some way by Southern powers and interests. For the South, the election of Lincoln signified a loss of control over the destiny and institutions of the South brought on by the now unfettered hostility of the North against the South.

This chapter is organized in the following fashion: first, I provide a brief review of the relevant events outlined in the previous chapter; second, I divide the remaining states of the South into three analytically distinct categories (the early seceders, the late seceders, and the non-seceders), providing an examination of the forces at work within each section of the South, and how these forces contributed to early secession, late secession, or remaining in the Union. These categories have cultural and geographic analogs. The early seceders are the other states of the Deep South. The late seceders are the states of the Upper South, and the non-seceders are the states of the Border South. By expanding my analytic gaze, I provide a more complete account of the contours of the decisions to secede or remain in the Union and the timing of those decisions. This, in turn, provides analytical leverage that will help us understand the process of secession in other contexts, even in the contemporary world.

In the first section, I examine the secession of the states that withdrew from the Union more or less immediately after South Carolina. These six states—Mississippi, Florida, Alabama, Georgia, Louisiana, and Texas—constitute the group I call the early seceders. The forces operative within each one of these states were qualitatively similar to those in South Carolina, although planter dominance was slightly less complete in these states than in South Carolina.[1] However, while there was virtual unanimity on the question of secession in South Carolina, there was a lack of unanimity among the other early seceders. Despite this lack of unanimity, support for secession was strong enough to allow secession to take place.

The second group of states I examine are the late seceders: Virginia, Arkansas, Tennessee, and North Carolina. These states seceded only after the shelling of Fort Sumter and Lincoln's proclamation calling up of troops to quell the rebellion. The logic of secession for the late seceders was profoundly different from the logic of secession among the early seceders. Planter-politician dominance was less thorough in these states and slavery was less common, compared to South Carolina and the early seceders (see Tables 3.4, 3.5, 3.6, and 3.7). Incidence of slaveholding was considerably less widespread among the delegates and representatives in the conventions and legislatures of the Upper South than in those of the Deep South. These states did not secede because of the potential threat to slavery posed by the election of Abraham Lincoln—if protecting themselves against this *potential* threat had been the primary goal of the decision-makers in these states, they would have seceded at the same time as the states of the Deep South. Instead, the states of the Upper South seceded only once the Lincoln administration demonstrated that it was an actual threat to the interests, identity, and freedom of the South by calling troops to participate in an invasion of the soil of the South to coerce the seceded states. After Sumter and Lincoln's proclamation, the potential confrontation between North and South became very real. While Upper South political actors did not consider the election of Lincoln alone a justification for secession, they would neither provide troops to put down the Southern "rebellion," nor consent to the coercion of the seceded states. The overt act of which so many spoke before and during the secession crisis had finally taken place, prompting these states to follow the seceded states in withdrawing from the Union. Although slavery was not the issue that justified secession, this institution played a role in establishing a common identity between the Deep South and Upper South states.

At the end of this chapter, I examine the slave states that did not secede: Maryland, Missouri, Kentucky, and Delaware. Even more than the states of the Upper South, the Border States were precariously balanced between North and South. These four states were Northern in many respects; the attitudes and orientations of their populations and their industrial capacities indicated a certain "Northern-ness," but they were also slaveholding states. While Deep South cotton went overseas, the importance of Northern markets for Border South products gave these states a strong stake in maintaining ties with the North. Political and economic forces within each of the non-seceding states snuffed out the desire for secession and kept them safe for the Union. These states were so populous, and their industrial output so large compared to the Deep South and the Upper South, that William Freehling has recently argued that the failure of these states to secede and vigorously support the Confederate cause was fatal to the prospect of maintaining the Confederate nation from its inception.[2] (Ironically, had South Carolina and the Deep South industrialized, they may have been more successful in their execution of the war, but if the Southern economy had diversified, secession would likely not have been necessary and the war may never have come.[3]) Finally, the slaveholders of these states did not hold sway in the halls of these states' governments, and the institution of slavery affected a comparatively small proportion of the population. In South Carolina and Mississippi, nearly 50 percent of the white population belonged to slave-owning families. In Delaware, it was less than 5 percent. The limited extent of slave-ownership had the added effect of eliminating the fear of dependence and the fear of political dominance of freed slaves that was so common in high-slaveholding areas.

Unlike my analysis of South Carolina, in which I relied on qualitative rather than quantitative evidence, my examination of the course followed by the rest of the South focus on the available quantitative data in election results, the dates of elections and other significant decisions, and the demographic characteristics of the states. This reliance on election results, in particular, may seem peculiar—especially because the story of South Carolina's secession was told with relatively few such results. As I pointed out in earlier chapters, the vast majority of political positions in South Carolina were made by legislative appointment, not by election. Compared to other states in the Union, there were simply fewer elections in South Carolina. Second, given the lack of two-party competition within South Carolina and the relative unanimity on fundamental issues among the population and politicians of South Carolina, the election results that do exist for South Carolina are essentially meaningless. In general, the elections that did take place are not significant because they do not represent two or more divergent perspectives vying for popular support. Finally, uncontested elections were common in South Carolina. Thus, even when there was an election, there was usually no particularly useful data to be examined. For example, more than 66 percent of all elections to the House of Representatives in the state of South Carolina between 1824 and 1860 were uncontested.[4] With few exceptions, the same is true of other elections held within the state. Political elites, who were also the state's economic elite, selected who would run for office, and the electorate had only to ratify that decision.

This distinctive characteristic of South Carolinian politics demonstrates the extent to which South Carolina had achieved virtual unanimity of opinion on political questions and the extent to which the political elites were the sole movers of politics within the state. Unlike South Carolina, election results in the other states are significant, first, because, they were widely contested, and, second, because there is a connection between votes cast for Southern Democratic presidential nominee John C. Breckenridge and support for secession. McCrary, et. al, wrote, "two thirds of the secessionist vote came directly from Breckenridge supporters."[5] Thus, examining the extent of support for Breckenridge may help to account for the support (or lack thereof) for secession in the convention elections that eventually took place in many of the states of the South. It is, therefore, imperative to make use of the widely available election results for elections in the pre-secession South.

THE EARLY SECEDERS

The factors contributing to secession among the early seceders were similar to the factors operating within South Carolina. The states of the Deep South were institutionally similar to South Carolina in the extent of the power of the legislature, the weakness of the governor, and, most importantly, the strength of the slaveholding interests.[6] In each there were strong—even overwhelming—pressures to secede once proper justification could be made of it. Despite a range of similarities, these states differed from South Carolina in that they were not willing to lead the movement for secession.

As with South Carolina, the fundamental factor influencing the decision of the early seceders was the threat the election of Lincoln posed to the institution of slavery, which, in turn, was a threat to the inviolable household of the slaveholders and to the slaveholders' political supremacy. Save for the fact that the other states of the Deep South were unable to initiate the secession movement, the landscape of secession among the early seceders looked very much like the landscape of secession in South Carolina. But their task was considerably easier than that of South Carolina. South Carolina took the lead; the early seceders merely followed. When states of the Deep South did secede, they did so because of the threat to slavery and because South Carolina paved the way, altering the strategic context in which these states made their decisions.

MISSISSIPPI

Mississippi was the second state to secede from the Union. It was on the forefront of the fight for Southern rights for a long time, although it never went to the same extremes as South Carolina. While Mississippi opposed South Carolina's actions during the nullification crisis,[7] it was a leading force behind the Nashville Convention, and it was one of the few states to send a full, regular delegation to the convention.[8] Mississippi even made preparations for a state convention during the latter crisis, but a late convention date was ultimately decided upon—much to the chagrin of South Carolinian secessionists.⁹ Thanks to the passage of the Georgia Platform, the possibility of cooperative secession had passed; only the most foolhardy state would have considered unilateral secession after December 1850. As the agitation surrounding the compromise measures waned, there appeared to be a sea change in public opinion, moving away from secessionism, demonstrated by the 1852 election of unionist Henry Foote to the position of governor. When the Mississippi convention finally met, its members committed the state to abide by the Compromise of 1850, which had been passed 16 months earlier.¹⁰

Cotton and slavery were dominant forces in Mississippi, just as they were in South Carolina, but there were important differences. Though a slave state, Mississippi had moved much further along the road to democratization than South Carolina. Citizens were able to vote for a much larger variety of political positions within the state, and—most notably—its citizens were permitted to participate in the election of the president. Thus, not only was there a stronger tradition of citizen input into the government, but two-party competition was present to a significant degree.¹¹ Although there was strong support for secession in 1860–61, the mere presence of a two-party competition meant Mississippi would never have unanimity on the question of secession.

In the 1860 presidential election, Southern Democrat John C. Breckenridge won 40,768 votes to Bell's 25,045 votes and Douglas' 3,282 votes. But because the selection of presidential electors was given to the people, and not to the legislature, the state's governing body was not in session once it was known that Lincoln had been elected, and it was not scheduled to meet in regular session until the beginning of January. For the state to take full advantage of the excitement caused by Lincoln's election and the opportunity presented by the prospect of South Carolina's unilateral movement, Mississippi would have to make a number of important decisions before the legislature met in regular session. On 14 November 1860, Governor Pettus exercised his executive authority, calling the legislature into special session beginning 26 November 1860. On 29 November, the legislature approved a bill calling for a 20 December 1860 election of a convention that would meet beginning 7 January 1861. The secessionists won this election, with 16,800 of the 29,018 of the votes cast for candidates whose positions were publicly known. The cooperationist candidates received 12,218 votes, and there were approximately 12,000 votes cast for candidates whose positions were not known.¹² Even if every unknown vote was cast for a candidate who supported secession, Mississippi did not enjoy the same unanimity on secession that appeared to exist in South Carolina.

The debate over secession in Mississippi was a debate over how best to protect slavery. Some felt that slavery was best protected outside of the Union, where the South could manage its own domestic affairs. Others felt slavery was best protected by staying in the Union. As Rainwater noted,

"Both of these groups regarded the benefits of the Union as secondary to the preservation of slavery, which was the support of the state's social and economic system."[13]

By the time the Mississippi secession convention met on 7 January 1861, South Carolina had been an independent republic for over two weeks. Although the state was willing to follow South Carolina out of the Union, Mississippi, like many states in the South, long desired true cooperative secession; it had supported a Southern Convention in the aftermath of John Brown's raid. Once the time for secession drew near, and it seemed that Mississippi was on the verge of insisting upon true cooperation, which was the same error that had devastated earlier movements, Governor Gist of South Carolina cautioned Governor Pettus of Mississippi against seeking a Southern Convention. Gist argued, "the Border and non-acting States would outvote us and thereby defeat action."[14] Despite the comparatively narrow victory for the secessionists in the convention election, the state heeded Gist's advice: The ordinance of secession was passed in convention on 9 January 1861, by a vote of 85 to 15. With South Carolina *and* Mississippi now out of the Union, the conceit that unilateral secession equaled cooperation had become a reality.

FLORIDA

In 1860, Florida was a minor state playing a minor role in national politics. Among the slave states, Florida's population was larger than Delaware's alone. Typical of other Southern states, Florida representatives supported the elements of the Compromise of 1850 that were favorable to the South and opposed the elements that were favorable to the North. Generally, though, political actors in this state desired to get beyond the divisiveness of the debate over the compromise and agreed to support its principles.[15] Florida sent delegates to the Nashville Convention, but only in an unofficial capacity.[16]

Perhaps due to its small population or its shorter history, or because it sits on the geographic periphery of the U.S., there was little interest in Florida's actions. The path of Florida was not looked at with the same interest as the path of Georgia or Virginia. There was little doubt that Florida would follow South Carolina out of the Union; indeed, in his reply to Governor Gist's letter, Florida's governor was the *only* governor to claim that the secession of a single state was a sufficient condition for the secession of Florida. With South Carolina and Mississippi already outside the Union, it was virtually inconceivable that Florida would remain in the Union.

Like Mississippi, and, in fact, like every other state of the South, Florida had moved further along the road to democratization than had South Carolina. Florida gave the selection of members of the Electoral College to the voting population of the state, which helped to establish and maintain two-party competition within the state. Traditionally, the second party was the

Whig Party, but in the 1860 presidential election, the Constitutional Union Party (the most recent incarnation of the Whig Party) played that role. The existence of two-party competition in Florida meant that Florida, like Mississippi and unlike South Carolina, would not enjoy unanimity on the question of secession.

Like the other states of the Deep South, Floridians cast their ballot overwhelmingly for the Southern Democratic candidate, John C. Breckenridge, giving him all of the state's presidential electors. Although the Whig Party had virtually no chance to win, it still garnered substantial support in the presidential election getting 4,736 votes to Breckenridge's 8,157 votes.[17] Without the obligation to select presidential electors, the Florida legislature would not meet in regular session until 26 November 1860. This proved to be early enough to take advantage of public excitement over the outcome of the election. On 30 November 1860, the legislature passed a bill calling for a convention election to be held on 22 December 1860, for a convention to meet beginning 3 January 1861. Historian David Potter claimed that support for cooperationist candidates in the convention election was between 36 percent and 43 percent.[18] Despite this strong showing by cooperationist forces, on 10 January 1861, a mere one day after Mississippi's ordinance of secession was passed, and more than 20 days after South Carolina's ordinance was passed, the Florida convention adopted an ordinance of secession by a lopsided vote of 62 to 7.

ALABAMA

Though radical compared to the states of the Upper and Border South, Alabama was never as radical as South Carolina. South Carolina's effort at nullifying federal tariffs was supported by a small proportion of Alabama's population, but it never enjoyed the same level of support there as it did in South Carolina.[19] During the crisis in 1850, Alabama ultimately decided to affirm the principles of the Georgia Platform, declaring that the Compromise of 1850 was sufficient to warrant continued membership in the Union.[20] Further encroachments on Southern rights would be necessary if secession were ever to be accomplished. Through the late antebellum period, support for unionism in Alabama, although not overwhelming, was significant. It was the continued presence of this unionism that made it difficult for those like Alabama secessionist William Yancey to realize the goal of unilateral secession. Even as the election of Lincoln appeared certain, unionism remained a significant force.[21]

Although South Carolina had the distinction of being the first state to secede, Alabama made the first formal call for a convention in the likely event that a Republican was elected to the presidency in 1860. In December 1859, the State of Alabama's Senate Committee on Federal Relations passed a resolution that declared that, if the Republican Party candidate were elected president by the North, a convention of the state would be assembled "to consider, determine, and do whatever in the opinion of said convention the rights, interests, and honor of the State of Alabama require to be done for their protection."[22] The convention law passed both houses of the state legislature and received the governor's approval on 24 February 1860. But by the time it was clear that Lincoln was to be the next president, the state backed down from what would have been an action in advance of even South Carolina, justifying its pause on a technicality.[23] Although there was a national election on 6 November 1860, in which Lincoln was clearly victorious, Alabama's governor claimed that the election would not take place constitutionally until members of the Electoral College cast their ballots more than a month after the popular election. Despite the fact that it backed down from initiation, Alabama signaled its intention to take the election of Lincoln as a significant threat. (Moreover, Alabama's backing down from its original forward position may have actually worked to strengthen South Carolina's resolve to secede separately, which, in all probability was a necessary condition of the creation of a Southern Confederacy.)

Not surprisingly, Alabama voted for Breckenridge in the presidential election. Of 90,503 votes cast for the president, Breckenridge received 49,019 of them, or approximately 54 percent of the vote. Bell received 27,827 votes, and Douglas received 13,657 votes (approximately 31 percent and 15 percent of the vote respectively). Again, like the other states of the South, Alabama experienced significant two-party competition, with Bell and Douglas, the so-called "conservative" candidates in the election, winning 46 percent of the state's total vote. While the state had backed off from a commitment to hold a convention if Lincoln was elected, Alabama's governor declared that once the election was constitutional, the state would hold an election on 24 December 1860, for a state convention that would meet beginning 7 January 1861.[24] Despite its caution, the state made arrangements to secede, if not first, then at least early.

The 24 December 1860 election for convention delegates demonstrated significant support for unilateral secession, but the state was far from unanimous on the question. The total vote for the separate state secessionists was 35,693 out of 63,874 votes cast, or approximately 56 percent of the votes. The cooperationists garnered 28,181 votes, or 44 percent of the votes cast. This result translated into a convention composed of 54 unilateral secessionists and 46 cooperative secessionists. This proportionality of election results to convention composition can be attributed to the regional concentration of support for cooperation and secession. In general, the unilateral secessionists came from the southern and central region of the state, while the cooperationists were from the North. Historian Denman hypothesized that Northern cooperationism originated from northern Alabama's reliance on Tennessee as an outlet for its goods. Cooperative action—not unilateral secession—was the only way to guarantee the market's continued availability.[25]

In convention, recognizing the futility of opposing secession, supporters of cooperation agreed to support unilateral secession to maintain the appearance of unanimity. Moreover, events in other states of the South, and secession in South Carolina, Mississippi, and Florida, convinced those who were initially committed to cooperation to support unilateral secession. On 11 January 1861, Alabama's ordinance for immediate secession passed by a vote of 61 to 39. Fifteen of the 39 who voted against the ordinance eventually attached their signature to the document.[26] Unilateral secession in the South saw three victories in three days.

GEORGIA

Georgia exhibited typical Southern ambivalence about the 1828 and 1832 tariffs and South Carolina's remedy to them. Like most Southern states, Georgia opposed protective tariffs, believing they were detrimental to the free trade upon which the agricultural states depended. Still, this state saw nullification as "rash and revolutionary."[27] They condoned neither the tariffs nor the remedy proposed by South Carolina.[28] This ambivalence came out again during the 1850 crisis. Playing perhaps the most important role in the crisis, at the end of 1850, the state convention of Georgia passed the Georgia Platform, which effectively demobilized secessionist sentiment in the South. This platform stated that while Georgia would adhere to the Compromise of 1850, it would meet further encroachments on Southern rights with vigorous opposition—with "a disruption of the Union," if necessary.

Conservatism in Georgia was more entrenched than in any other of the Deep South states. Turning unilateral secession into cooperative secession and a Southern Confederacy was only as strong as the least willing state; that is, the successful creation of a Southern Confederacy depended upon states less committed to secession than South Carolina. The momentum for secession seen in December 1860 and January 1861 could easily be stalled by the caution of a single state. If there was one state that could produce a meaningful and significant pause in the process of secession, it was Georgia. There was no expectation that the states of the Upper South would secede during the winter crisis. The Deep South states had, after all, agreed to meet in Montgomery, not Richmond, to form their new nation. In fact, the Deep South strategy of sequential exit depended upon the unwillingness of the Upper South to secede for some time. The mass of unseceded states would provide the seceded states with a territorial *cordon sanitaire* between the North and the Deep South, as well as a moderate voice in Washington to prevent the federal government from doing something rash,[29] but if Georgia decided to adopt a conservative position during the winter of 1860–61, the movement for a Southern Confederacy would be fatally wounded. Fehrenbacher speculated, "if only three or four states had seceded, such a feeble effort might well have ended peaceably in failure."[30] Thus, Georgia's secession may well have been crucial to the success of the movement.

Divisions between unionism and secessionism in Georgia can be seen in the election results of the 1860 presidential election. Of the 106,717 votes cast in the presidential election of 1860, 52,176 (or 48.9 percent) were cast for Southern Democrat John C. Breckenridge. There were 42,960 votes cast for the Constitutional Union ticket, and 11,581 were cast for Stephen Douglas. In other words, more than half of the votes cast in Georgia went to so-called "conservative" candidates.

Although Georgia's legislature convened relatively early in the movement (7 November 1860), it was never assumed that this early convening would translate into an initiation of the movement for secession; Georgia was too divided to initiate the movement. Soon after assembling, news reached the capital of Georgia that Lincoln was elected president of the U.S. The same Georgia Platform that demobilized secession in 1850 pledged the state to resistance in the event of further Northern encroachments on Southern rights. Would they live up to their promise? If so, could the state be relied upon to commit itself to secession, as it had promised? Or would the state seek some form of resistance short of secession? At the foundation of these debates was a question of whether or not the constitutional election of a president could be considered just cause for secession.

The path Georgia followed guaranteed it would secede unilaterally. On 20 November 1860, the legislature passed a bill designating a 2 January 1861 election for a convention that would meet beginning 16 January 1861. In the election for the convention, 44,152 of the 85,784 votes—or only 51 percent of the votes—were cast for candidates supporting immediate secession. The cooperationists had 41,632 votes (or slightly less than 49 percent of the total vote). There is, it should be noted, considerable historical debate over who actually won the election: In response to an inquiry, Governor Brown of Georgia claimed that "the delegates to the convention who voted for the ordinance of secession were elected by a clear majority . . . of 13,120 votes."[31] This claim is deceptive, however, because in the seceding states of the South there was a tendency for those who ran as cooperationists to support secession once it seemed inevitable in order to maintain the veneer of unanimity. Reading back election results does not provide a good indication of the level of support for unilateral secession or cooperation during the campaign. Despite this controversy, Georgia's convention adopted an ordinance of secession on 19 January 1861, by a comparatively close vote of 166 to 130.[32] The most important piece of the Deep South puzzle had been put in place. What remained to be seen now was if the remaining states of the Deep South would follow suit.

LOUISIANA

Thanks to its commercial ties to the North, and to New York in particular, Louisiana was regarded as one of the more conservative states of the Deep South. These commercial connections may have made Louisiana loath to play an active role during the crisis in 1850. Louisiana was one among a handful of Southern states not to send any representatives to the Nashville Convention in 1850. This did, however, not prevent the newly elected governor of Louisiana at this time, Joseph Marshall Walker, from threatening to disrupt the Union if the federal government trampled Southern Rights.[33]

In the 1860 presidential election, of the 50,510 votes cast, 22,681 (or 45 percent) were for Southern Democratic candidate John C. Breckenridge. The Constitutional Union candidate was in a close second with 20,204 votes, while Stephen Douglas received 7,625 votes. As with Georgia, over half of all votes cast were for "conservative" candidates.

On 11 December 1860, the state legislature passed a bill calling for a 7 January 1861 election for a convention to meet beginning 23 January 1861. The popular vote for the convention was 20,214 votes (or 52 percent) for secessionist candidates and 18,451 votes (or 48 percent) for cooperationist candidates. Despite the relative closeness of the vote, events in other states had, by this time, made unilateral secession inevitable. Dumond noted that it was "of little consequence, so far as secession was concerned, which set of candidates received the majority of votes."[34] Cooperation originally meant some form of Southern Convention, but thanks to the unilateral secession of South Carolina—followed by Mississippi, Florida, Alabama, and Georgia—cooperation now meant unilateral secession. By this time, to fail to secede unilaterally was to fail to cooperate. Despite the close presidential vote and the close convention vote, under these new circumstances, the convention voted to secede from the Union by a lopsided vote of 113 to 17.

TEXAS

Although Texas was one of the few states to actually send a full slate of delegates to the Nashville Convention, and despite the fact that a portion of the passed compromise measures constituted a reduction of Texas' territory, the citizens and leadership of the state supported the Compromise of 1850.[35] Then-Senator Sam Houston of Texas was one of only a few who voted for all elements of the compromise. Houston was governor of the state during the 1860–61 secession crisis, and in spite of his steadfast unionism, the state managed early secession from the Union.

In the 1860 presidential election, Texans voted overwhelmingly for the Breckenridge ticket. The Republican and Northern Democratic tickets of Lincoln and Douglas did not even appear on the ballot. Breckenridge received 47,548 of the 62,986 votes cast, or a full 75.5 percent of the vote.[36]

Being on the periphery of the Union, the path of Texas, like the path of Florida, was not regarded as being as important as the path followed by Georgia, for example. Still, the path followed by Texas showed the extent to which supporters of secession were willing to go in order to achieve their political ends. Up to this point, even Deep South governors who did not support secession recognized the necessity of calling a convention of the people to keep apace of events and avoid the ire of citizens desiring immediate action. Governor Sam Houston of Texas was the exception to this general rule; displaying an uncommon devotion to the Union, Houston did not and would not call the legislature into special session to consider a convention law. Secessionists, however, were unwilling to concede Houston's attempt to stall the movement. Because of Houston's opposition, Texan secessionists were forced to follow a path outside of normal politics to call a convention of the people. Asserting the right of the people to meet in convention in a number of public speeches held throughout the state, Texan secessionists declared that a convention would meet beginning 28 January 1861. Elections were to be held 8 January 1861, though some counties held their elections earlier.[37] Results for this election appear to be as inconsequential as the election in South Carolina. Cooperationist candidates were, for the most part, not up for election to the convention.[38] Thinking that the legislature would resent the secessionists' usurpation of its authority, and to put the brakes on the secession movement, Houston called the legislature into session in January. Rather than putting the brakes on secession, however, the legislature gave quick approval to the convention, stipulating only that the convention's decision be affirmed by a popular referendum.[39]

Once the convention met, it declared, by a vote of 152 to six, that it was "the deliberate sense of this Convention that the State of Texas should separately secede from the Union."[40] On 1 February 1861, after the ordinance of secession was drafted, the convention voted 166 to eight to secede from the Union. Overwhelming support for secession among the citizens of Texas convinced Governor Houston to lend his symbolic support to secession by attending the ratification of the ordinance. In the February referendum, of the 57,337 votes cast, fully 44,317 (or 77 percent) were for secession. Only 13,020 votes (less than 23 percent) were cast against the actions of the convention. Nowhere else in the South, expect perhaps South Carolina, was secession as popular.[41] That it occurred later than the other states of the Deep South can probably be attributed to Houston's opposition to it.

Lincoln saw Houston's opposition to secession as an opportunity to stem the tide of secession and keep Texas in the Union. After ascending to the presidency, Lincoln offered Governor Houston 70,000 troops to help keep Texas in the Union. Following the advice of his advisors, Houston declined the offer.[42] Although he disapproved of the actions of his state and even tried to prevent it from seceding, he was not willing to participate in coercion to keep the state in the Union.

Following the secession of Texas (the last of the Deep South states to withdraw from the Union), the momentum of the movement was spent. At this point, the Upper South, which eventually seceded, did not have an issue behind which a successful movement could be mobilized. For the time being, the pressing issue shifted from secession to the creation of a new government for the seceded states. They met in Montgomery, Alabama, to prepare a constitution and select a president.

THE LATE-SECEDERS

The Upper South had long been the home of the moderate advocates of Southern rights. The Upper South had ties to the North profound enough to moderate what, in the Deep South, had, by late 1860, become profound anti-Northern sentiment, verging on paranoia. Perhaps the central difference between these two groups of states was the importance of the institution of slavery and the extent to which slave interests dominated these states. While the Upper South states of Virginia, Arkansas, Tennessee, and North Carolina were slave states, slavery was not the critical institution there that it was in the Deep South. In 1860, Virginia had more slaves than any other state, but slaves accounted for less than 31 percent of the state's total population. Slaves in these four states accounted for only slightly more than 30 percent of all slaves in the U.S. Furthermore, incidence of slaveholding was far less extensive in the Upper South as in the Lower South. While the slaveholders of these states still held a disproportionately large share of political power, political power was shared with the non-slaveholder to a greater extent here than in the Deep South. In South Carolina, for example, only 16 of 169 secession convention delegates (less than 10 percent) held no slaves; in Arkansas, 30 of 77 convention delegates (or almost 40 percent) held no slaves (see Figure 5.1).[43]

Because the institution and its advocates were less influential in Upper South states, because the link between political power and slaveholding was less firmly established, and because of economic links to the North, the mere election of Lincoln was not enough convince the political elites of these states of the need for secession. To be sure, the slaveholding interests pressed for early radical action, but these interests did not enjoy the

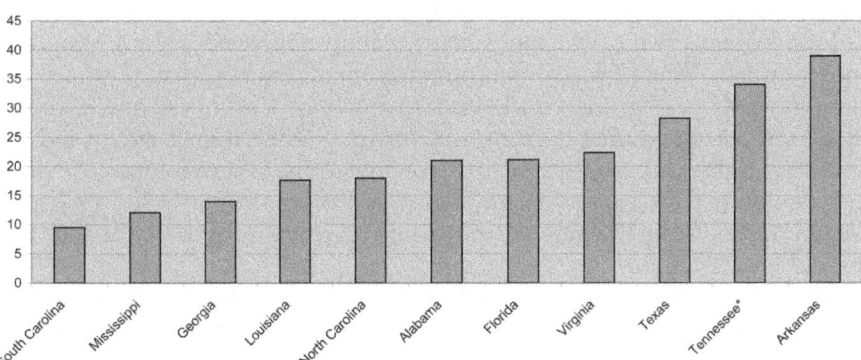

Figure 5.1 Percentage of convention seats held by non-slaveholders in secession conventions (or state legislature) 1860–61. *Secession was accomplished in Tennessee's legislature, not in convention.
Source: Wooster (1962).

near-monopoly of power enjoyed by the slaveholding interests in the Deep South; thus, these efforts were not successful. For most of the political elites, and for the populations of the Upper South states, Lincoln's constitutional election did not provide justification for secession. Where the as-yet-unrealized threat to slavery did not mobilize the population, coercion of a seceded state might. While Upper South politicians tended to believe that the election of Lincoln, in and of itself, provided no justification for secession, these states remained committed to a definition of states' rights that precluded condoning—let alone participating in—the coercion of the seceded states. For these late seceders, secession followed the imperative to take sides, not the imperative to protect slavery.

VIRGINIA

Throughout the antebellum era, Virginia occupied a rather unusual position; Virginia was to the whole South what Georgia was to the Deep South. The support of Virginia was widely thought to be necessary to any successful movement to assert and protect Southern rights. As a rule, Virginia was more conservative than the states that implored it to lead the movement for the protection of Southern rights. Virginia eventually seceded, but not on the issue that drove the Deep South out of the Union. Virginia only seceded once it came time to pick sides in the inevitable conflict between the Republican administration and the seceding states of the Deep South.

Although the resolutions condemning the Alien and Sedition Acts, which provided justification for nullification, emanated from Virginia (and Kentucky), Virginia did not support South Carolina's efforts to put state interposition, or nullification, into practice.[44] Virginia demonstrated a similar ambivalence in its response to the Compromise of 1850. It saw the compromise "as a necessity rather than as a fair judgment."[45] This state's response to John Brown's raid on Harper's Ferry merely confirmed its long-standing conservatism. When Brown's actions prompted South Carolina to send a commissioner to Virginia in an effort to convince Virginia of the need for concerted action against current and future Northern encroachments on Southern rights and safety, Virginia welcomed the commissioner (the former moderate Christopher Memminger), but ultimately refused to participate in the Southern Conference that South Carolina proposed, fearing that its goal was disunion.[46]

The two-party system remained much stronger in Virginia than in the Deep South. The state was one of only three states to gives its Electoral College votes to Constitutional Union candidate John Bell, who won by a narrow margin, getting 74,681 votes to Breckenridge's 74,323 votes. Douglas received only 16,290 votes, and Lincoln received a handful of votes.[47]

Acting on pressure from legislators, Governor Letcher agreed to call the legislature into special session on 7 January 1861. Among the legislature's first actions was the passage of a resolution opposing coercion.[48] The state also promised that "if all efforts at redress failed, Virginia would go with the South,"[49] but it was not about to take the decision to secede lightly. Before Virginia would secede, every effort at peacefully resolving the dispute between the sections had to be made. On 19 January 1861, the Virginia legislature passed a law calling for a 4 February 1861 election for a convention that would meet beginning 13 February 1861. Although proposed, the effort to allow the people to decide whether to hold the convention failed. However, the people were given the option of deciding whether the decision of the convention should be submitted to the people for ratification. Unlike the convention election in South Carolina, in which opposition to secession was weak or absent, the convention election in Virginia was heavily contested because of pockets of enduring Unionism within the state. Unionism was so strong in the western counties of this state that they eventually seceded from Virginia and formed the state of West Virginia, which was the last slave state admitted to the Union.[50] In the early February elections, the secessionists won only about 30 of the 152 seats in the convention. The question of putting the decision of the convention to the people easily passed by 100,536 votes to 45,161 votes. On the same day that the states of the Deep South were in Montgomery, Alabama forming the Confederate States of America, the people of Virginia made it clear that they would not be joining the Confederate states any time soon. Prior to Lincoln's proclamation, Virginia's convention acted with caution. As long as the *status quo* was maintained, convention members saw no reason to secede.

At the same time Virginia was preparing to hold a convention, it recommended that all of the states of the Union meet in order to formulate a compromise that would establish new terms for the Union, bring the seceded states back into the Union, and avert the possibility of war. Although the Crittenden Compromise had already failed, hopes were high that some sort of compromise could be approved. The same day the seceded states of the Deep South met in Montgomery to form a new country and the same day the citizens of Virginia voted for convention delegates, delegates from 21 of 33 states met in Washington to save the Union. The recommendations of the conference departed little from what Crittenden recommended.[51] Not surprisingly, Congress did not consider them.

On 4 April 1861 (one month after Abraham Lincoln had taken office, and two months after the CSA was formed), Lewis Harvey, a pre-proclamation secessionist, moved that the convention submit an ordinance of secession to the people in the up-coming May elections. This motion was decisively defeated by a vote of 90 to 45.[52] After this defeat, secessionists were resigned to the fact that Virginia would not secede unless external events forced a revolution in this state's thinking, or unless the other Upper South states seceded—an event that may have compelled Virginia to leave the Union.[53]

On 10 April 1861, South Carolinian political elite Langdon Cheves wrote that Virginia "will do nothing until there is <u>declared</u> war & she has no choice but to be friend or <u>enemy</u>."[54] On 15 April 1861 the prospect of war became a reality. Three days after Confederate forces initiated the shelling of Fort Sumter in Charleston Harbor, President Lincoln issued a proclamation that called up 75,000 troops from the state militias to quell the Southern insurrection. Before the proclamation, conservative Virginians could argue that a Republican administration could be endured by the slaveholding states of the South. The proclamation not only proved that remaining in the Union was inconsistent with the maintenance of slavery, but that remaining in the Union was inconsistent with a commitment to Southern rights, honor, and dignity, and that the Union posed a threat the very principles it was created to uphold. The precarious middle ground, which the Upper South and Border South states were content to occupy while the *status quo* was maintained, was no longer tenable. As delegate to the Virginia secession convention James Dorman noted, the "issue presented is of a fight and the question simply is 'which side will you take?'"[55]

Virginia picked sides two days after the proclamation was issued: On 17 April 1861, Virginia's constituent convention voted to secede from the Union by a vote of 88 to 55. The convention's action, however, as mandated in the convention election more than two months earlier, would have to be ratified by a popular referendum. The transformation of opinion on secession had changed so thoroughly that after the ordinance passed, a South Carolinian in Virginia wrote that he did "not believe one thousand votes could be obtained in the state to remain in the Union."[56] On 23 May 1861, the people ratified the convention's actions by a lopsided vote of 125,950 to 20,373.[57] Ominously, opposition to secession was concentrated in the northwest counties of the state, a mountainous Up Country region in which the institution of slavery was not deeply entrenched.

Even at this late date, secession was driven by interests and identity tied to the institution of slavery. The proximate cause of secession in Virginia was the grievance associated with the prospect of coercion in the Southern states; Virginia did not secede in order to provide protection to slavery. With the issuance of the proclamation, Southerners, even those who initially opposed secession, became convinced that Lincoln and his Republican Party meant to wage war on the South. Virginia (and the rest of the Upper South) would not consent to this and decided to secede from the Union. Still, the Southern identity that they were trying to protect was inextricably linked to the institution of slavery.

ARKANSAS

Like many states in the South, Arkansas experienced divisions within the state between moderates, who supported remaining in the Union, and radicals, who supported secession. During the 1850 crisis, despite a determined set of actors who wished to see the state secede from the Union at this time, the political leadership of Arkansas supported the compromise.[58] Arkansas was represented in the Nashville Convention, but not by a full, regularly elected delegation.

During the 1860 presidential election, the voting population of Arkansas voted predominantly for the Southern Democrat, Breckenridge. He received 28,732 (or 53.2 percent) of the 54,053 votes cast. Bell received just over 20,000 votes, and Douglas received just over 5,000 votes.

The state legislature of Arkansas met in regular session on 10 November 1860. Given the strong divisions within the state, this early meeting did not translate into early secession. As elsewhere, upon the election of Lincoln, the state's slaveholding interests were quick to call for secession, but the balance of power in the state was not in the hands of the radical, slaveholding interests. For the majority of the state's population and political actors, the election of Lincoln did not provide a sufficient justification for secession. Still, the forces in favor of protecting Southern interests, if not through secession, were strong enough that on 22 December 1860, the state House of Representatives passed a bill calling for a convention. After some balking, the Senate followed suit on 15 January 1861. The election for the convention was to be held on 18 February 1861 and the convention was to meet beginning 4 March 1861. The convention law passed by the Arkansas legislature allowed the citizens of Arkansas to vote for or against holding a convention at the same time they elected delegates to it. This provision put a unionist in the somewhat awkward position of "opposing the convention and advocating his own election to it."[59] Notwithstanding this awkwardness, there was a strong desire on both sides to hold a convention "to express the will of the people."[60] Convention advocates won with a vote of 27,412 to 15,826. The vote for delegates was slightly closer: Unionist candidates received 23,626 votes, while secessionist candidates received 17,927 votes.[61]

On 4 March 1861, the Arkansas convention assembled to determine the state's path. In general, the convention was conservative, voting down the Hanly Plan, according to which the convention would pass an ordinance of secession and submit it to the people in referendum, by the comparatively close vote of 35 to 39. Rather than attempting to thrust secession on the people of the state only to have them vote it up or down, the convention tried a different tack. Soon after the defeat of the Hanly Plan the convention passed a motion to determine "the sense of the people of the state on the question of 'cooperation' or 'secession.'"[62] The state was to hold a referendum on secession on 5 August 1861. Arkansans did not have to wait until August to decide the fate of their state and its relationship to the Union, however. Following the shelling of Sumter and Lincoln's issuance of the proclamation, the president of the Arkansas convention ordered the convention to reconvene on 6 May 1861.

Opposition to coercion was stronger than loyalty to the Union; thus, on the first day of reconvening, the convention passed an ordinance of secession by a lop-sided vote of 65 to five. Seeking unanimity, the president of the convention asked the opposition to reconsider their vote. Four of the five votes against secession decided to throw their support behind the move. With this, Arkansas became the second state from the Upper South to join the Confederacy.

TENNESSEE: UNCONVENTIONAL SECESSION

Over the course of the antebellum period, Tennessee acted like a typical Upper South state. This state could not condone Northern encroachment on Southern rights, but it would not adopt the radical standard of resistance. Members of Congress from Tennessee tended to support most of the elements of the Compromise of 1850 and to oppose the radical factions in the Nashville Convention, desiring instead "that secession talk be ended and the compromise be accepted."[63] Political leaders in Tennessee hoped that the sectional mistrust that plagued the Union since the introduction of the Wilmot Proviso would subside; they were aware, however, that it probably would not.[64] Tennessee was caught between North and South in its devotion to the Union, but the Union to which they were devoted was undergoing a number of fundamental transformations that would alter the state's calculations.

In the 1860 presidential election, Tennessee was one of only a handful of states in which the Constitutional Union Party won a plurality of the votes cast. Of the 146,106 votes cast, 69,728 (or almost 48 percent) were cast for John Bell. Breckenridge was in a close second, with 65,097 votes, while Douglas won only 11,281 votes. Two-party competition was obviously alive and well in Tennessee.

Nowhere in the Upper South was the path of secession as interesting and unorthodox as in Tennessee. Although there were great differences in timing, almost every seceding state followed a fundamentally similar path: a convention bill was passed by the state legislature, elections were held, and the members of the convention voted, either before the shelling of Fort Sumter or after, to adopt an ordinance of secession from the Union. In Tennessee, the secession ordinance was passed, not in convention, but by the state legislature.

On 7 January 1861, the Tennessee legislature convened in special session to determine the state's course of action. By this time, South Carolina had already seceded, and the Deep South states were poised to secede. Tennessee was in the typical Upper South position. Political actors in this state did not want to secede from the Union over the mere election of Lincoln, but Tennessee was not willing to condone the coercion of the Southern states that had already seceded. Recognizing that the rights of the South needed to be protected, and that some practical measures had to be taken to protect them, on 19 January 1861, the Tennessee legislature passed an act calling for a convention of the people of the state. As in Arkansas, the law that was passed stipulated that the election of delegates to the convention would be accompanied by a referendum on the question of whether the convention should meet at all. The convention bill also stipulated that the convention's actions would be subject to the approval of the people in a referendum.

Unlike Arkansas, however, the people of Tennessee voted 69,387 to 57,978 against holding a convention during the February election. Although there appears to have been general opposition to holding a convention at this time, the decision not to do so was aided by the nearly unanimous opposition to it in the eastern portion of the state. The voting citizens of Tennessee cast 88,803 votes for unionist candidates, while votes cast for secessionists numbered only 24,749. To say the least, the prospects for secession in Tennessee appeared bleak. It was not until Fort Sumter was fired on and the issuance of Lincoln's proclamation that popular opinion in Tennessee shifted from conditional unionism to immediate secessionism. Indeed, the shift was so swift and thorough that the state rejected the convention as the means by which to accomplish secession. After receiving Lincoln's proclamation calling up state militias, the governor of Tennessee sent a formal letter refusing to allow the state's militia to coerce South Carolina and declared that the state legislature would reconvene on 25 April 1861. Once in session, the legislature proceeded in secret. On 6 May 1861, in secret session, the legislature passed an ordinance of secession, subject to ratification by the citizens of Tennessee in a June 8 referendum. On May 7, the legislature approved a military alliance with the Confederate States of America, essentially securing secession prior to the people's ratification of it.

While the citizens of eastern Tennessee continued their opposition to secession, the middle and western section of Tennessee came out strongly for secession in the referendum. The total vote in the state was 104,913 for secession and 47,238 against. Only eastern Tennessee returned a majority against secession. Although they were formally free to vote for maintaining the Union, many Union men were afraid to do so out of fear of reprisal from secessionists.[65] Given the determined action of the state legislature, a stronger Union vote may have caused conflict within the state. Thus, secession was accomplished in Tennessee on the same issue that it was accomplished in the rest of the Upper South, but in a markedly different manner.

NORTH CAROLINA: THE LAST STATE SECEDES

North Carolina was never the firebrand that its sister state was. North Carolinians tended to oppose protectionist tariffs passed by the federal government, but they also opposed the doctrine of nullification.[66] During the nullification crisis, Andrew Jackson was confident that he could, if needed, raise troops from North Carolina to enforce federal laws in South Carolina.[67] Presaging future conservatism, North Carolina was one of the many Southern states not represented in the Nashville Convention of 1850.[68] On the Compromise of 1850, this state supported the principles outlined in the Georgia Platform. North Carolinians believed that the compromise was not perfect, but that it was sufficient for North Carolina to remain in the Union.[69]

Of the 96,712 votes cast in the presidential election of 1860, John C. Breckenridge won a majority of them, with 48,846 (or 50.5 percent of the vote). John Bell came in second place, with 45,129 votes, and Douglas won only 2,737 votes.

Long after the states of the Deep South had seceded, or taken the necessary steps to secede, North Carolina only managed to make a first attempt at secession. On 29 January 1861, the state legislature called for a convention election to be held on 28 February 1861. The convention law contained provisions similar to the laws passed by Arkansas and Tennessee. In the election, the people would elect members of the convention while deciding whether the convention should be held at all. The law also provided that anything decided by the convention had to be submitted to the people for ratification.

Thanks to the initial optimism surrounding the Washington Peace Conference, the people voted narrowly against holding a convention, with 47,323 against the convention and 46,672 for (a difference of merely 651 votes out of more than 90,000 votes). The superfluous election for delegates saw a decided victory for unionist candidates. According to Joseph Sitterson, "Of the one hundred and twenty delegates chosen, forty-two were secessionists, twenty-eight conditional Unionists, and fifty unconditional Unionists."[70] As in other states, citizens of regions in North Carolina with the highest proportion of slaves were more likely than others to vote for delegates supporting secession, but these counties were still evenly divided on the question.[71] Unionist victories in the Upper South, most notably in Virginia, undoubtedly influenced actions in North Carolina. Sitterson claimed, "The election of a Union majority to the Virginia Convention strengthened Union influence, for many were convinced that the action of Virginia would determine the course to be followed by North Carolina."[72] Both states appear to have assumed that there was a way to find new terms in the Union.

In the aftermath of Fort Sumter and Lincoln's Proclamation, not to mention the failure of Congress to take up the proposals of the Washington Peace Conference, the governor of North Carolina, incredulous at the request for troops to put down the Southern rebellion, called the state legislature into special session beginning 1 May. Making his intention to have North Carolina side with the Confederacy clear, this request was accompanied by a call to capture federal forts and armories within the state. Because external events radically altered the relationship between North and South and made coercion a virtual certainty, when the legislature convened on 1

May 1861, it moved quickly to pass a bill to call a convention of the people. Unlike their fellow Southerners in Tennessee, North Carolinians felt that the state convention was the proper forum in which secession should occur. Attempts to amend the convention bill to require a ratification of the convention's decision by the people failed. The convention bill passed unanimously in the House; there were only three dissenters in the Senate, and this mild dissent seemed to have been based upon a desire to submit the decision to the people, not upon opposition to secession.[73] The convention election was held on 13 May 1861, and the convention assembled 20 May 1861. In both, secession triumphed.

Given the altered political context after the shelling and Lincoln's proclamation, political divisions within the state no longer centered on secessionism versus unionism; unionism had perished. Instead, division centered on the character of the action North Carolina was preparing to take. At issue was whether there was a right of secession or whether secession should be considered revolution (the pre-political right of the politically wronged). The revolutionists were not willing to concede that secession was constitutional and the secessionists did not believe the course of action they intended to follow was revolution. Although commonly referred to as revolution in the South, supporters of secession believed there was a right to secede implicit in the constitution, meaning that it was not, strictly speaking, revolution. Ultimately, North Carolina decided against "revolution" and instead seceded from the Union according to the implicit principles of the constitution: it rescinded the state's ratification of the Constitution of the U.S.

This tier of states held in common the view that the election of Lincoln did not in itself provide justification for secession. They were conservative and willing to wait until the Lincoln administration committed an overt act against Southern interests before acting. Every state in this tier, however, was united behind a refusal to consent to the coercion of the seceded states. They would not secede while there was no need to take sides. Once the choice was changed from the option of either unionism or secessionism to fighting against the North or against the South, however, the choice this group of states felt they had to make was obvious, and they acted quickly. South Carolina had been right all along: Any attempt to coerce a seceded state would dissolve the Union.

THE NON-SECEDERS: BORDER SOUTH STATES LOOK NORTH

The states of the Deep South had an interest in maintaining slavery that was so profound that the mere election of a president who might pose a threat the institution (by not consenting to its expansion, for example) justified secession. In the Upper South, the issue was not slavery *per se*, but with (or against) whom the states would fight once the simmering sectional conflict boiled over. The Border South had neither the same interest in slavery as the

Table 5.1 Per Capita Value of Manufactured Goods Produced in 1860, by State

State	Per Capita value of manufactured goods
Rhode Island	233
Massachusetts	208
California	180
Connecticut	178
New Hampshire	115
New Jersey	114
Pennsylvania	100
New York	98
Delaware	88
Maine	61
Maryland	61
Oregon	57
Ohio	52
Vermont	46
Michigan	44
Wisconsin	36
Missouri	35
Illinois	34
Kentucky	33
Virginia	32
Indiana	31
Louisiana	22
Nebraska	21
Iowa	21
Minnesota	20
Florida	17
North Carolina	17
Tennessee	16
Georgia	16
South Carolina	12
Alabama	11
Texas	11
Mississippi	8
Arkansas	7

Source: http://fisher.lib.virginia.edu/cgi-local/censusbin/census/cen.pl?year=860. Accessed January 3, 2001.

Deep South nor the same connection to the Deep South that the Upper South had. Its cultural compass pointed North rather than South in the conflict between the sections. Most importantly, slavery was not as indispensable an institution in this part of the South as it was in the Deep South and in parts of the Upper South.[74] Furthermore, the industrial capacity of the Border South states was comparable to that of the Old Northwest, rather than the South (see Table 5.1). The economies of the Border South were more diversified than the Upper South and the Deep South. The Border South produced more industrial goods than the states of the Deep South, which were primarily agricultural. In addition, commercial ties to the North were stronger in the Upper South simply by virtue of geography. The following section briefly examines the path followed by the non-seceding states of the South in the secession winter and spring of 1860–61.

MISSOURI

From the beginning, Missouri was a battleground over which (and in which) the pro- and anti-slavery forces fought. Missouri's application for admission into the Union as a slave state precipitated one of the early conflicts over slavery in the Union. This conflict led to the establishment of the balance rule according to which slave state and free states were admitted to the Union in pairs in order to maintain equal representation of each section into the Senate, which would allow each section to have veto over policies unfriendly to its interests.[75] The state played no part in South Carolina's earlier confrontations with the Union. Missouri, moreover, was uniquely important because of the Missouri river and its situation on the Mississippi River. Union trade—both domestic and international—depended upon access to these rivers.

Missouri was the only state in which a plurality of the electorate voted for Douglas, which under the winner-take-all rules of the American electoral system gave Douglas this state's entire slate of Electoral College votes. (Although Lincoln won the plurality of the vote in New Jersey, New Jersey gave a portion of its presidential electors to Douglas.) Of the 165,518 votes cast in the 1860 presidential election, Douglas received 58,801 (or 35.5 percent) of them. Bell came in a very close second, with 58,372 votes, while Breckenridge came in third, with more than 31,000 votes; Lincoln was fourth, with just over 17,000 votes.

The actions of Missouri's state legislature in the face of Lincoln's election demonstrate the state's conservatism. On 31 December 1860, the radical-controlled state legislature met. Given the significance of the recent election, the legislature's highest priority was determining an appropriate course of action. Deep South radicalism and Upper and Border South conservatism certainly informed the decision that was about to be made by the Missouri legislature. On 21 January 1861, the governor of Missouri signed a bill into law calling for 18 February 1861 elections for a convention that would meet beginning 28 February 1861. The bill stipulated that the people of Missouri approve any movement made by the convention in a referendum.

Radicals may have held sway in the legislature, but radicalism did not dominate the state. Of the approximately 140,000 votes cast for convention delegates, only 30,000 of them went to radical candidates. The unionist votes were split between unconditional unionists, who would never have supported secession, and conditional unionists, who might have thrown their support behind secession if circumstances warranted. According to one estimate, conditional unionism dominated the state.[76] Given this, Missouri was not about to be compelled to secede from the Union by the election of Lincoln or by the secession of Deep South states. What remained to be seen was whether Missouri would consent to the coercion of the seceded states of the South.

The convention passed a number of resolutions (drawn up by the committee on federal relations) that affirmed Missouri's conservative position. They stated that Missouri had no cause to secede from the Union, that the conflict between the sections ought to be solved according to the principles outlined in the Crittenden Compromise, and that any attempt at coercion would result in civil war. On the last point, they were careful not to say whether the state would fight should hostilities arise.[77] An effort by a radical in the convention to promise Missouri to the South was soundly defeated.[78]

After adopting these resolutions, the convention adjourned, agreeing to meet again in December, but subject to recall, should events require it. Unlike states of the Upper South, Lincoln's proclamation did not strengthen secessionist support; nor did it lead to the immediate recall of the convention. The convention finally met again on 25 July 1861, but by this time the secessionists had withdrawn from it, leaving it more firmly in the hands of unionists than before. Members voted to depose a number of elected officials in the state and replace them with those more favorable to the Union. While pro-union forces were placed in governmental positions, a pro-southern government operated in exile in the Confederacy for the duration of the war. Like other Border States, Missouri existed between the extremes of each section. For these states, the war was not only a savage conflict between the sections, but also a conflict that took place among the citizens of the state.

KENTUCKY

Henry Clay, the author of the Compromise of 1850, was from Kentucky. With Clay, Kentuckians supported the Compromise of 1850.[79] Straddling North and South, Kentucky felt the interests of both slave and free labor.

Prior to the commencement of the War Between the States, Abraham Lincoln is supposed to have said that, while he hoped to have God on his side, he must have Kentucky. No state that remained in the Union was more evenly divided between North and South than Kentucky. Birthplace of both American presidents, Abraham Lincoln and Jefferson Davis, and bordered by three slave states and three free states, Kentucky felt the conflict between North and South in a way that could not be comprehended by states that sat at the extremes of either side of the Mason-Dixon line. Kentucky was important as such, but it was also important because Union control of Kentucky assured Union control of the Ohio River, which was an important resource for trade.

In the 1860 presidential election, Kentucky was one of only three states in which Constitutional Union candidate John Bell won a plurality of the votes cast. Of the 146,216 votes cast in Kentucky, 66,051 votes (or 45 percent) were cast for Bell. Douglas was in second place, with 53,163 votes, while Breckenridge earned a somewhat surprising third place with 25,638 votes.

Kentucky's legislature met on 17 January 1861, after many of the Deep South states had seceded, and 20 March 1861, after Lincoln was inaugurated. Ultimately, Kentucky never called a state convention to consider secession. Although Lincoln's proclamation precipitated secession in the states of the Upper South, the calling up of troops did not galvanize secessionists in Kentucky. In this state, the conflict was not between secessionists and unionists, but between those who desired that Kentucky remain neutral and those who thought Kentucky should choose sides. Wooster noted, "the majority of the former [pro-neutralists] were unionists," and "the majority of the latter [anti-neutralists], secessionists."[80] After the legislature convened, it adopted neutrality. For his part, Lincoln facilitated the maintenance of neutrality by promising to refrain from invading or occupying the state while it remained neutral. The strategy worked, and as the war progressed Kentucky's unionism also progressed.

MARYLAND

In the 1860 presidential election, Maryland's presidential electors went for John C. Breckenridge, but a majority of the votes were cast for conservative candidates Bell and Douglas. Of the 92,502 votes cast, 42,482 (or 46 percent) were for Breckenridge; Bell received 41,760 votes, Douglas received 5,966 votes, and Lincoln received 2,294 votes.

Maryland was unique among the Border South states, if only in regards to the geographical positions of the state and the capital of the U.S. Maryland's future was inextricably intertwined with the future of Virginia. If Maryland's position on secession could be summarized, it was simply this: "Wait for Virginia."[81] The prospect of this state's secession put the Union in a peculiar position: If Virginia *and* Maryland left the Union, Washington, DC would be surrounded by Confederate territory. Obviously, both states could not be permitted to secede from the Union.

In the immediate aftermath of secession in the Deep South, Maryland's unionist governor, Thomas Hicks, stubbornly refused to call the legislature into session. After Sumter and the Proclamation, however, he relented. Consequently, the legislature of Maryland met on 26 April 1861. On the same day that the legislature met, however, federal forces initiated their occupation of the state. Under these circumstances, it was inexpedient and unadvisable for the legislature to consider calling a convention. Occupation did not, however, prevent legislators from initiating a failed movement to limit the power of the unionist governor of the state.[82] Both Houses of the legislature passed resolutions advocating Northern recognition of the Confederacy and decrying the military occupation of the state.

Because keeping this state in the Union was central to maintaining and protecting the federal capital, Maryland had to remain in the Union regardless of the preferences of its citizens. Lawrence Denton claimed that the "secession movement in Maryland probably would have been successful if Marylanders had been free to choose, because a majority of her people favored the South."[83] Or, as another noted, the "state of Maryland was kept in the Union, largely because the people who wanted to take it out of the Union were thrown into jail."[84] Given the path followed by the rest of the Border South, it seems more likely that Maryland would have decided to remain in the Union. (Eventually, the people of Maryland did choose the Union, but this choice was constrained by the knowledge that choosing otherwise might result in imprisonment.)

DELAWARE

Suspicion in Delaware of ideas and actions originating in South Carolina had an extensive history. To Delaware, the South Carolinian doctrine of nullification was dangerous. Unlike most of the other slave states, Delaware did not even pay lip service to anti-tariff sentiment during the nullification crisis. Manufacturing was an increasingly important element in the American economy, and Delaware was part of this larger trend. Thus, the principle of protection was not inimical to the interests of this state.[85] In the crisis of 1850, Delaware supported the compromise and refused to attend the Nashville Convention.[86]

In the 1860 presidential election, Breckenridge won a plurality, receiving 7,337 of the 16,039 votes cast; Bell came in second, with 3,864 votes; Lincoln came in third, with 3,815 votes, while Douglas earned a surprising fourth place with 1,023 votes.

While Delaware was a Border State and a slave state, the certainty with which the political leaders of Delaware confronted the secession crisis contradicts what we have come to expect from the slave states—especially those whose Electoral College votes went to Breckenridge. When Delaware's legislature convened on 1 January 1861, it passed a motion expressing "unqualified disapproval" of secession as a remedy to the grievances that the South confronted.[87] Perhaps the best demonstration of its position as a Border South state was its enthusiasm for the failed (and largely ignored) Washington Peace Conference: Delaware sent a full slate of delegates to this failed attempt at saving what remained of the Union and bringing the seceded states back into the Union.[88] When a commissioner from the seceded state of Georgia spoke in Delaware's legislature and asked the state to join the Confederate States of America, the legislature responded by passing a resolution asking Georgia to reconsider its actions.[89] After the legislature adjourned, not even Lincoln's proclamation compelled the governor to ask it to reconvene. As Wooster noted, "Delaware like Maryland was safe for the Union,"[90] although in Delaware, military occupation was not necessary to keep the state in the Union.

CONCLUSION

The secession of South Carolina was a necessary condition for the secession of both the Deep South and the Upper South, although the logic of secession within each set of states was different. Whatever inclinations there were in states of the Deep South to secede first, none of these states were willing to risk the ignominy of initiating the movement. Once South Carolina seceded, the strategic context of choice was fundamentally altered. The cooperation that was almost universally sought in the Deep South could now be had, ironically, through the unilateral secession of the other states of the Deep South. South Carolina felt it had nothing to lose by seceding—and everything to gain. Their gamble (and it was a gamble) paid off: The secession of South Carolina was followed by the secession of the rest of the Deep South and, eventually, most of the other slave states.

The shelling of Fort Sumter and Lincoln's Proclamation intervened between the secessions of South Carolina and the Deep South and the secessions of the states of the Upper South, but this tipping in favor of secession in the Upper South was only possible if South Carolina seceded. If this state had not seceded, possession of the federal forts would not have been an issue, Fort Sumter would not have been fired on, and Lincoln would not have felt the need to call up troops: There would have been no rebellion to quell. The strategic context in which the Upper South states seceded was markedly different from the context in which the Deep South states seceded. In both cases, however, South Carolina's actions were crucial. Without this state's action, the dream of a Southern Confederacy would never have become a reality. This is, in fact, the way the state saw itself (see Figure 5.2—the secession banner).[91] The secession banner hung in Institute Hall while the secession convention met.

The states of the Deep South did not need guns trained in one direction or another order to support secession. In fact, secession in these states

132 *Federalism, Secession, and the American State*

occurred shortly after the commander-in-chief of the armed forces promised them that no force would be used. Political actors within these states found the justification for secession in the significance of the election of Lincoln. For the Upper South seceders, the mere fact of Lincoln's election did not provide justification for secession. Once Lincoln revealed he was willing to coerce a seceded state, the states of the Upper South were prepared to choose sides in the conflict.

Figure 5.2 From the Collections of the South Carolina Historical Society.

The divisions that the Upper South experienced on the question of Union versus secession were even more pronounced in the Border South; this group of states was unwilling to secede upon the election of Lincoln, and while there was some outrage at the anticipated coercion of the seceded states, that outrage did not translate into a grievance level sufficient to justify secession.

Secession (or non-secession) occurred in each group for very different reasons. In one, it was the threat to slavery; in another, it was the threat of war. For the Border South, neither the threat to slavery nor the threat of war was enough to push them out of the Union. The outcome of this was multi-faceted: There was a war that resulted in the death of over 600,000 Americans, and four million Americans who were in bondage were given a freedom that was not formalized until late into the twentieth century. The U.S. had previously been pulled in different directions, one section favoring agriculture and a limited state, the other section favoring industry and an activist state; the outcome of the Civil War was a decided victory for free labor, industrialism, and an activist state. It was this transformation that has led observers to call the Civil War the second American Revolution.[92]

6 The Past and Future of Federalism and Secession

Between the formation of the American Union and the beginning of the Civil War, the American state was transformed from being a limited state, the institutional capacity of which was restricted by principle, by design, and by a variety of formal and informal mechanisms to a consolidated state controlled by a single section and a single political party. This transformation both reflected and allowed a transformation to the political economy of the nation. This second American Revolution signaled a new dominance of an industrial economy over the older agricultural economy, of the North over the South, and of free labor over slave labor.

In this book, I have constructed an account of how the institutional design of the American state contributed to the likelihood of secession. A design that provides constituent units with a high level of institutional capacity and autonomy, and that confers separate constitutional sovereign status to constituent units, is more prone to secession than a design in which the center maintains a monopoly on constitutional authority and on legitimate violence and where the location of sovereignty is relatively uncontested. Simply put, the costs of secession are lowered when state institutions are in place and can carry over to the new state after secession. All of these conditions were present in the pre-Civil War U.S. The federal state was so weak in the antebellum period that it was hardly an exaggeration to claim "there was no state." The arrow does not point in only one direction, however: Conferring separate constitutional existence on the constituent units of a political union can work to ease secessionist pressures by meeting the autonomist desires of constituent units and providing a safety valve that prevents regional crises and conflicts from spreading to the entire political union.

I have attempted to account for the desire to mobilize against the *status quo* and the reasons that mobilization took the form of secession. I have also attempted to account for the sequence by which secession took place in the South, including the decision of South Carolina to lead off and the timing of that decision. A strong grievance level explains the decision to pursue remedial action, but the decision to pursue secession rather than another solution is explained by the institutional design of the state. This design accounts for the long history of state challenges to central state authority, and the gradual development of a belief in the right to secede. Thus, limited central state functionality combined with expansive constituent state functionality explains the long tradition of challenging central state authority and the ability to maintain limited central government over time. Federalism in the U.S. meant that the locus of sovereignty would be contested. States could, and often did, claim that they were sovereign and that the Union was a mere compact between the states to be adhered to or abandoned as circumstances merited. Moreover, the very practice of federalism meant that political withdrawal from the central state could occur with minimal disruption and the carryover of state functionality.

I concentrated on South Carolina's challenge to central state authority in two crucial episodes prior to the successful movement for secession in South Carolina: the nullification crisis of 1832–33 and the first secession crisis of 1850–52. During these episodes, South Carolina articulated a position of state sovereignty and states' rights. The state developed its radical program to protect and maintain states' rights and to limit the power and the extent of the federal government's authority and a strategy that it would use in order to meet future challenges to Southern rights.

Although some political leaders during the first crisis advocated secession, the issue in 1832–33 was not secession, but rather state interposition—a position underpinned by the idea of state sovereignty. Because South Carolina felt it was the victim of the federal government's protective tariff policies that resulted in depressed international trade, higher prices on goods required by South Carolinians, and the discriminatory redistribution of federal monies, and because the political actors of the state believed that the foundation of federal tariff policies was a federal government overstepping its established constitutional authority, the state of South Carolina attempted to nullify the law that established the tariff. Better to challenge the center over tariffs, an issue on which South Carolinians hoped they could find allies in both sections of the Union, South Carolinians reasoned, than over the much more contentious issue of slavery, an issue for which the South would have a hard time finding Northern allies.

South Carolina's victory in getting tariff rates reduced came at a cost: states of the North and South widely regarded South Carolina as excessively radical and desiring of the destruction of the Union. South Carolinians realized they could not necessarily count on the other states of the South to cooperate with them in a confrontation with the center. The nullification crisis was followed by years of simmering conflict between the center and South Carolina. Sectional conflict did not boil over, however, until the crisis over the territories acquired from Mexico. At issue was whether these new American territories would be open to slavery. While compromise measures were being debated and passed in the center, the South—significantly, not the whole South—met in Nashville to determine what was to be done about the latest attack on Southern rights.

The convention accomplished little more than revealing the extent to which there was no South. While South Carolina was making arrangements to secede separately, the state of Georgia met in convention and produced the Georgia Platform, revealing to the world that the most important of the potentially radical Deep South states would adhere to the principles outlined in the Compromise of 1850. Georgia's actions ended the possibility of secession at this time.

Unwilling to admit, or even recognize, defeat, the state of South Carolina moved forward with its plans to hold a convention that would have the purpose of withdrawing South Carolina from the Union. The initial victory won by unilateral secessionists was muted by the eventual and decisive victory of cooperationists. Neither cooperative nor unilateral secession would take place in the first secession crisis: South Carolina's secession convention was held, but did not vote to secede. The most the convention could manage was an assertion of the existence of the right of secession; a right which few doubted existed at that time.[1]

In 1860, the simmering sectional conflict once again boiled over. With John Brown's raid, the sectional dismemberment of the Democratic Party, and the victory of Republican Abraham Lincoln in the presidential election, the radical states of the Deep South became convinced that *something* had to be done. South Carolina's efforts at bringing about true cooperative secession failed early enough in the movement that the state recognized that it could not rely on the other states of the South to act in cooperation with it. With Lincoln's victory—made possible by demographic changes in the Union that contributed to relative decline in the power of the South—South Carolina, uniquely situated to perceive a strong level of grievance and to act early, followed a course of action that assured the unilateral secession of the state. Though risky, the action followed by South Carolina was strategically sound: since the South, such as it was, was divided on the question of how best to protect Southern and slave interests, South Carolinian and other Southern elites believed unilateral secession was the only way to guarantee the creation of a Southern, slaveholding Confederacy. The soundness of this logic and this strategy was demonstrated by what followed South Carolina's unilateral secession: the unilateral secession of the remaining states of the Deep South.

The timing of secession among the states of the Deep South indicates that these states seceded for reasons that were qualitatively similar to the reasons behind South Carolina's secession; the timing of secession in the Upper South indicates that these states seceded for different reasons. The threat to slavery posed by Lincoln's election, combined with South Carolina's willingness to initiate the movement, determined the path followed by the Deep South; the Upper South would not secede to protect slavery, but would secede once the likelihood of war between North and South was demonstrated. In each case, secession was determined by a grievance, but set of states seceded for a different set of reasons. The states of the Border

The Past and Future of Federalism and Secession

South never felt a grievance strong enough to warrant secession; thus, they never seceded.

The construction of an issue that could justify secession explains the timing of secession by the political elite of South Carolina. That issue was the election of a Republican president. Once Lincoln had been elected, South Carolinians merely had to fulfill the promise they made: to secede first and alone. Thanks to the impending threat of war following the shelling of Fort Sumter and Lincoln's proclamation calling up troops to quell the Southern rebellion, the states of the Upper South followed suit and seceded from the Union, though the logic of secession was different in these states than in the states of the Deep South. The Border South states never seceded, despite the threat of war and the perceived threat to slavery. In this book, therefore, I have constructed an account of the decision to secede, the timing of that decision, and the sequence by which secession was accomplished following the election of Lincoln. I have done this with sensitivity to the way in which the federal institutional structure complicates (and facilitates) the decision pursue radical collective action.

THE PARADOX OF FEDERALISM: THE FUTURE OF FEDERALISM?

Establishing a link between federalism and secession is nothing new. There is a developing and expanding literature that does precisely this. Federalism is adopted to prevent, reduce, or eliminate secessionist sentiment and to provide an escape valve that keeps regional conflict at the regional level. But federalism has a paradoxical impact—sometimes encouraging secession, other times discouraging it. The research done here can suggest something about the fate of federations and the advisability of exporting federal institutions to societies that are or might be in conflict. To conclude this work, let me use the arguments presented in this research to briefly consider two other cases of secessionist movements in Québec and Scotland and Wales.

In Canada, federalism was adopted in order to accommodate the French fact on the ground in Canada. Federalism was a compromise between creating a highly centralized state and maintaining separate existence, with its attendant dangers. Contrary to states' goals of adopting federalism in the first place, federalism has influenced the development and expression of secessionist sentiment in the province of Québec.[2] While there are different interpretations of the Canadian Confederation, variations on compact theory continue to be central.[3] Compact theory plays a central role in describing the grievance animating the desire to alter the *status quo* in Québec, but the normative justification for secession has shifted from secession as a state's right to secession justified by the principle of national self-determination.[4] Like the states of the antebellum American South, the Québec state today has relatively a high degree of institutional capacity, giving it the ability to secede with minimal disruption of state function. Events in Québec indicate that both citizens and political leaders believe that there is a right to secession. While federal rules governing secession have been challenged within Québec, the federal government has specified the conditions in which secession is permissible, further legitimizing secession as a grievance remediation strategy. Furthermore, there are political parties that compete (often very successfully), at both the provincial and federal levels, which are firmly committed to an independent Québec. These parties, however, are challenged by a federalist-nationalist alternative at every level. There is, in other words, division among the population and political elites in Quebec regarding the how best to protect the social, economic, and political attributes of Québec's national identity. As long as this condition is maintained, secession will continue to be difficult to accomplish. With institutional structures in place that make secession feasible and with provincial and federal policies that have legitimated secession as a policy, the most important missing element in the quest for secession in Québec is a grievance strong enough to mobilize a sufficient level of secessionist support. Such a grievance must be serious enough to convince a clear majority (possibly a super-majority) of the Québécois to support secession via a referendum. Despite the razor-thin margin of victory by the federalist forces in the 1995 referendum on secession, secessionist forces in Québec seem to be unable to garner the support of even a simple majority of the Québécois.

The case of Québec demonstrates the paradoxical impact of federalism. Placing the considerable autonomy of the province alongside an accommodative federal government means that the forces in favor of secession will continue to have significant barriers in front of achieving their ends. Only once the population of Québec perceives a sufficiently high grievance level will secession be possible. I argued earlier that nothing animates secession like a threat to survival. While the decimation of the French language will, most likely, not endanger the life of even one individual, it is the most essential element of Québec cultural identity. A threat to these sets of institutions may convince a clear majority of the Québécois that secession is necessary. Another more political grievance is also conceivable. Québec is a more collective society than the more individualist rest of Canada. It is possible to find a sufficient grievance by challenging the collective policies of Québec by a government that doesn't have a significant constituency in Québec. This suggests, at the very least, that the grievance driving support for secession is highly political and socially constructed. Until such time that a strong enough grievance is developed, the threat of secession will continue to be used as a negotiating tool to wrest concessions from the center.[5]

While there are similarities between the South and Québec, there are differences, too. Unlike the Southern states of the Union, Québec is a single province; thus my discussion of sequencing in secession may not apply—at the very least, it will not apply in the same way it did in the South. However, there may be something to be gained by examining the potential for clashes among the hard-line secessionists of Québec and the federal government (and the influence such a conflict could have in brining about sequential exit by convincing moderates to support secession). Were a small, secessionist subsection of Québec's population to provoke a confrontation with Ottawa, soft-secessionists and Québec's substantial number of federalist-nationalists might come out in support of the radicals. Thus, sequencing strategies may still play a role in the success or failure of secession in Québec, but that role would be markedly different in Québec than it was in the slave states of the U.S.

This project can also provide insight into the potential for secession in Great Britain. Of particular import are the institutional and constitutional changes that have taken place in Scotland and Wales. The devolution of some political authority to local parliaments in Scotland and Wales signals a significant alteration in the institutional design of the British state. This state may not be federal, but neither is it wholly unitary. Granting limited autonomy to the two regions through their local parliaments may be a first step in the development of substantial state institutional capacity at the regional level in Scotland and Wales. If this institutional capacity grows over time, it would help to ease a transition to independence, should there ever be a grievance strong enough to animate support for secession among the population. We see the paradox playing out: The same institutional innovations that are intended to maintain the territorial integrity of Great Britain may help to dissolve it along national boundaries.

While not unchallenged, there are secessionist activists in place in both Scotland and Wales in local, national, and supranational political institutions. Those advocating outright independence have significant, but not overwhelming, support, especially in Scotland. The boundaries of Scotland and Wales are currently firmly established; if the movement for secession matures, however, we may begin to hear about partition among the unionists in these regions. What is lacking in these two regions is a strong grievance that could animate secessionist sentiment. Indeed, the center's willingness to devolve authority can be seen as a firm argument in favor of maintaining continued union. However, should a future government attempt to limit or remove that autonomy, and if such limitations can be framed in a way that make them look like a threat to Scotland's or Wales's cultural survival, then a recentralizing movement could provide a grievance strong enough to bring about secession, especially now that each region has representative institutions in place. Like Québec, sequencing may not play as important a role in Great Britain as it did in the Southern U.S.; however, it may be possible for the most radical among secessionist groups to precipitate a conflict with the center that would increase support for secession among moderates. As in the Southern U.S., the successful secession of one unit might have the effect of strengthening the resolve of those in another to pursue secession.

A LESS PERFECT UNION?

In the political history recounted in this book, secession provides little to recommend it: It was sought by a reactionary, racist, and tyrannical minority to protect the privileged position they occupied, and it lead to a long and destructive war. Still, it's certainly worth considering whether secession—or a looser version of local autonomy and loosened Union—can help countries that are stuck in (or locked into) an inferior equilibrium.[6] Would increased local or regional autonomy help the U.S. deal with grid-lock in the center wrought by seemingly incommensurable preferences held by the population? Would a looser federal union in Belgium aid that country in getting beyond its seemingly perennial stalemate? Possibly, but the devil is in the details and the context.

Federalism means centralization and decentralization at the same time. Finding the balance that allows these territorially oppositional institutions to persist over time is not easy, even when the divisions within a polity are merely political. Federalism and secession are intrinsically intertwined. Thanks to the persistence of the threat of secession in the current international system and the violence that so often accompanies the threat and the act, secession remains an important subject of political research. This book has attempted to fill in a number of gaps in our understanding of the process and dynamic of secession. I have accomplished this task through an analysis of an under-studied, but historically important, case of secession. The case-specific analysis of the American South is persuasive and, at the same time, has generated novel insight into the process of secession wherever (and whenever) it might occur.

Notes

NOTES TO CHAPTER 1

1. This is a paraphrase of Shearer Davis Bowman, "Antebellum Planters and Vormarz Junkers in Comparative Perspective," *American Historical Review* 85, no. 4 (1980): 805.
2. Let there be no mistake: the central freedom that South Carolinians were trying to protect by seceding was tyranny over African slaves.
3. John Ashworth, *Slavery, Capitalism, and Politics in the Antebellum Republic* (New York: Cambridge University Press, 1995); Charles A. and Mary R. Beard. *The Rise of American Civilization* 2 vols. (New York: The Macmillan Company, 1927); Richard Franklin Bensel, *Yankee Leviathan: The Origins of Central State Authority in America, 1859–1877* (Cambridge: Cambridge University Press, 1990); Barrington Moore, *Social Origins of Dictatorship and Democracy: Lord and Peasant in the Making of the Modern World* (Boston: Beacon Press, 1966).
4. Donald L. Horowitz, *Ethnic Groups in Conflict* (Berkeley: University of California Press, 1985); John McGarry and Brendan O'Leary, *The Politics of Ethnic Conflict Regulation* (London and New York: Routledge Press, 1993); Ralph R. Premdas, "Secessionist Movements in Comparative Perspective," in Ralph R. Premdas, S.W.R. Samarasinghe, and Alan B. Anderson, eds. *Secession Movements in Comparative Perspective* (New York: St. Martin's Press, 1990), 12–31; Allen Buchanan, "Federalism, Secession, and the Morality of Inclusion," *Arizona Law Review* 37 (1995): 53–63.
5. With respect to grievance, "losses loom larger than the corresponding gains," according to Robert Jervis, "Political Implications of Loss Aversion," *Political Psychology* 13, no. 2 (1992): 187. See also Geoffry Taubman, "Nationalism, Loss-Gain Framing and the Confederate States of America," *Nations and Nationalism* 3, no. 2 (1994): 251–271.
6. John R. Wood, "Secession: A Comparative Analytical Framework," *Canadian Journal of Political Science* 14, no. 1 (1981): 107–134; Michael Hechter, "The Dynamics of Secession," *Acta Sociologica* 35, no. 4 (1992): 367–373; Horowitz, *Ethnic Groups*; Kisangani N. Emizet and Vicki L. Hesli, "The Disposition to Secede: an Analysis of the Soviet Case," *Comparative Political Studies* 27 (1995): 493–536; Stephane Dion, "Why is Secession Difficult in Well-Established Democracies? Lessons from Quebec," *British Journal of Political Science* 26 (1996): 269–283.
7. Jan Erk, "Does Federalism Really Matter?," *Comparative Politics* 39, no.1 (2006): 103–120; Jan Erk, "Federalism as a Growth Industry," *Publius: the Journal of Federalism* 37, no. 2 (2007): 262–278; Jan Erk and Wilfried

Swenden, eds., *New Directions in Federalism Studies* (London: Routledge, 2009).
8. Mikhail Filippov, Peter C. Ordeshook, and Olga Shvetsova, *Designing Federalism: A Theory of Self-Sustainable Federal Institutions* (Cambridge: Cambridge University Press, 2004).
9. Ugo Amoretti and Nancy Bermeo, eds., *Federalism and Territorial Cleavages* (Baltimore, MD: Johns Hopkins University Press, 2004).
10. Henry E. Hale, "Divided We Stand: Institutional Sources of Ethnofederal State Survival and Collapse," *World Politics* 56 (2004): 165–193; Henry E. Hale, "The Double-Edged Sword of Ethnofederalism: Ukraine and the USSR in Comparative Perspective," *Comparative Politics* 40, no. 2 (2008): 293–312; Michael Hechter and Dina Okamoto, "Political Consequences of Minority Group Formation," *Annual Review of Political Science* 4 (2001): 189–215.
11. Dawn Brancati, "Decentralization: Fueling the Fire or Dampening the Flames of Ethnic Conflict and Secessionism," *International Organizations* 60 (2006), 651–685; Jan Erk and Lawrence M. Anderson, eds., *The Paradox of Federalism* (London: Routledge Press, 2010).
12. Dwight L. Dumond, *The Secession Movement: 1860–1861* (New York: The Macmillan Company, 1931); William W. Freehling, *The Reintegration of American History: Slavery and the Civil War* (New York: Oxford University Press, 1994); David M. Potter, *The Impending Crisis: 1848–1861* (New York: Harper and Rowe, 1976). For exceptions, see William W. Freehling, *The Road to Disunion, Volume II: Secessionists Triumphant* (New York: Oxford University Press, 2007) and Hudson Meadwell and Lawrence Anderson, "Sequence and Strategy in the Secession of the American South," *Theory and Society* 37, no. 3 (2008): 199–227.
13. Paul Pierson, *Politics in Time* (Princeton, NJ: Princeton University Press, 2004) and Alexander George and Andrew Bennett, *Case Studies and Theory Development in the Social Sciences* (Cambridge, MA: MIT Press, 2005).
14. Calvin C. Jillson, *Constitution Making: Conflict and Consensus in the Federal Convention of 1787* (New York: Agathon Press, 1988); Jack Knight and Lee Epstein, "On the Struggle for Judicial Supremacy," *Law and Society Review* 30, no. 1 (1996), 87–120; William Riker, *The Strategy of Rhetoric: Campaigning for the American Constitution* (New Haven: Yale University Press, 1966); Barry Weingast, *Institutions and Political Commitment: A New Political Economy of the American Civil War Era* (Unpublished Manuscript, Hoover Institution, Stanford University, 1996).
15. Peter Hall, *Governing the Economy: The Politics of State Intervention in Britain and France* (New York: Oxford University Press, 1986); Junko Kato, "Review Article: Institutions and Rationality in Politics—Three Varieties of New-Institutionalists," *British Journal of Political Science* 26, no. 4 (1996): 553–582; James G. March and Johan P. Olsen, "The New Institutionalism: Organizational Factors in Political Life," *American Political Science Review* 78, no. 3 (1984), 734–749. Theda Skocpol, "Why I am an Historical Institutionalist," *Polity* 28, no. 1 (1995), 103–106; Sven Steinmo, Kathleen Thelen, and Frank Longstreth, eds., *Structuring Politics: Historical Institutionalism in Comparative Analysis* (Cambridge and New York: Cambridge University Press, 1992).
16. Kathleen Thelen, "Historical Institutionalism in Comparative Politics," *Annual Review of Political Science* 2 (1999): 371.
17. See William D. Porter, *State Sovereignty and the Doctrine of Coercion, by the Hon. Wm. D. Porter; Together with a Letter from Hon. J.K. Paulding, Former Sec. Of Navy. Right to Secede by "States"*. [1860 Association Tract

No. 2] (Charleston, SC: Evans and Cogswell, 1860); Troup, *To the People of the South. Senator Hammond and the Tribune*. [1860 Association Tract No. 3] (Charleston, SC: Evans and Cogswell, 1860).
18. Elections in South Carolina tended to be insignificant. Most were uncontested.

NOTES TO CHAPTER 2

1. Elizabeth R. Varon, *Disunion! The Coming of the American Civil War, 1789–1859* (Chapel Hill: University of North Carolina Press, 2008).
2. Donald Livingston, "The Secession Tradition in America," in David Gordon, ed. *Secession, State and Liberty* (New Brunswick, NJ: Transaction Publishers, 1988), 1–34. Livingston describes the existence of a "secession tradition" in the U.S. Writing from an anti-statist perspective, Livingston believes this tradition should be used to provide an effective check on the authority of the central state.
3. Douglass North, *Structure and Change in Economic History* (New York: Norton, 1981), 21. See also Bob Jessop, *State Theory: Putting States in their Place* (University Park, PA: Pennsylvania State University Press, 1990) and Max Weber, *Economy and Society* 3 vols. New York: Bedminster Press, 1968). For further discussion of theories of the state, see Michael Mann, "The Autonomous Power of the State: Its Origins, Mechanisms and Results," *European Journal of Sociology* 25, no. 2 (1984): 185–213; Michael Mann, "Nation-States in Europe and Other Continents: Diversifying, Developing, Not Dying," *Daedalus* 122, no. 3 (1993): 115–140; and Michael Mann, *Sources of Social Power, Volume 2* (Cambridge and New York: Cambridge University Press, 1993).
4. Theda Skocpol, "State Formation and Social Policy in the United States," *American Behavioral Scientist* 35, nos. 4/5 (1992): 568.
5. See, especially, Charles Tilly, ed., *The Formation of National States in Western Europe* (Princeton, NJ: Princeton University Press, 1975). But also see Ernest Barker, *The Development of Public Services in Western Europe* (Hamden, CT: Archon Books, 1966); Hudson Meadwell, "Breaking the Mould? Quebec Independence and Secession in the Developed West," in Sukumar Periwal, ed. *Notions of Nationalism* (Budapest and New York: Central European University Press, 1995), 129–152; Hudson Meadwell, "Institutional Design and State-breaking in North America," in David Carment, John F. Stack Jr., and Frank Harvey, eds. *The International Politics of Quebec Secession. State-making and State-breaking in North America* (Westport, CT and London: Praeger Publishers, 2001), 11–32. For criticisms and qualifications, see Thomas Ertman, *Birth of the Leviathan: Building States and Regimes in Medieval and Early Modern Europe* (New York: Cambridge University Press, 1997) and Hendrik Spruyt, *The Sovereign State and its Competitors: An Analysis of Systems Change* (Princeton, NJ: Princeton University Press, 1994).
6. J.P. Nettl, "The State as a Conceptual Variable," *World Politics* 20, no. 4 (1968): 559–592.
7. Nettl, "The State," 579.
8. Mann, "Autonomous Power," 198.
9. Tilly, *The Formation of National States*.
10. This is not to suggest that war was wholly absent in North America, or that the U.S. did not engage in wars during this period; it did: the War of Independence, the War of 1812, and the war with Mexico. Rather, my point is that

there was a relative absence of war in North American compared to Europe. See, for example, Erik Goldstein, *Wars and Peace Treaties: 1816–1991* (London: Routledge Press, 1992) and Melvin Small and J. David Singer, *Resort to Arms: International and Civil Wars, 1816–1980* (Beverly Hills, CA: Sage Publications, 1982). Disagreeing is William Riker, *Federalism: Origin, Operation, Significance* (Boston and Toronto: Little, Brown and Company, 1964).

11. Daniel H. Deudney, "The Philadelphian System: Sovereignty, Arms Control, and Balance of Power in the American States-Union, circa 1787–1861," *International Organization* 49, no. 2 (1995): 191–228.
12. Nettl, "The State," 568.
13. Walter Dean Burnham quoted in Robert Keohane, "Associative American Development, 1776–1860: Economic Growth and Political Disintegration," in John Gerard Ruggie, ed. *The Antinomies of Interdependence: National Welfare and the International Division of Labor* (New York: Columbia University Press, 1983), 84. Italics are in Keohane's work. See also Pierre Birnbaum, *States and Collective Action: The European Experience* (Cambridge: Cambridge University Press, 1988); Alexis De Tocqueville, *Democracy in America* 2 vols. (New York: Vintage Books, 1990); Deudney, "The Philadelphian System"; Eric Nordlinger, *On the Autonomy of the Democratic State* (Cambridge, MA and London: Harvard University Press, 1981). For an alternate view, see Andrew Vincent, *Theories of the State* (Oxford and New York: Basil Blackwell, 1987).
14. Constitution of the United States. Article VI, Clause 2; Leslie Friedman Goldstein, "State Resistance to Authority in Federal Unions: The Early United States (1790–1860) and the European Community (1958–94)," *Studies in American Political Development* 11, no. 1 (1997): 149–189.
15. Charles Bright and Susan Harding, eds., *State-Making and Social Movements: Essays in History and Theory* (Ann Arbor: University of Michigan Press, 1984), 121–122.
16. Peter B. Knupfer, *The Union as It Is: Constitutional Unionism and Sectional Compromise, 1787–1861* (Chapel Hill: University of North Carolina Press, 1991).
17. Deudney, "The Philadelphian System," 192.
18. Theodore Lowi, *The End of Liberalism: The Second Republic of the United States*, second ed. (New York: W.W. Norton & Company, 1979), 272. See also Bensel, *Yankee Leviathan* and Stephen Skowronek, *Building a New American State* (New York: Cambridge University Press, 1982).
19. Lee W. Eysturlid, "'An Opportunity to Show their Epaulets and Feathers': The South Carolina Militia During the First Secession Crisis, 1848–1851," *Armed Forces and Society* 20, no. 2 (1994), 303–316; Jean Martin Flynn, *The Militia in Antebellum South Carolina Society* (Spartanburg, SC: The Reprint Company, 1991); John E. Jessup, ed. in chief, and Louise B. Ketz, executive ed., *Encyclopedia of the American Military* 3 vols. (1994); Allan R. Millett and Peter Maslowski, *For the Common Defense: A Military History of the United States of America* (New York and London: The Free Press, 1994); Walter Mills, *Arms and Men: A Study in American Military History* (New York: G.P. Putnam's Sons, 1956); William Riker, *Soldiers of the States* (Washington: DC: Public Affairs Press, 1979); Charles Reginald Schrader, ed., *Reference Guide to the United States Military History* vol. 2 (New York: Facts on File, 1993).
20. Clement Eaton, "Censorship of Southern Mails," *American Historical Review* 48, no. 2 (1943): 266–280.
21. Emphasis is mine.

22. See the Hayne-Webster debates for a debate between those holding national and confederal interpretations of the Union. See the first two speeches by Hayne and Webster respectively in *Register of Debates* 1830. Senate, 21st Congress, 1st Session, pages 31–35 and *Register of Debates* 1830. Senate, 21st Congress, 1st Session, pages 35–41. For a contemporary articulation of the national view, see Samuel H. Beer, *To Make A Nation: The Rediscovery of American Federalism* (Cambridge, MA: Harvard University Press, 1993).
23. Beer, *To Make a Nation*, 23.
24. Alexander Hamilton, James Madison, and John Jay, *Federalist Papers* (New York: Penguin Books, 1961), 244.
25. The Seventeenth Amendment provided for direct election of Senators by a state's electorate. Even before the passage of the Seventeenth Amendment, many states gave their citizens a voice in the election of their Senators, but it was not until the passage of this Amendment that this rule was formalized and nationalized. By 1860, South Carolina was the only state in which the state legislature selected its U.S.Senators without input from the people.
26. John R. Alden, *A History of the American Revolution* (New York: Da Capo, 1969).
27. The Kentucky Resolutions can be found in Henry Steele Commager, ed., *Documents of American History*, seventeenth edition (New York: Appleton-Century-Crofts, 1963), 178–179. Italics are in original.
28. Commager, *Documents of American History*, 184.
29. Herman V. Ames, ed., *State Documents on Federal Relations: The States and the United States* (New York: Da Capo Press, 1970), 16.
30. Ames, *State Documents on Federal Relations*, 17.
31. Ames, *State Documents on Federal Relations*, 19.
32. Karl Marx and Friedrick Engels, *The Civil War in the United States*, (New York: International Publishers, 1961); Weingast, *Institutions and Political Commitment*; Barry Weingast, "Political Stability and Civil War: Institutions, Commitment and American Democracy," in Robert H. Bates, Avner Greif, Margaret Levi, Jean-Laurent Rosenthal, and Barry R. Weingast, eds. *Analytic Narratives* (Princeton, NJ: Princeton University Press, 1998), 148–193.
33. Ames, *State Documents on Federal Relations*, 85.
34. Carl J. Vipperman, *William Lowndes and the Transition of Southern Politics: 1782–1822* (Chapel Hill, NC: University of North Carolina, 1989).
35. David Potter, *The South and the Sectional Conflict* (Baton Rouge: Louisiana State University Press, 1968), 75–76.
36. Bensel, *Yankee Leviathan*, 13, noted that the Southern devotion to states' rights had to be pragmatic, rather than ideological, given the strong central state created by the Confederate States of America. My general claim—that states' rights discourse was not unique to the South and that state's rights was defensively adopted when states were displeased with policies emanating from the center—does not preclude the fact that there were those Southerners who were ideologically infused with a doctrine of states' rights. These anti-statist and anti-federal tendencies remain in the Union to this day.

NOTES TO CHAPTER 3

1. Edgar, *South Carolina*, 311.
2. South Carolina's Constitution can be found in Francis Newton Thorp, *The Federal and State Constitutions, Colonial Charters, and other Organic Laws of the States, Territories, and Colonies Now or Heretofore Forming The*

United States of America (Washington, DC: Government Printing Office, 1909), 3258–3269.
3. James Henry Hammond to Edmund Ruffin, 10 October 1845 quoted in William W. Freehling, *The Road to Disunion, Volume I: Secessionists at Bay, 1776–1854* (New York: Oxford University Press, 1990), 223.
4. Ralph Wooster, *The People in Power: Courthouse and Statehouse in the Lower South, 1850–1860* (Knoxville, TN: University of Tennessee Press, 1969), 49.
5. Chalmers Gaston Davidson, *The Last Foray, The South Carolina Planters of 1860: A Sociological Study* (Columbia, SC: University of South Carolina Press, 1971), 75.
6. Greenberg, "Representation and the Isolation."
7. William A. Schaper, *Sectionalism and Representation in South Carolina* (Washington, DC: American Historical Association, 1901), 436.
8. These figures include those ineligible to vote because of age.
9. Schaper, *Sectionalism and Representation*, 446. Representation in the South Carolina Legislature and, by extension, any South Carolina Convention, was distributed not only by population, but also by wealth. The Constitution of South Carolina, as amended in 1808, stated, "The house of representatives shall consist of one hundred and twenty-four members, to be apportioned among several election districts of the State, according to the number of white inhabitants contained, and the amount of taxes raised by the legislature . . . In assigning representatives to the several districts of the State, the legislature shall allow one representative for every sixty-second part of the whole number of white inhabitants in the State; and one representative also for every sixty-second part of the whole taxes raised by the whole legislature of the state." This can be found in Thorpe, *The Federal and State Constitutions*, 3258–3269. This gave wealth, including wealth in slaves, as much representation in the House as the white, voting population. With the Senate already skewed to the wealthy Low Country, organizing the House in this way further entrenched the political power of the planter class in South Carolina.
10. United States Department of Commerce. Bureau of the Census, *The Statistical History of the United States: From Colonial Times to the Present* (New York: Basic Books, Inc., Publishers, 1975), 1071.
11. Richard P. McCormick, *The Second American Party System: Party Formation in the Jacksonian Era*, (Chapel Hill, NC: University of North Carolina Press, 1966), 14 claimed, "Party formation was most directly conditioned not by divisions in Congress nor by explicit doctrinal issues but rather by the contest for the presidency." According to this model, in the absence of competition for the presidency, South Carolina did not develop a strong party system such as existed in the rest of the United States. See also James M. Banner, Jr., "The Problem of South Carolina," in Stanley Elkins and Eric McKitrick, eds. *The Hofstadter Aegis, A Memorial* (New York: Alfred A. Knopf, 1974), 60–93; William Nisbet Chambers, and Walter Dean Burnham, *The American Party System: Stages of Political Development* (London and New York: Oxford University Press, 1967); and Michael F. Holt, *The Political Crisis of the 1850s* (New York: John Wiley and Sons, 1978).
12. South Carolina, perhaps stinging from the success of the Compromise of 1850 and its own failure to secede, did not participate in the Democratic Convention of 1852. See Congressional Quarterly, Inc., *Congressional Quarterly's Guide to U.S. Elections*, (Washington, DC: Congressional Quarterly Inc., 1975).
13. Laurence M. Keitt to unknown, 19 September 1855, Laurence Massillon Keitt letters, Manuscript Collection, Duke University, Durham, North Carolina.

14. John C. Calhoun to Joseph W. Lesesne, 19 July 1847, Joseph W. Lesesne Papers, Southern Historical Collection, University of North Carolina at Chapel Hill, Chapel Hill, North Carolina.
15. Although the immediate source for this desire for unanimity was the South Carolinian experience during the nullification crisis, this state always engaged in a unique form of politics that was distinguished by widespread consensus on fundamental political issues. Central to the South Carolinian political philosophy was the desire to maintain "personal independence." See Robert M. Weir, "'The Harmony We Were Famous For': An Interpretation of Pre-Revolutionary South Carolina Politics," *William and Mary Quarterly* 26, no. 4 (1969): 474.
16. Banner, "The Problem of South Carolina."
17. Lacy K. Ford, *Origins of Southern Radicalism: The South Carolina Upcountry, 1800–1860* (New York: Oxford University Press, 1988), viii.
18. Charleston *Mercury*, 3 November 1860.
19. Congressional Quarterly, Inc., *Guide*.
20. Kenneth S. Greenberg, *The Second American Revolution: South Carolina Politics, Society, and Secession, 1776–1860* (Ph.D. diss. University of Wisconsin, 1976), 174.
21. Greenberg, *Second American Revolution*, 174.
22. *Ibid.*, 104. See also Rogers, "South Carolina Federalists."
23. Henry Lesene, *The Making of a Southern Research University: The University of South Carolina, 1940–1990* (Ph.D. diss. University of South Carolina, 1998), 1. See also Davidson, *The Last Foray*, and Rogers, "South Carolina Federalists."
24. Goldstein, "State Resistance," noted that no less than 10 Northern states had, in effect, nullified the fugitive slave element of the Compromise of 1850. Northern states' actions exacerbated the existing tension between the slave and the free states, further setting the stage for the coming conflict.
25. Freehling, *Disunion Vol. 1*, 254.
26. A tariff collected for revenue purposes will be lower than a tariff collected for protection. The purpose of a protective tariff is not to collect revenue, and can, therefore, be prohibitively high.
27. *Register of Debates*. 1833. Senate, 22nd Congress, 2nd Sess. Pages 519–553.
28. Frederic Bancroft, *Calhoun and the South Carolina Nullification Movement* (Baltimore, MD: The Johns Hopkins Press, 1928); Chauncey Samuel Boucher, *The Nullification Controversy in South Carolina* (Chicago: University of Chicago Press, 1916).
29. Eugene Genovese, *The Political Economy of Slavery* (New York: Random House, 1967), 159.
30. Keohane, "Associative American Development," 61; Douglass North, *The Economic Growth of the United States 1790–1860* (New York: W.W. Norton and Company, 1966), 76, 233.
31. W. Hardy Wickwar, *300 Years of Development Administration in South Carolina* (Columbia, SC: University of South Carolina Bureau of Governmental Research and Service, 1970), 89.
32. Drew Gilpin Faust, *James Henry Hammond and the Old South: A Design for Mastery* (Baton Rouge: Louisiana State University Press, 1982), 46; William W. Freehling, *Prelude to Civil War: The Nullification Controversy in South Carolina 1816–1836* (New York: Oxford University Press, 1992), 48.
33. Freehling's seminal work on nullification serves as the primary exemplar of this interpretation of nullification. On a contemporaneous discussion of the link between nullification and slavery, see the letters from Robert W.

Barnwell to Robert Barnwell Rhett in John Barnwell, "Hamlet to Hotspur: Letters of Robert Woodward Barnwell to Robert Barnwell Rhett," *South Carolina Historical Magazine* 77, no. 4 (1976), 236–256. J.P. Ochenkowski, "The Origins of Nullification in South Carolina," *The South Carolina Historical Magazine* 83, no. 2 (1982), 121–153 offers a different interpretation of nullification.

34. Daniel Wallace, *The Political Life and Services of the Hon. R. Barnwell Rhett, of South Carolina. By "a Contemporary." (The Late Hon. Daniel Wallace.) And also, his Speech at Grahamville, S.C. July 4, 1859* (Nd), 19. See also Walter B. Edgar, *South Carolina: A History* (Columbia, SC: University of South Carolina Press, 1998), 330.
35. The questionable commitment of non-slaveholding Southerners to slavery played a large role in the account of secession in Freehling's, *Reintegration*.
36. Southern tariff strategies are outlined in F.W. Taussig, *The Tariff History of the United States* (New York: Capricorn, 1962), 88–89.
37. Taussig, *Tariff History*, 102.
38. In convention, each district and parish had a delegation equal to its total representation in the State House of Representatives and State Senate.
39. Richard Hofstadter, *The American Political Tradition* (New York: Knopf, 1962).
40. Pauline Maier, "The Road Not Taken: Nullification, John C. Calhoun, and the Revolutionary Tradition in South Carolina," *The South Carolina Historical Magazine* 82, no. 1 (1981): 15.
41. Edgar, *South Carolina*, 332.
42. Calhoun quoted in Ross M. Lence, ed., *Union and Liberty: The Political Philosophy of John C. Calhoun* (Indianapolis: Liberty Fund, 1992), 383–384. Italics are in original.
43. Taussig, *Tariff History*, 109.
44. *Ibid.*, 110.
45. The "American System" referred to a set of policies advocated by the Whig Party. It included protective tariffs, internal improvements, a strong national bank, and distribution of proceeds from federal land sales to the states. Those who opposed this system were concerned that a strong and active federal government would reduce the independence of the states.
46. State of South Carolina, *Journal of the Convention of the People of South Carolina: Assembled at Columbia on the 19th of November, 1832, and again, on the 11th of March, 1833* (Columbia, SC: Printed from the Original by A.S. Johnston, Printer to the Convention, 1832–33), 28. For more on the link between the American System, protectionism, and consolidation, see Calhoun's *South Carolina Exposition*, which can be found in Lence, *Union and Liberty*.
47. It is no surprise that Freehling's seminal work on this episode is titled *Prelude to Civil War*. This was South Carolina's first major confrontation with the federal government, and the lessons learned from this episode would help to inform the strategy used to accomplish secession. For many, mobilization for secession really began with this dispute over tariff level in the 1820s.
48. This was not the case in 1860, however, when the state was unified behind secession: Stephanie McCurry, *Masters of Small Worlds: Yeoman Households, Gender Relations, and the Political Culture of the Antebellum South Carolina Low Country* (New York: Oxford University Press, 1995), 297. See also Lillian Kibler, "Unionist Sentiment in South Carolina in 1860," *Journal of Southern History* 4, no. 3 (1938), 346–66. Largely absent were the divisions experienced by South Carolina during nullification and the first secession crisis.

49. Edgar, *South Carolina*, 335.
50. Rob Y. Hayne, "Letters on the Nullification Movement in South Carolina, 1830–1834," *The American Historical Review* 6, no. 4 (1901): 736–765.
51. "The conclusion is irresistible that what they—Jefferson & Madison meant as simply declaratory, the South Carolinians determined to be operative . . ." Alfred Huger to Wickham, 2 June 1858, Alfred Huger Papers, Manuscript Collection, Duke University, Durham, North Carolina.
52. State of South Carolina, *Journal of the Convention . . . 1832*, 58.
53. *Ibid.*, 28.
54. *Ibid.*, 33.
55. *Ibid.*, 48.
56. *Ibid.*, 60, emphasis in original.
57. Commager, *Documents of American History*, 262–226, italics in original.
58. In analyzing the conflicts between the center and the state of South Carolina, one cannot fail to notice the difference between Jackson's response and Buchanan's response to South Carolinian challenges. Both found the South Carolina doctrine to be unconstitutional; however, the manner in which each perceived their duty was radically different. Jackson declared that he would not consent to the destruction of the Union. Buchanan believed he had no power to prevent it.
59. George McDuffie to Armistead Burt, 19 February 1833, George McDuffie Papers, Manuscript Collection, Duke University, Durham, North Carolina.
60. Freehling, *Road to Disunion Vol. 1*, 293.
61. Robert Fogel, *Without Consent or Contract: The Rise and Fall of American Slavery* (New York: Norton, 1989), 297.
62. Calhoun's defense of minority rights fits in nicely with the minority rights discourse of the founders: protecting the interests of the wealthy.
63. Calhoun quoted in Lence, *Union and Liberty*, 35.
64. Vukan Kuic, "John C. Calhoun's Theory of the 'Concurrent Majority,'" *American Bar Association Journal* 69 (1983), 482–486.
65. Thomas B. Alexander, "The Civil War as Institutional Fulfillment," *The Journal of Southern History* 47, no. 1 (1981): 3–32.
66. Calhoun's ideas are presented in Lence, *Union and Liberty*, 275–277.
67. George C. Rogers, "South Carolina Federalists and the Origins of the Nullification Movement," *South Carolina Historical Magazine* 71, no. 1 (1970): 17–32.
68. Edgar, *South Carolina*, 336; Freehling, *Reintegration*, 278–279.
69. Chauncey Samuel Boucher, "The Ante-bellum Attitude of South Carolina Towards Manufacturing and Agriculture," *Washington University Studies* 3, no. 2 (1916): 243–270.
70. The term "revolution" is used advisedly. There were no fewer than two ways to understand the position of the South Carolina secessionists: One was that they were acting according to an implicit constitutional right to withdraw from a compact when its terms have been violated. By this view, the actions undertaken were not revolutionary but constitutional, loosely understood. A second view is that the actions taken by South Carolina were not founded in a constitutional right, but rather in a reserved revolutionary right of the people to replace one government for another. According the *Declaration of Independence*, "whenever any government became destructive of these ends [the security of the rights of life, liberty and the pursuit of happiness] it is the right of the people to alter or abolish it."
71. Ames, *State Documents on Federal Relations*, 180.
72. *Ibid.*, 181.
73. *Ibid.*, 183.

74. According to Peter Aranson, "Calhoun's Constitutional Economics," *Constitutional Political Economy* 2, no. 1 (1991): 31–52, John C. Calhoun's early political commitments should be characterized as nationalist. This was not at all uncommon for South Carolinian political elites. By the time of nullification, he adopted a defensively sectionalist position. See also John L. Conger, "South Carolina and the Early Tariffs," *The Mississippi Valley Historical Review* 5, no. 4 (1919): 415–433.
75. Chauncey Samuel Boucher, "The Annexation of Texas and the Bluffton Movement in South Carolina," *Mississippi Valley Historical Review* 6, no. 1 (1919), 3–33.
76. William Barney, *The Road to Secession* (New York and London: Praeger Publishers, 1972), 117. Italics are in original.
77. Eric H. Walther, *The Fire-Eaters* (Baton Rouge and London: Louisiana State University Press, 1992).
78. Barney, *The Road to Secession*, 117.
79. *Congressional Globe*, 29th Congress, 1st Sess., page 1217.
80. *Congressional Globe*, 29th Congress, 2nd Sess., appendix page 315.
81. David Duncan Wallace, *The History of South Carolina* 3 vols. (New York: The American Historical Society, 1934), 116.
82. Emerson David Fite, *The Election of 1860* (New York: The Macmillan Company, 1911), 92.
83. This claim is based on the assumption that slave labor was best suited for certain agricultural enterprises, but not for industrial work, and that industrialization was a threat to slavery. Barney, *Road to Secession*, 29, formulated it this way: "The price of industrialization seemed to be the end of slavery."
84. *Congressional Globe*, 31st Congress, 2nd Sess., Appendix, page 317.
85. *Congressional Globe* 1850. 31st Cong., 1st Sess., page 451.
86. *Congressional Globe* 1850. 31st Cong., 1st Sess., page 452.
87. Potter's, *The Impending Crisis*, 90, chapter about the Compromise of 1850 is titled the "Armistice of 1850."
88. *Ibid.*, 113.
89. *Ibid.*, 116.
90. Nathaniel Beverley Tucker to James Henry Hammond, 17 July 1850, 21 September 1850, Nathaniel Beverley Tucker Papers, Manuscript Collection, Duke University, Durham, North Carolina. In the second letter, Tucker argued that South Carolina was able to secede because of the homogeneity of its population. Moreover, the states bordering South Carolina would not allow anything bad to befall the state if it decided to secede. In addition to all of these arguments, Tucker suggested that action should be taken immediately, because times were good. He wrote, "The time of action is not when you are fasting, but when you are full." South Carolina was "full" at this point, and Tucker believed that if she remained in the Union, the federal government would make sure that the state would never be full again.
91. Potter, *The Impending Crisis*.
92. The Diary of Benjamin Franklin Perry, volume 2, 14 September 1850, Southern Historical Collection, University of North Carolina at Chapel Hill, Chapel Hill, North Carolina.
93. Michael F. Holt, *The Rise and Fall of the American Whig Party* (New York and Oxford: Oxford University Press, 1999), 608.
94. Commager, *Documents of American History*, 324, italics added.
95. John Barnwell, *Love of Order: South Carolina's First Secession Crisis* (Chapel Hill, NC: University of North Carolina Press, 1982), 145.

96. Chauncey Samuel Boucher, "The Secession and Co-operation Movements in South Carolina, 1848 to 1852," *Washington University Studies* 5, no. 2 (1918): 67–138.
97. Edgar, *South Carolina*, 344.
98. Diary Entry, 13 October 1851, Matthew J. Williams Information and Papers, Manuscript Collection, Duke University, Durham, North Carolina.
99. Barnwell, *Love of Order*, 181.
100. Diary Entry, 15 October 1851, Matthew J. Williams Information and Papers, Manuscript Collection, Duke University, Durham, North Carolina. E. W. Rhett to Robert Barnwell Rhett, Robert Barnwell Rhett Papers, 17 October 1851, South Carolina Historical Society, Charleston, South Carolina.
101. David Flavel Jamison to unknown, 8 June 1860, David Flavel Jamison Papers, Manuscript Collection, Duke University, Durham, North Carolina.
102. Barnwell, *Love of Order*, 163.
103. This series of articles by Rutledge was reproduced in pamphlet form in Rutledge, *Separate State Secession Practically Discussed in a Series of Articles Published Originally in the Edgefield Advertiser* (Edgefield, SC: Advertiser Print, 1982). See also D.H. Hamilton, *An Oration Upon the Policy of Separate Secession, Delivered at Bluffton, South Carolina, on the 4th July, 1851* (Charleston, SC: Steam Power Press of Walker and James, 1851).
104. Rutledge, *Separate State Secession*, 26.
105. Ibid., 23. Similar confidence was seen in the second secession crisis. Robert Barnwell Rhett indicated South Carolina's desire to form an alliance with Great Britain, and if Great Britain did not wish for one, they would look for another European partner. Rhett's confidence is related in a letter from British Consul Robert Bunch to Lord John Russell found in "Despatch from the British Consul at Charleston to Lord John Russell, 1860," *American Historical Review* 18, no. 4 (1913), 783–787.
106. Lewis Malone Ayer, Jr., *An Address on the Question of Separate State Secession, to the People of Barnwell District* (Charleston, SC: Steam Power Press of Walker and James, 1851).
107. Armistead Burt, *Southern Rights and Co-operation, Documents. No. 3. Letter from the Hon. Armistead Burt. [to Capt. Thos. B. Byrd, and others]* (N.d.), 6.
108. Laura A. White, *Robert Barnwell Rhett: Father of Secession* (Gloucester, MA: Peter Smith, 1931), 239.
109. A.P. Aldrich to James Henry Hammond, 11 November 1851, James Henry Hammond Papers, Manuscript Collection, Library of Congress, Washington, DC.
110. W.W. Boyce, *Letter from W.W. Boyce to the Hon. John P. Richardson, President of Southern Rights Associations of South Carolina.* (1852).
111. Carol Bleser, ed., *Secret and Sacred: The Diaries of James Henry Hammond, a Southern Slaveholder* (New York: Oxford University Press, 1988), 251–252.
112. State of South Carolina, *Journal of the State Convention of South Carolina Together with the Resolution and Ordinance Held in 1852* (Columbia, SC: Johnson and Davis, Printers to the Convention, 1852), 18.
113. William L. Barney, *The Secessionist Impulse: Alabama and Mississippi in 1860* (Princeton, NJ: Princeton University Press, 1974).
114. Meadwell and Anderson, "Sequence and Strategy," 215.
115. Echoing what most of the South felt about the admission of California, unionist B.F. Perry stated, "The admission of California is wrong . . . but in it there is no violation of the Constitution or point of honor." This is found in

152 *Notes*

The Diary of Benjamin Franklin Perry, vol. 2, 14 September 1850, Southern Historical Collection, University of North Carolina at Chapel Hill, Chapel Hill, North Carolina.
116. B.F. Perry to F.W. Pickens, 27 June 1857, Benjamin Franklin Perry Papers, Southern Historical Collection, University of North Carolina at Chapel Hill, Chapel Hill, North Carolina.
117. Boucher, "The Secession and Cooperation Movements," 138.
118. Greg Craven, *Secession: The Ultimate States Right* (Carlton, Victoria: Melbourne University Press, 1986).

NOTES TO CHAPTER 4

1. William Henry Trescott to William Porcher Miles, 8 February 1859, William Porcher Miles Papers, Southern Historical Collection, University of North Carolina at Chapel Hill, Chapel Hill, North Carolina.
2. William Henry Trescott to William Porcher Miles, 8 February 1859, William Porcher Miles Papers, Southern Historical Collection, University of North Carolina at Chapel Hill, Chapel Hill, North Carolina.
3. Keith T. Poole and Howard Rosenthal, *Congress: A Political-Economic History of Roll Call Voting* (New York and Oxford: Oxford University Press, 1997).
4. [Preston S. Brooks], *Disunion Document, No. 1. Speech of Honorable Preston S. Brooks. Delivered at Columbia, South Carolina, Aug. 29, 1856* (Boston: John P. Jewett & Co., 1856), 8. The pamphlet in which this speech appears was published in the North in order to demonstrate the extent to which Southerners were responsible for the troubles confronting the Union. Brooks, thanks to his caning of Sumner, is called an "assassin."
5. Henry Hardy Perritt, *Robert Barnwell Rhett: South Carolina Secession Spokesman* (Ph.D. diss. University of Florida, 1954), 293–294 noted that the Southern secessionists' "plans for a campaign to bring on secession in 1860 . . . included an opening speech by Rhett." This speech can be found in the Charleston *Mercury* 7 July 1859 and in Wallace, *The Political Life*.
6. Wallace, *The Political Life*; Charleston *Mercury* 7 July 1859.
7. *Ibid.*
8. *Ibid.*
9. *Ibid.*
10. *Ibid.*
11. James Henry Hammond to William Brown Hodgson, 24 January 1847, James Henry Hammond Letters, Manuscript Collection, Duke University, Durham, North Carolina.
12. David Flavel Jamison to unknown, 8 June 1860, David Flavel Jamison Papers, Manuscript Collection, Duke University, Durham, North Carolina.
13. Potter, *The South and the Sectional Conflict*, 204.
14. Potter, *The Impending Crisis*.
15. See Freehling, *Reintegration*, for an interesting interpretation of the Vesey case.
16. Rutledge, *Separate State Secession*.
17. Stephen Channing, *Crisis of Fear: Secession in South Carolina* (New York: Simon and Schuster, 1970), 58–59
18. William Porcher Miles to Christopher G. Memminger, 15 January 1860, Christopher G. Memminger Papers, Southern Historical Collection, University of North Carolina, Chapel Hill, North Carolina.
19. For evidence of Memminger's cooperationist credentials, see *Speech of Mr. Memminger at a Public Meeting of the Friends of Cooperation in the Cause*

of Southern Rights, held in Charleston, September 23, 1851, for the purpose of nominating delegates to the Southern Congress (Charleston, SC: Steam Power Press of Walker and James, 1851). See also Harry Hammond to James Henry Hammond, 9 December 1850, Hammond, Bryan and Cummings Families, South Caroliniana Library, University of South Carolina, Columbia, South Carolina.
20. Resolutions of the South Carolina Legislature quoted in Henry D. Capers, *The Life and Times of C. G. Memminger* (Richmond, VA: Everett Waddey Co., 1893), 241–242.
21. Resolutions of the South Carolina Legislature quoted in Capers, *The Life and Times*, 241–242.
22. *Ibid.*
23. Christopher G. Memminger to William Porcher Miles, 27 December 1859, William Porcher Miles Papers, Southern Historical Collection, University of North Carolina, Chapel Hill, North Carolina.
24. Christopher G. Memminger to William Porcher Miles, 3 January 1860, William Porcher Miles Papers, Southern Historical Collection, University of North Carolina, Chapel Hill, North Carolina.
25. Text of his address can be found in Christopher G. Memminger, *Doc. No. LVIII. Address of the Hon. C.G. Memminger, Special Commissioner from the State of South Carolina, before the Assembled Authorities of the State of Virginia, January 19, 1860* (1860).
26. Ollinger Crenshaw, "Christopher G. Memminger's Mission to Virginia, 1860," Journal of Southern History 8, no. 3 (1942), 334–349 considered this question, but determined that it cannot be definitively answered. Memminger may have gone to Virginia to attempt to save the Union, but the conditions under which it could be saved would never have been acceptable to the North. Unionist proclamations may have betrayed an ulterior secessionist motive. Chauncey Samuel Boucher, "South Carolina and the South on the Eve of Secession, 1852 to 1860," *Washington University Studies* 6, no. 2 (1919): 133 noted that it is difficult to determine what South Carolina wanted when it passed resolutions sending a commissioner to Virginia and calling for funds to protect the state. In the latter instance, the state failed to mention whether protecting the state would be done inside or outside the Union.
27. William Porcher Miles to Christopher G. Memminger, 18 January 1860, Christopher G. Memminger Papers, Southern Historical Collection, University of North Carolina, Chapel Hill, North Carolina.
28. Christopher G. Memminger to Robert Barnwell Rhett, 28 January 1860, Christopher G. Memminger Papers, Manuscript Collection, Library of Congress, Washington, DC.
29. Harold S. Schultz, *Nationalism and Sectionalism in South Carolina 1852–1860* (Durham, NC: Duke University Press, 1950), 203.
30. Christopher G. Memminger to William Porcher Miles, 24 January 1860, William Porcher Miles Papers, Southern Historical Collection, University of North Carolina, Chapel Hill, North Carolina.
31. Christopher G. Memminger to William Porcher Miles, 6 February 1860, William Porcher Miles Papers, Southern Historical Collection, University of North Carolina, Chapel Hill, North Carolina.
32. William Porcher Miles to Christopher G. Memminger, 3 February 1860, William Porcher Miles Papers, Southern Historical Collection, University of North Carolina, Chapel Hill, North Carolina.
33. *Acts of Alabama* 1859–60, pages 658–97, quoted in Clarence P. Denman, *The Secession Movement in Alabama* (Montgomery, AL: Alabama State Department of Archives and History, 1933), 79.

34. Clarence P. Denman, *The Secession Movement in Alabama*, 92.
35. An account of events can be found in Austin L. Venable, "The Conflict Between the Douglas and Yancey Forces in the Charleston Convention," *Journal of Southern History* 8, no. 2 (1942), 226–241. Dean Yarwood, "A Failure in Coalition Maintenance: The Defection of the South Prior to the Civil War," in Sven Groennings, E.W. Kelley, and Michael Leiserson, eds. *The Study of Coalition Behavior: Theoretical Perspectives and Cases from Four Continents*, (New York: Holt, Rinehart and Winston, Inc., 1970), 226 wrote that "effective secession" can be dated from the time the delegates from the Southern states bolted from the convention in Charleston.
36. In his unpublished autobiography, Robert Barnwell Rhett claimed that he offered the following deal to Col. John Richardson of Illinois, confidante of Douglas: "[G]ive us an endorsement of the decision of the Supreme Court of the United States, in the Dred Scott case, and we will give you the whole South for Mr. Douglas; but fail to do this, and the South leaves you, the democratic party will be divided, and Mr. Douglas defeated." This quote is found in "Political Writings: Fragments and appendix to Robert Barnwell Rhett's Autobiography," Robert Barnwell Rhett Papers, South Carolina Historical Society, Charleston, South Carolina. This story may be true, but it is doubtful that Rhett could deliver on his offer. He was hated in the South almost as much as Douglas.
37. As always, the Cincinnati Platform was subject to sectional interpretation, with each section reading it in a way that was consistent with their wider political commitments.
38. Southern Democratic Platform of 1860 found in Commager, *Documents of American History*, 366.
39. Democratic Party Platform of 1860 found in *Ibid.*, 365–366.
40. Potter, *Impending Crisis*, 410. Surprising as it may be, the entire South Carolina delegation to the Charleston Convention did not bolt the convention with the rest of the Southern states. This makes more sense when it is made clear that the South Carolina delegation to the convention was actually strongly unionist. B.F. Perry, one of the only Unionists left in the state in 1860, was one of the three who did not bolt with the rest. See Channing, *Crisis of Fear*, 204n., and Roy Franklin Nichols, *The Disruption of American Democracy* (New York: The Free Press, 1948).
41. Fite, *The Election of 1860*, 108.
42. Thomas B. Alexander, "The Civil War as Institutional Fulfillment," *The Journal of Southern History* 47, No. 1 (1981), 20.
43. Seymour Martin Lipset, *Political Man: The Social Bases of Politics* (Garden City, New York: Doubleday & Company, Inc., 1959), 346.
44. William Henry Gist to Governor Thomas Moore, 5 October 1860, William Henry Gist Papers, South Caroliniana Library, University of South Carolina, Columbia, South Carolina.
45. Governor Ellis to William Henry Gist, 25 October 1860, William Henry Gist Papers, South Caroliniana Library, University of South Carolina, Columbia, South Carolina.
46. Governor Ellis to William Henry Gist, 25 October 1860, William Henry Gist Papers, South Caroliniana Library, University of South Carolina, Columbia, South Carolina.
47. Thomas Moore to William Henry Gist, 26 October 1860, William Henry Gist Papers, South Caroliniana Library, University of South Carolina, Columbia, South Carolina.

48. John J. Pettus to William Henry Gist, 26 October 1860, William Henry Gist Papers, South Caroliniana Library, University of South Carolina, Columbia, South Carolina.
49. Joseph E. Brown to William Henry Gist, 31 October 1860, William Henry Gist Papers, South Caroliniana Library, University of South Carolina, Columbia, South Carolina.
50. Joseph E. Brown to William Henry Gist, 31 October 1860, William Henry Gist Papers, South Caroliniana Library, University of South Carolina, Columbia, South Carolina.
51. A.B. Moore to William Henry Gist, 25 October 1860, William Henry Gist Papers, South Caroliniana Library, University of South Carolina, Columbia, South Carolina.
52. M. S. Perry to William Henry Gist, 9 November 1860, William Henry Gist Papers, South Caroliniana Library, University of South Carolina, Columbia, South Carolina.
53. The hope, according to the letters Gist received, went something like this: If South Carolina secedes, Florida and Mississippi will follow. If Florida, Mississippi, and South Carolina secede, Alabama will follow. South Carolina, Florida, Mississippi, and Alabama were not quite the grand Southern confederacy that South Carolina hoped for, but it was a good start and would provide adequate protection for slavery.
54. Charleston *Mercury*, 3 November 1860.
55. All quotes are taken from Charleston *Mercury*, 3 November 1860.
56. Robert Barnwell Rhett Papers, Political Writings (call number 11/357/6), South Carolina Historical Society, Charleston, South Carolina.
57. North, *Structure and Change*.
58. Republican Party Platform of 1860 in Commager, *Documents of American History*, 363–364.
59. Republican Party Platform of 1860 in *ibid*.
60. The total proportion would have been higher had Zachary Taylor, of Louisiana, by way of Virginia and Kentucky, not died after a little over one year in office.
61. Barnwell, *Love of Order*.
62. Dwight L. Dumond, *Antislavery Origins of the Civil War in the United States* (Ann Arbor: University of Michigan Press, 1939) and J.G. de Roulhac Hamilton "Lincoln's Election an Immediate Menace to Slavery," *American Historical Review* 37, No. 4 (1932): 700–711.
63. Robert William Fogel and Stanley L. Engerman, *Time on the Cross: The Economics of American Negro Slavery* (Boston and Toronto: Little, Brown and Company, 1974), 243.
64. Arthur C. Cole, "Lincoln's Election an Immediate Menace to Slavery in the States," *The American Historical Review* 36, no. 4 (1931), 740–767; John G. Van Deusen, *Economic Bases of Disunion in South Carolina* (New York: Columbia University Press, 1928).
65. Carl Russel Fish, "Removal of Officials by the President of the United States," *American Historical Association Annual Report* 1 (1899), 67–86; Fish, "Lincoln and the Patronage," *American Historical Review* 8, no. 1 (1902), 53–69; Fish, *The Civil Service and the Patronage* (New York: Longmans, Green, and Co., 1905).
66. Clement Eaton, "Censorship of Southern Mails," *American Historical Review* 48, no. 2 (1943), 266–280.
67. Gerald Cullinan, *The Post Office Department* (New York: Frederick A. Praeger, Publishers, 1968).

68. [John Townsend,] *The South Alone Should Govern the South. And African Slavery Should be Controlled by those only who are Friendly to it. [1860 Association Tract No. 1]* (Charleston, NC: Evans and Cogswell, 1860).
69. George C. Rogers, *Generations of Lawyers: A History of the South Carolina Bar* (Columbia, SC: The South Carolina Bar Foundation, 1992), 43. According Mary Boykin Chesnut, *A Diary from Dixie*, Ben Ames Williams, ed., (Cambridge: Harvard University Press, 1980), Magrath was one of the people sent to the state legislature to pressure it into taking action.
70. William Kauffman Scarborough, ed., *The Diary of Edmund Ruffin, volume 1 Toward Independence October, 1856–April 1861* (Baton Rouge and London: Louisiana State University Press, 1972), 485n.
71. Charles Edward Cauthen, *South Carolina Goes to War: 1860–1865* (Chapel Hill, NC: University of North Carolina Press, 1950), 54. *State of South Carolina House Journal, called session*, (November 1860), 18–19.
72. M.W. Gary, *Remarks of M.W. Gary, Esq., of Edgefield, in the House of Representatives, Nov. 9, 1860. In the House of Representatives, Nov. 9, 1860. On Mr. Trenholm's Resolutions (1860)*, 7.
73. Gary, *Remarks*, 7.
74. Scarborough, *The Diary of Edmund Ruffin*, 487.
75. Potter, *Impending Crisis*, 490.
76. Charleston *Mercury*, Saturday, 10 November 1860. Recounting a secession rally featuring prominent citizens of South Carolina and Georgia, the writer noted the following: "Were our Representatives at Columbia at the meeting last night . . . they would no longer falter or hesitate over what their constituents so ardently desire them to accomplish."
77. Both the intention of Georgia to hold a convention and the story of Toombs' resignation were reported in Charleston *Mercury*, Saturday, 10 November 1860.
78. Potter, *Impending Crisis*, 490. For an extended discussion of the military miscalculations on both sides, see Emory M. Thomas, *The Dogs of War: 1861* (New York: Oxford University Press, 2011).
79. Edward McPherson, *The Political History of the United States of America During the Great Rebellion, 1860–1865* (New York: Da Capo Press, 1865), 37.
80. Charles Edward Cauthen, "South Carolina's Decision to Lead the Secessionist Movement," *North Carolina Historical Review* 18, no. 4 (1941): 369.
81. Speech of John Cunningham in the South Carolina House of Representatives, 10 November 1860, reported in Charleston *Daily Courier*, 12 December 1860.
82. *State of South Carolina Senate Journal, called session* (November 1860), 22; *State of South Carolina House Journal, called session* (November 1860); Cauthen, "South Carolina's Decision"; McCarter's Journal, Manuscript Collection, Library of Congress, Washington, DC.
83. McCarter's Journal, Manuscript Collection, Library of Congress, Washington, DC; see also Charleston *Mercury*, Saturday, 10 November 1860.
84. John Berkley Grimball to Elizabeth Grimball, 12 November 1860, John Berkley Grimball Papers, Manuscript Collection, Duke University, Durham, North Carolina.
85. Maxcy Gregg to Robert Barnwell Rhett, 14 September 1858, Robert Barnwell Rhett Papers, South Carolina Historical Society, Charleston, South Carolina.
86. James Henry Hammond, *Selections from the Letters and Speeches of the Hon. James H. Hammond, of South Carolina*. With an Introduction and notes by Clyde N. Wilson, Published for the Southern Studies Program,

Notes 157

University of South Carolina (Spartanburg, SC: The Reprint Company, 1978).
87. Carol Bleser, ed., *Secret and Sacred: The Diaries of James Henry Hammond, a Southern Slaveholder* (New York: Oxford University Press, 1988), 206.
88. James Henry Hammond to Legislature of South Carolina, November 1860, James Henry Hammond Papers, South Caroliniana Library, University of South Carolina, Columbia, South Carolina.
89. James Henry Hammond to Legislature of South Carolina, November 1860, James Henry Hammond Papers, South Caroliniana Library, University of South Carolina, Columbia, South Carolina.
90. James Henry Hammond to Legislature of South Carolina, November 1860, James Henry Hammond Papers, South Caroliniana Library, University of South Carolina, Columbia, South Carolina.
91. James Henry Hammond to Marcellus Hammond, 12 November 1860, James Henry Hammond Papers, Library of Congress, Manuscript Collection, Washington, DC.
92. Jon L. Wakelyn, "The Changing Loyalties of James Henry Hammond: A Reconsideration," *South Carolina Historical Magazine* 75, no. 1 (1974), 1–13. See Lawrence T. McDonnell, "Struggle Against Suicide: James Henry Hammond and the Secession of South Carolina," *Southern Studies* 22, no. 2 (1983), 109–137 for a compelling account of Hammond's decision not to fight secession.
93. Rosser H. Taylor, "Boyce-Hammond Correspondence," *Journal of Southern History* 3, no. 3 (1937): 348.
94. A.P. Aldrich to James Henry Hammond, 25 November 1860, James Henry Hammond Papers, Manuscript Collection, Library of Congress, Washington, DC.
95. A.P. Aldrich to James Henry Hammond, 25 November 1860, James Henry Hammond Papers, Manuscript Collection, Library of Congress, Washington, DC.
96. A.P. Aldrich to James Henry Hammond, 25 November 1860, James Henry Hammond Papers, Manuscript Collection, Library of Congress, Washington, DC.
97. A.P. Aldrich to James Henry Hammond, 25 November 1860, James Henry Hammond Papers, Manuscript Collection, Library of Congress, Washington, DC.
98. A.P. Aldrich to James Henry Hammond, 25 November 1860, James Henry Hammond Papers, Manuscript Collection, Library of Congress, Washington, DC.
99. A.P. Aldrich to James Henry Hammond, 25 November 1860, James Henry Hammond Papers, Manuscript Collection, Library of Congress, Washington, DC.
100. Nichols, *Disruption*, 375. See also John G. Nicolay and John Hay, *Abraham Lincoln: A History Volume Two* (New York: The Century Co., 1890), 317–318.
101. Charleston *Mercury* 3 November 1860.
102. Nicolay and Hay, *Abraham Lincoln*, 315–327.
103. John Bassett Moore, ed., *The Works of James Buchanan* vol. 11 (Philadelphia and London: J.B. Lippincott Company, 1910), 9.
104. Moore, *James Buchanan*, 18; Governor Gist of South Carolina actually received word of Buchanan's view on secession and coercion before the 3 December address in a 19 November 1860 letter from Thomas Drayton. Nicolay and Hay, *Abraham Lincoln*, 323, argued that this gave South Carolina the ability to plan its actions well in advance.

105. Moore, *James Buchanan*, 7.
106. *Ibid.*, 8.
107. McCurry, *Small Worlds*, 297. See also Kibler, "Unionist Sentiment." Scarborough, *Edmund Ruffin*, 493, reported that on 12 November 1860, firsthand witness of South Carolinian attitudes Edmund Ruffin noted, "Every opinion is favorable to the action of the legislature. Since I have been here, I have not heard of a dissenting opinion, either from or of man or woman in S.C."
108. Potter, *Impending Crisis*, 494–495.
109. James W. Gettys, "Mobilization for Secession in Greenville District," *Proceedings and Papers of the Greenville Historical Society 1975–1979* 6 (1981): 50–66; Lillian Kibler, *Benjamin F. Perry: South Carolina Unionist* (Durham, NC: Duke University Press, 1946), 343. Ralph Wooster, *The Secession Conventions of the South* (Princeton, NJ: Princeton University Press, 1962), 15.
110. James Louis Petigru to Susan P. King, 10 November 1860, Vanderhorst Papers, South Carolina Historical Society, Charleston, South Carolina.
111. Chesnut, *Diary from Dixie*, 63.
112. Ford, *Southern Radicalism*, 371.
113. Cauthen, *South Carolina*, 75.
114. Edgefield *Advertiser* 12 December 1860.
115. Charleston *Mercury*, 26 November 1860.
116. New York *Tribune*, 13 December 1860.
117. [F.J. Moses,] "How South Carolina Seceded," *The Nickell Magazine* (1897), 345–351.
118. May Spencer Ringold, "Robert Newman Gourdin and the '1860 Association'," *Georgia Historical Quarterly* 55, no. 4 (1971): 501–509.
119. *Ibid.*, 42. See also Ringold, "Robert Newman," 502.
120. Rogers, *Generations*, 41–45.
121. Rogers, *Generations*, 43.
122. [Townsend], *The South Alone*, 15.
123. Lacy K. Ford, "Republics and Democracy: The Parameters of Political Citizenship in Antebellum South Carolina," in Clyde N. Wilson and David R. Chesnut, eds. *The Meaning of South Carolina History* (Columbia, SC: University of South Carolina Press, 1991), 121–145; Mark D. Kaplanoff, "Charles Pinckney and the American Republican Tradition," in Michael O'Brien and David Moltke-Hansen, eds. *Intellectual Life in Antebellum Charleston*, (Knoxville, TN: University of Tennessee Press, 1986), 85–122.
124. Whitemarsh B. Seabrooke to Governor John Quitman, 14 July 1851, Whitemarsh B. Seabrook Papers, Southern Historical Collection, University of North Carolina at Chapel Hill, Chapel Hill, North Carolina. Similar words are used in W.C. Daniel to Robert Gourdin, 9 December 1860, Robert N. Gourdin Papers, Manuscript Collection, Duke University, Durham, North Carolina.
125. Lacy K. Ford, "Republican Ideology in a Slave Society: The Political Economy of John C. Calhoun," *The Journal of Southern History* 54, no. 3 (1988): 405–424.
126. Potter, *Impending Crisis*, 513.
127. Clarence P. Denman, *The Secession Movement in Alabama* (Montgomery, AL: Alabama State Department of Archives and History, 1933), 112 wrote, "[T]he ostensible purpose of these commissioners was to advise and consult with the other states, but their real mission was to influence them to secede."
128. *Ibid.*, 112; Dumond, *Secession Movement*, 139–140.

129. State of South Carolina, *Journal of the Convention of South Carolina Held in 1860, 1861, and 1862, Together With the Ordinances, Reports, Resolutions* (Columbia, SC: R.W. Gibbes, Printer to the Convention, 1862), 461–466.
130. State of South Carolina, *Journal of the Convention . . . 1860, 1861, and 1862*, 467–476.
131. *Ibid.*
132. According to Kenneth M. Stampp, *The Peculiar Institution: Negro Slavery in the American South* (London: Eyre and Spottiswoode, 1956), one of the central purposes of slavery was to control labor.
133. Hinton Rowan Helper, *The Impending Crisis of the South, How to Meet it* (Cambridge, MA: The Belknap Press of Harvard University Press, 1968).
134. David Y. Thomas, "Southern Non-Slaveholders in the Election of 1860," *Political Science Quarterly* 26, no. 2 (1911), 222–237.
135. Freehling, *Reintegration*, 116; McCurry, *Small Worlds*.
136. Edgar, *South Carolina*, 294.
137. Norma Basch, *Framing American Divorce* (Berkeley, Los Angeles, and London: University of California Press, 1999); Stephanie McCurry, "The Politics of Yeoman Households in South Carolina," in Catherine Clinton and Nina Silber, eds. *Divided Houses: Gender and the Civil War* (New York: Oxford University Press, 1992), 22–42.
138. Paul F. Paskoff and Daniel J. Wilson, *The Cause of the South: Selections from De Bow's Review, 1846–1867* (Baton Rouge and London: Louisiana State University Press, 1982); Henry William Ravenel Journal Entry, 8 November 1860, Henry William Ravenel Journal, South Caroliniana Library, University of South Carolina at Columbia, Columbia, South Carolina.
139. Ford, *Southern Radicalism*.
140. *Congressional Globe*. Senate. 35th Congress, 1st Sess., page 962.
141. Thomas, "Southern Non-Slaveholders."
142. White, *Robert Barnwell Rhett*, 140.
143. Boucher, "South Carolina and the South."
144. William W. Freehling, *The South Vs. The South: How Anti-Confederate Southerners Shaped the Course of the Civil War* (New York: Oxford University Press, 2001), 21.
145. Barney, *Secessionist Impulse*, 229.
146. Hammond recounted that in "a speech made at Barnwell C.H. some two years ago, I said that 'I regarded this union as a policy and not a principle.'" This quote is taken from Hammond's November 1860 letter to the South Carolinian legislature. James Henry Hammond to Legislature of South Carolina, November 1860, James Henry Hammond Papers, South Caroliniana Library, University of South Carolina, Columbia, South Carolina.
147. In 1850 Mississippi's Governor Quitman is quoted in Philip M. Hamer, *The Secession Movement in South Carolina, 1847–1852* (New York: Da Capo Press, 1971), 88–89 as saying: "The secession of a Southern state would startle the whole South, and force the other states to meet the issue plainly; it would present practical issues, and exhibit everywhere a widespread discontent than politicians have imagined." In 1860, Quitman's words became a reality.

NOTES TO CHAPTER 5

1. Greenberg, "Representation and the Isolation."
2. Freehling, *The South vs. the South*.
3. Leonard Price Stavisky, "Industrialism in Ante Bellum Charleston," *Journal of Negro History* 36, no. 3 (1951), 302–322.

4. Congressional Quarterly, Inc., *Congressional Quarterly's Guide to U.S. Elections* (Washington, DC: Congressional Quarterly inc., 1975).
5. Peyton McCrary, Clark Miller and Dale Baum, "Class and Party in the Secession Crisis: Voting Behavior in the Deep South, 1859–1861," *Journal of Interdisciplinary History* 8, no. 3 (1978): 457. This article was a reaction to Lipset, *Political Man*, who claimed that support for secession came predominantly from supporters of presidential candidate John Bell of the Constitutional Union party.
6. Ralph Wooster, *The People in Power: Courthouse and Statehouse in the Lower South, 1850–1860* (Knoxville, TN: University of Tennessee Press, 1969).
7. Freehling, *Road to Disunion*, 265.
8. Potter, *Impending Crisis*, 104.
9. *Ibid.*, 125; White, *Robert Barnwell Rhett*, 112.
10. Potter, *Impending Crisis*, 129.
11. McCormick, *Second American Party*.
12. Potter, *Impending Crisis*.
13. Percy Lee Rainwater, *Mississippi: Storm Center of Secession* (Baton Rouge: Otto Claitor, 1938), 219.
14. Dumond, *Secession Movement*, 137.
15. Charlton W. Tebeau, *A History of Florida* (Coral Gables, Florida: University of Miami Press, 1971), 175–176.
16. Potter, *Impending Crisis*, 104.
17. Wooster, *Secession Conventions*, 68.
18. Potter, *Impending Crisis*, 496.
19. Freehling, *Road to Disunion*, 204, 265; William Warren Rogers, ed., *Alabama: The History of a Deep South State* (Tuscaloosa: University of Alabama Press, 1994), 136.
20. Rogers, *Alabama*, 161.
21. Lewy Dorman, *Party Politics in Alabama from 1850 through 1860* (Tuscaloosa: University of Alabama Press, 1995).
22. *Ibid.*, 79; Rogers, *Alabama*, 181.
23. The rationale behind Alabama's retreat from leading the movement for secession is discussed in the previous chapter.
24. Rogers, *Alabama*, 183.
25. Denman, *Secession Movement*.
26. Wooster, *Secession Conventions*, 59n.
27. Freehling, *Road to Disunion*, 265.
28. Kenneth Coleman, ed., *A History of Georgia* (Athens: University of Georgia Press, 1991), 134.
29. Charleston *Mercury*, 10 March 1860; S.L. Burn to C.L. Burn, 12 November 1860, Burn Family Papers, South Caroliniana Library, University of South Carolina at Columbia, Columbia, South Carolina.
30. Don E. Fehrenbacher, *The South and Three Sectional Crises* (Baton Rouge and London: Louisiana State University Press, 1980), 5.
31. Potter, *Impending Crisis*, 496n.
32. William W. Freehling and Craig M. Simpson, eds. *Secession Debated: Georgia's Showdown in 1860* (New York: Oxford University Press, 1992).
33. Charles Edwards O'Neill, *Louisiana, A History* (Arlington Heights, IL: Forum Press, 1984), 124.
34. Dumond, *Secession Movement*, 208.
35. Ben H. Procter, *Not Without Honor: The Life of John H. Reagan* (Austin: University of Texas Press, 1962), 74.

36. Edward McPherson, *The Political History of the United States of America During the Great Rebellion, 1860–1865* (New York: Da Capo Press, 1972), 1.
37. Wooster, *Secession Conventions*, 124.
38. Earl Wesley Fornell, *The Galveston Era: The Texas Crescent on the Eve of Secession* (Austin: University of Texas Press, 1961), 290; Potter, *Impending Crisis*, 497.
39. Fornell, *Galveston Era*, 290–291; Wooster, *Secession Conventions*, 124.
40. Wooster, *Secession Conventions*, 129.
41. William J. Donnelly, "Conspiracy or Popular Movement: The Historiography of Southern Support for Secession," *North Carolina Historical Review* 42, no. 1 (1965), 70–84.
42. Walter Beunger, *Secession and the Union in Texas* (Austin: University of Texas Press, 1984), 3. George Creel, *Sam Houston, Colossus in Buckskin* (New York: Cosmopolitan Book Corporation, 1928), 331–332. Donald Day and Harry Herbert Ullom, eds., *The Autobiography of Sam Houston* (Norman: University of Oklahoma Press, 1954), 270.
43. Wooster, *Secession Conventions*, 20, 161.
44. Freehling, *Road to Disunion*, 204, 265; Alfred Huger to Wickham, 2 June 1858, Alfred Huger Papers, Manuscript Collection, Duke University, Durham, North Carolina.
45. Avery O. Craven, *The Growth of Southern Nationalism, 1848–1861* (Baton Rouge: Louisiana State University Press, 1953), 103.
46. Henry T. Shanks, *The Secession Movement in Virginia, 1847–1861* (Richmond, VA: Garrett and Massie Publishers, 1934), 97–99.
47. Ibid., 117.
48. Ibid., 144.
49. Ibid., 145.
50. Michael P. Riccards, "Lincoln and the Political Question: The Creation of the State of West Virginia," *Presidential Studies Quarterly* 27, no. 3 (1997), 549–564.
51. The Crittenden Compromise refers to a set of measures proposed by Senator Crittenden of Tennessee. If successful, the compromise would have added an unamendable amendment to the Constitution that would have reestablished the Missouri Compromise line, but preemptively prohibiting slavery above the line and recognizing slavery below the line. Congress did not approve the Compromise. Even if it had, Lincoln would not have supported the extension of slavery. The Crittenden Peace Resolutions can be found in Commager, *Documents of American History*, 369–370.
52. Wooster, *Secession Conventions*, 147; Shanks, *Secession Movement*, 190.
53. Shanks, *Secession Movement*, 198.
54. Langdon Cheves to Charlotte McCord Cheves, 10 April 1861, The West Manuscripts, South Carolina Historical Society, Charleston, South Carolina. Emphasis is in original.
55. Daniel W. Crofts, *Reluctant Confederates: Upper South Unionists in the Secession Crisis* (Chapel Hill, NC: University of North Carolina Press, 1989), 337.
56. James. M. Schreckhise to unknown, 20 April 1861, James. M. Schreckhise Papers, Manuscript Collection, Duke University, Durham, North Carolina.
57. Wooster, *Secession Conventions*, 149.
58. James M. Woods, *Rebellion and Realignment: Arkansas's Road to Secession* (Fayetteville, AR: University of Arkansas Press, 1987), 48–49.
59. Ibid., 122.
60. Wooster, *Secession Conventions*, 157.

61. James Ford Rhodes, *History of the United States from the Compromise of 1850* (New York: The Macmillan Company, 1953), 381–382; Wooster, *Secession Conventions*, 157.
62. Wooster, *Secession Conventions*, 164.
63. Robert E. Corlew, *Tennessee: A Short History* (Knoxville, TN: University of Tennessee Press, 1990), 273.
64. Corlew, *Tennessee*, 272–273.
65. Crofts, *Reluctant Confederates*, 346.
66. Joseph C. Sitterson, *The Secession Movement in North Carolina* (Chapel Hill, NC: University of North Carolina Press, 1939), 31.
67. Boucher, *Nullification*, 241.
68. Sitterson, *Secession Movement*, 63.
69. *Ibid.*, 74.
70. *Ibid.*, 223.
71. *Ibid.*
72. *Ibid.*, 222.
73. Wooster, *Secession Conventions*, 195.
74. Dumond, *Secession Movement*.
75. Weingast, "Political Instability."
76. Wooster, *Secession Conventions*, 226.
77. Walter Harrington Ryle, *Missouri: Union or Secession* (Nashville, TN: George Peabody College for Teachers, 1931), 221.
78. Wooster, *Secession Conventions*, 233.
79. Thomas D. Clark, *A History of Kentucky* (Lexington, KY: John Bradford Press, 1960), 308.
80. Wooster, *Secession Conventions*, 216–217, felt that the pro and con position on neutrality was analogous to secessionism and unionism, respectively. James M. McPherson, *Battle Cry of Freedom: The Civil War Era* (New York: Oxford University Press, 1988), 294 noted, "in theory, neutrality was little different from secession." The neutralist position was, like secession, based upon the proposition of state sovereignty. Further, in practice, the Confederates were given a considerable about of room to operate within the state of Kentucky, both in terms of recruiting soldiers for the confederate cause and in terms of funneling trade to the Confederate States through its territory.
81. Lawrence M. Denton, *A Southern Star for Maryland: Maryland and the Secession Crisis, 1860–1861* (Baltimore, MD: Publishing Concepts, 1995), 60.
82. There were extra-legislative efforts of the sort seen in Texas to force the holding of a convention, but these efforts ceased once it became evident that the governor would have to call a convention of the people.
83. Denton, *Southern Star*, 113.
84. Bruce Catton, *Reflections on the Civil War* (New York: Berkley Books, 1982), 33.
85. John Thomas Scharf, *History of Delaware: 1609–1888* (Philadelphia: L.J. Richards, 1888), 317.
86. Potter, *Impending Crisis*, 104.
87. Wooster, *Secession Conventions*, 254.
88. The Washington Peace Conference was an effort initiated by Virginia to save the Union. The Conference recommended a series of constitutional amendments that were virtually identical to those recommended by Crittenden. Congress failed to act of these recommendations.
89. Wooster, *Secession Conventions*, 255.
90. *Ibid.*

91. The secession banner hung in Institute Hall in Charleston when the ordinance of secession was adopted. It now hangs in the South Carolina Historical Society. In the banner, the Southern Republic is built from 15 blocks, representing the 15 slave states, with South Carolina as the keystone. This illustrates both the confidence that South Carolinians had that their efforts would compel the entire slave South to secede and a sense of the state's importance in securing the creation of a Southern confederacy.
92. Moore, *Social Origins*; Greenberg, *Second American Revolution*.

NOTES TO CHAPTER 6

1. Cole, "Lincoln's Election."
2. Lawrence M. Anderson, "Federalism and Secessionism: Institutional Influences on Nationalist Politics in Québec," *Nationalism and Ethnic Politics* 13, no. 2 (2007): 187–211; Hudson Meadwell, "The Politics of Nationalism in Quebec," *World Politics* 45, no. 2 (1993): 203–241.
3. Paul Romney, "Provincial Equality, Special Status and the Compact Theory of Canadian Confederation," *Canadian Journal of Political Science* 32 (1999): 21–40.
4. Hudson Meadwell, "Secession, States and International Society," *Review of International Studies* 25, No. 3 (1999), 371–387.
5. Charles F. Doran, "Will Canada unravel?," *Foreign Affairs* 75, no. 5 (1996), 97–109.
6. Beth V. and Robert M. Yarbrough, "Unification and Secession: Group Size and 'Escape from Lock-In'," *Kyklos* 51, no. 2 (1998): 171–195.

References

UNPUBLISHED SOURCES

Manuscripts Department, Perkins Library, Duke University, Durham, North Carolina

Nathaniel Beverley Tucker Papers
Matthew J. Williams Papers
Alfred Huger Papers
George McDuffie Papers
David Flavel Jamison Papers
John Berkley Grimball Papers
James M. Schreckhise Papers
Robert N. Gourdin Papers
Laurence Massillon Keitt letters

Manuscripts Division, Library of Congress, Washington, DC

James Henry Hammond Papers
McCarter's Journal
C.G. Memminger Papers

South Carolina Historical Society, Charleston, South Carolina

Vanderhorst Family Papers
Robert Barnwell Rhett Papers
Cheves, The West Manuscripts

Manuscripts Division, South Caroliniana Library, University of South Carolina, Columbia, South Carolina

James Henry Hammond Papers and Diary
William Henry Gist Papers
Hammond, Bryan and Cummings Papers
Burn Family Papers
Henry William Ravenel Journals

Southern Historical Collection, University of North Carolina at Chapel Hill, Chapel Hill, North Carolina

Christopher G. Memminger Papers
William Porcher Miles Papers
Benjamin F. Perry Papers
Benjamin F. Perry Diaries
Whitemarsh B. Seabrook Papers
Joseph W. Lesesne Papers

PUBLISHED SOURCES

Pamphlets

Ayer, Lewis Malone Jr. *An Address on the Question of Separate State Secession, to the People of Barnwell District.* (Charleston, SC: Steam Power Press of Walker and James, 1851).

Boyce, W.W. *Letter from W.W. Boyce to the Hon. John P. Richardson, President of Southern Rights Associations of South Carolina.* (1852).

Brooks, Preston S. *Disunion Document, No. 1. Speech of Honorable Preston S. Brooks. Delivered at Columbia, South Carolina, Aug. 29, 1856.* (Boston: John P. Jewett & Co., 1856).

Burt, Armistead. *Southern Rights and Co-operation, Documents. No. 3. Letter from the Hon. Armistead Burt. [to Capt. Thos. B. Byrd, and others].* (N.d.)

Gary, M.W. *Remarks of M.W. Gary, Esq., of Edgefield, in the House of Representatives, Nov. 9, 1860. In the House of Representatives, Nov. 9, 1860. On Mr. Trenholm's Resolutions.* (1860).

Hamilton, D.H. *An Oration Upon the Policy of Separate Secession, Delivered at Bluffton, South Carolina, on the 4th July, 1851.* (Charleston, SC: Steam Power Press of Walker and James, 1851).

Porter, William D. *State Sovereignty and the Doctrine of Coercion, by the Hon. Wm. D. Porter; Together with a Letter from Hon. J.K. Paulding, Former Sec. Of Navy. Right to Secede by "States".* [1860 Association Tract No. 2] (Charleston, SC: Evans and Cogswell, 1860).

Rutledge. *Separate State Secession Practically Discussed in a Series of Articles Published Originally in the Edgefield Advertiser.* (Edgefield, SC: Advertiser Print, 1851).

Speech of Mr. Memminger at a Public Meeting of the Friends of Cooperation in the Cause of Southern Rights, held in Charleston, September 23, 1851, for the purpose of nominating delegates to the Southern Congress. (Charleston, SC: Steam Power Press of Walker and James, 1851).

[Townsend, John]. *The South Alone Should Govern the South. And African Slavery Should be Controlled by those only who are Friendly to it.* [1860 Association Tract No. 1] (Charleston, SC: Evans and Cogswell, 1860).

Troup. *To the People of the South. Senator Hammond and the Tribune.* [1860 Association Tract No. 3]. (Charleston, SC: Evans and Cogswell, 1860).

Wallace, Daniel. *The Political Life and Services of the Hon. R. Barnwell Rhett, of South Carolina. By "a Contemporary." (The Late Hon. Daniel Wallace.) And also, his Speech at Grahamville, S.C. July 4, 1859.* (N.d.)

Newspapers and other periodicals

Charleston *Daily Courier*
Charleston *Mercury*
Charleston *Standard*
Edgefield *Advertiser*
New York *Tribune*
Congressional Globe
Register of Debates

State of South Carolina Government Documents

State of South Carolina. South Carolina Legislature. House. *Journal of the House of Representatives of South Carolina.*
State of South Carolina. South Carolina Legislature. Senate. *Journal of the Senate of South Carolina.*
State of South Carolina. *Journal of the Convention of the People of South Carolina: Assembled at Columbia on the 19th of November, 1832, and again, on the 11th of March, 1833.* Columbia, SC: Printed from the Original by A.S. Johnston, Printer to the Convention, 1832–33.
State of South Carolina. *Journal of the State Convention of South Carolina Together with the Resolution and Ordinance Held in 1852.* Columbia, SC: Johnson and Davis, Printers to the Convention, 1852.
State of South Carolina. *Reports and Resolutions of the General Assembly of the State of South Carolina passed at the Annual Session of 1860.* Columbia, SC: R.W. Gibbes, State Printer, 1860.
State of South Carolina. *Journal of the Convention of South Carolina Held in 1860, 1861, and 1862, Together With the Ordinances, Reports, Resolutions.* Columbia, SC: R.W. Gibbes, Printer to the Convention, 1862.

SECONDARY SOURCES

[Moses, F.J.]. "How South Carolina Seceded." *The Nickell Magazine* (1897): 345–351.
Alden, John R. *A History of the American Revolution.* New York: Da Capo, 1969.
Alexander, Thomas B. "The Civil War as Institutional Fulfillment." *Journal of Southern History* 47, no. 1 (1981): 3–32.
American Historical Review. "Despatch from the British Consul at Charleston to Lord John Russell, 1860." *American Historical Review* 18, no. 4 (1913): 783–787.
Ames, Herman V., ed. *State Documents on Federal Relations: The States and the United States.* New York: Da Capo Press, 1970.
Amoretti, Ugo and Nancy Bermeo, eds. *Federalism and Territorial Cleavages.* Baltimore, MD: Johns Hopkins University Press, 2004.
Anderson, Lawrence M. "Federalism and Secessionism: Institutional Influences on Nationalist Politics in Québec." *Nationalism and Ethnic Politics* 13, no. 2 (2007): 187–211.
Aranson, Peter. 1991. "Calhoun's Constitutional Economics." *Constitutional Political Economy* 2, no. 1 (1991): 31–52

References

Ashworth, John. *Slavery, Capitalism, and Politics in the Antebellum Republic.* New York: Cambridge University Press, 1995.
Bancroft, Frederic. *Calhoun and the South Carolina Nullification Movement.* Baltimore, MD: The Johns Hopkins Press, 1928.
Banner, James M. Jr. "The Problem of South Carolina." In *The Hofstadter Aegis, A Memorial*, edited by Stanley Elkins and Eric McKitrick, 60–93. New York: Knopf, 1974.
Barker, Ernest. *The Development of Public Services in Western Europe.* Hamden, CT: Archon Books, 1966.
Barney, William. *The Road to Secession.* New York and London: Praeger Publishers, 1972.
Barney, William L. *The Secessionist Impulse: Alabama and Mississippi in 1860.* Princeton, NJ: Princeton University Press, 1974.
Barnwell, John. "Hamlet to Hotspur: Letters of Robert Woodward Barnwell to Robert Barnwell Rhett." *South Carolina Historical Magazine* 77, no. 4 (1976): 236–256.
Barnwell, John. *Love of Order: South Carolina's First Secession Crisis.* Chapel Hill, NC: University of North Carolina Press, 1982.
Basch, Norma. *Framing American Divorce.* Berkeley, Los Angeles, and London: University of California Press, 1999.
Beard, Charles A. and Mary R. *The Rise of American Civilization* 2 vols. New York: The Macmillan Company, 1927.
Bednar, Jenna. *The Robust Federation.* New York: Cambridge University Press, 2009.
Beer, Samuel H. *To Make A Nation: The Rediscovery of American Federalism.* Cambridge, MA: Harvard University Press, 1993.
Bensel, Richard Franklin. *Yankee Leviathan: The Origins of Central State Authority in America, 1859–1877.* Cambridge: Cambridge University Press, 1990.
Bermeo, Nancy. "The Import of Institutions." *Journal of Democracy* 13 (2002): 96–110.
Beunger, Walter. *Secession and the Union in Texas.* Austin: University of Texas Press, 1984.
Birnbaum, Pierre. *States and Collective Action: The European Experience.* Cambridge: Cambridge University Press, 1988.
Bleser, Carol, ed. *Secret and Sacred: The Diaries of James Henry Hammond, a Southern Slaveholder.* New York: Oxford University Press, 1988.
Boucher, Chauncey Samuel. *The Nullification Controversy in South Carolina.* Chicago: University of Chicago Press, 1916.
Boucher, Chauncey Samuel. "The Ante-bellum Attitude of South Carolina Towards Manufacturing and Agriculture." *Washington University Studies* 3, no. 2 (1916): 243–270.
Boucher, Chauncey Samuel. "The Secession and Co-operation Movements in South Carolina, 1848 to 1852." *Washington University Studies* 5, no. 2 (1918): 67–138.
Boucher, Chauncey Samuel. "South Carolina and the South on the Eve of Secession, 1852 to 1860." *Washington University Studies* 6, no. 2 (1919): 81–144.
Boucher, Chauncey Samuel. "The Annexation of Texas and the Bluffton Movement in South Carolina." *Mississippi Valley Historical Review* 6, no. 1 (1919): 3–33.
Bowman, Shearer Davis. "Antebellum Planters and Vormarz Junkers in Comparative Perspective." *American Historical Review* 85, no. 4 (1980): 779–808.
Brancati, Dawn. "Decentralization: Fueling the Fire or Dampening the Flames of Ethnic Conflict and Secessionism." *International Organizations* 60 (2006): 651–685.

Bright, Charles and Susan Harding, eds. *State-Making and Social Movements: Essays in History and Theory.* Ann Arbor: University of Michigan Press, 1984.
Buchanan, Allen. "Federalism, Secession, and the Morality of Inclusion." *Arizona Law Review* 37 (1995): 53–63.
Bunce, Valerie. *Subversive Institutions: The Design and the Destruction of Socialism and the State.* Cambridge and New York: Cambridge University Press, 1999.
Capers, Henry D. *The Life and Times of C. G. Memminger.* Richmond, VA: Everett Waddey Co., 1893.
Catton, Bruce. *Reflections on the Civil War.* New York: Berkley Books, 1982.
Cauthen, Charles Edward. "South Carolina's Decision to Lead the Secessionist Movement." *North Carolina Historical Review* 19 (1941): 360–372.
Cauthen, Charles Edward. *South Carolina Goes to War: 1860–1865.* Chapel Hill, NC: University of North Carolina Press, 1950.
Chambers, William Nesbit and Walter Dean Burnham. *The American Party System: Stages of Political Development.* London and New York: Oxford University Press, 1967.
Channing, Stephen. *Crisis of Fear: Secession in South Carolina.* New York: Simon and Schuster, 1970.
Chesnut, Mary Boykin. *A Diary from Dixie.* Ben Ames Williams, ed. Cambridge, MA: Harvard University Press, 1980.
Clark, Thomas D. *A History of Kentucky.* Lexington, Kentucky: John Bradford Press, 1960.
Cole, Arthur C. "Lincoln's Election an Immediate Menace to Slavery in the States." *American Historical Review* 36, no. 4 (1931): 740–767.
Coleman, Kenneth, ed. *A History of Georgia.* Athens: University of Georgia Press, 1991.
Commager, Henry Steele, ed. *Documents of American History,* seventeenth edition. New York: Appleton-Century-Crofts, 1963.
Conger, John L. "South Carolina and the Early Tariffs." *Mississippi Valley Historical Review* 5, no. 4 (1919): 415–433.
Congressional Quarterly, Inc. *Congressional Quarterly's Guide to U.S. Elections.* Washington, DC: Congressional Quarterly Inc, 1975.
Corlew, Robert E. *Tennessee: A Short History.* Knoxville, TN: University of Tennessee Press, 1990.
Cornell, Svante E. "Autonomy as a Source of Conflict: Caucasian Conflict in Theoretical Perspective." *World Politics* 54 (2002): 245–276.
Craven, Avery O. *The Growth of Southern Nationalism, 1848–1861.* Baton Rouge: Louisiana State University Press, 1953.
Craven, Greg. *Secession: The Ultimate States Right.* Carlton, Victoria: Melbourne University Press, 1986.
Creel, George. *Sam Houston, Colossus in Buckskin.* New York: Cosmopolitan Book Corporation, 1928.
Crenshaw, Ollinger. "Christopher G. Memminger's Mission to Virginia, 1860." *Journal of Southern History* 8, no. 3 (1942): 334–349.
Crofts, Daniel W. *Reluctant Confederates: Upper South Unionists in the Secession Crisis.* Chapel Hill, NC: University of North Carolina Press, 1989.
Cullinan, Gerald. *The Post Office Department.* New York: Frederick A. Praeger, Publishers, 1968.
Davidson, Chalmers Gaston. *The Last Foray, The South Carolina Planters of 1860: A Sociological Study.* Columbia, SC: University of South Carolina Press, 1971.
Day, Donald and Harry Herbert Ullom, eds. *The Autobiography of Sam Houston.* Norman: University of Oklahoma Press, 1954.

De Tocqueville, Alexis. *Democracy in America* 2 vols. New York: Vintage Books, 1990.
Denman, Clarence P. *The Secession Movement in Alabama.* Montgomery, AL: Alabama State Department of Archives and History, 1933.
Denton, Lawrence M. *A Southern Star for Maryland: Maryland and the Secession Crisis, 1860–1861.* Baltimore, MD: Publishing Concepts, 1995.
Deudney, Daniel H. "The Philadelphian System: Sovereignty, Arms Control, and Balance of Power in the American States-Union, circa 1787–1861." *International Organization* 49 (1995): 191–228.
Dion, Stephane. "Why is Secession Difficult in Well-Established Democracies? Lessons from Quebec." *British Journal of Political Science* 26 (1996): 269–283.
Donnelly, William J. "Conspiracy or Popular Movement: The Historiography of Southern Support for Secession." *North Carolina Historical Review* 42 (1965): 70–84.
Doran, Charles F. "Will Canada unravel?" *Foreign Affairs* 75, no. 5 (1996): 97–109.
Dorff, Robert H. "Federalism in Eastern Europe: Part of the Solution or Part of the Problem?" *Publius: The Journal of Federalism* 24 (1994): 99–114.
Dorman, Lewy. *Party Politics in Alabama from 1850 through 1860.* Tuscaloosa: University of Alabama Press, 1995.
Dumond, Dwight L. *The Secession Movement: 1860–1861.* New York: The Macmillan Company, 1931.
Dumond, Dwight L. *Antislavery Origins of the Civil War in the United States.* Ann Arbor: University of Michigan Press, 1959.
Eaton, Clement. "Censorship of Southern Mails," *American Historical Review* 48, no. 2 (1943): 266–280.
Edgar, Walter B. *South Carolina: A History.* Columbia, SC: University of South Carolina Press, 1998.
Emizet, Kisangani N. and Vicki L. Hesli. "The Disposition to Secede: An Analysis of the Soviet Case." *Comparative Political Studies* 27 (1995): 493–536.
Erk, Jan. "Does Federalism Really Matter?" *Comparative Politics* 39, no. 1 (2006): 103–120.
Erk, Jan "Federalism as a Growth Industry." *Publius: The Journal of Federalism*, 37, no. 2 (2007): 262–278.
Erk, Jan and Lawrence M. Anderson, eds. *The Paradox of Federalism.* London: Routledge Press, 2010.
Erk, Jan and Wilfried Swenden, eds. *New Directions in Federalism Studies.* London: Routledge, 2009.
Ertman, Thomas. *Birth of the Leviathan: Building States and Regimes in Medieval and Early Modern Europe.* New York: Cambridge University Press, 1997.
Eysturlid, Lee W. "'An Opportunity to Show their Epaulets and Feathers': The South Carolina Militia During the First Secession Crisis, 1848–1851." *Armed Forces and Society* 20 (1994): 303–316.
Faust, Drew Gilpin. *James Henry Hammond and the Old South: A Design for Mastery.* Baton Rouge: Louisiana State University Press, 1982.
Fehrenbacher, Don E. *The South and Three Sectional Crises.* Baton Rouge and London: Louisiana State University Press, 1980.
Filippov, Mikhail, Peter C. Ordeshook, and Olga Shvetsova. *Designing Federalism: A Theory of Self-Sustainable Federal Institutions.* Cambridge: Cambridge University Press, 2004.
Fish, Carl Russell. "Removal of Officials by the President of the United States." *American Historical Association Annual Report* 1 (1899): 67–86.
Fish, Carl Russell. "Lincoln and the Patronage." *American Historical Review* 8, no. 1 (1902): 53–69.

Fish, Carl Russell. *The Civil Service and the Patronage*. New York: Longmans, Green, and Co., 1905.
Fite, Emerson David. *The Election of 1860*. New York: The Macmillan Company, 1911.
Flynn, Jean Martin. *The Militia in Antebellum South Carolina Society*. Spartanburg, SC: The Reprint Company, 1991.
Fogel, Robert William. *Without Consent or Contract: The Rise and Fall of American Slavery*. New York: Norton, 1989.
Fogel, Robert William and Stanley L. Engerman. *Time on the Cross: The Economics of American Negro Slavery*. Boston and Toronto: Little, Brown and Company, 1974.
Ford, Lacy K. *Origins of Southern Radicalism: The South Carolina Upcountry, 1800–1860*. New York: Oxford University Press, 1988.
Ford, Lacy K. "Republican Ideology in a Slave Society: The Political Economy of John C. Calhoun," *The Journal of Southern History* 54, no. 3 (1988): 405–424.
Ford, Lacy K. "Republics and Democracy: The Parameters of Political Citizenship in Antebellum South Carolina." In *The Meaning of South Carolina History*, edited by Clyde N. Wilson and David R. Chesnut, 121–145. Columbia, SC: University of South Carolina Press, 1991.
Fornell, Earl Wesley. *The Galveston Era: The Texas Crescent on the Eve of Secession*. Austin: University of Texas Press, 1961.
Freehling, William W. *Prelude to Civil War: The Nullification Controversy in South Carolina 1816–1836*. New York: Oxford University Press, 1965.
Freehling, William W. *The Road to Disunion, Volume I: Secessionists at Bay, 1776–1854*. New York: Oxford University Press, 1990.
Freehling, William W. *The Reintegration of American History: Slavery and the Civil War*. New York: Oxford University Press, 1994.
Freehling, William W. *The South vs. The South: How Anti-Confederate Southerners Shaped the Course of the Civil War*. New York: Oxford University Press, 2001.
Freehling, William W. *The Road to Disunion, Volume II: Secessionists Triumphant*. New York: Oxford University Press, 2007.
Freehling, William W. and Craig M. Simpson, eds. *Secession Debated: Georgia's Showdown in 1860*. New York: Oxford University Press, 1992.
Genovese, Eugene. *The Political Economy of Slavery*. New York: Random House, 1967.
George, Alexander and Andrew Bennett. *Case Studies and Theory Development in the Social Sciences*. Cambridge, MA: MIT Press, 2005.
Gettys, James W. "Mobilization for Secession in Greenville District." *Proceedings and Papers of the Greenville Historical Society 1975–1979* 6 (1981): 50–66.
Ghai, Yash. "Autonomy as a Strategy for Diffusing Conflict." In *International Conflict Resolution after the Cold War*, edited by Paul C. Stern and Daniel Druckman, 483–530. Washington, DC: National Academy Press, 2000.
Goldstein, Erik. *Wars and Peace Treaties: 1816–1991*. London: Routledge, 1992.
Goldstein, Leslie Friedman. "State Resistance to Authority in Federal Unions: The Early United States (1790–1860) and the European Community (1958–94)." *Studies in American Political Development* 11 (1997): 149–189.
Gorenburg, Dmitry. 2003. *Minority Ethnic Mobilization in the Russian Federation*. Cambridge: Cambridge University Press.
Greenberg, Kenneth S. *The Second American Revolution: South Carolina Politics, Society, and Secession, 1776–1860*. Ph.D. diss. University of Wisconsin, 1976.
Greenberg, Kenneth S. "Representation and the Isolation of South Carolina, 1776–1860." *Journal of American History* 63, no. 3 (1977): 723–743.

Gurr, Ted Robert. *Peoples versus States: Minorities at Risk in the New Century.* Washington, DC: United States Institute of Peace Press, 2000.

Hale, Henry E. "Divided We Stand: Institutional Sources of Ethnofederal State Survival and Collapse." *World Politics* 56 (2004): 165–193

Hale, Henry E. "The Double-Edged Sword of Ethnofederalism: Ukraine and the USSR in Comparative Perspective." *Comparative Politics* 40, no. 2 (2008): 293–312.

Hall, Peter. *Governing the Economy: The Politics of State Intervention in Britain and France.* New York: Oxford University Press, 1986.

Hamer, Philip M. *The Secession Movement in South Carolina, 1847–1852.* New York: Da Capo Press, 1971.

Hamilton, Alexander, James Madison, and John Jay. *The Federalist Papers.* New York: Penguin Books, 1961.

Hamilton, J.G de Roulhac. "Lincoln's Election an Immediate Menace to Slavery." *American Historical Review* 37, no. 4 (1932): 700–711.

Hammond, James Henry. 1866. *Selections from the Letters and Speeches of the Hon. James H. Hammond, of South Carolina.* With an Introduction and notes by Clyde N. Wilson. Published for the Southern Studies Program, University of South Carolina. Spartanburg, SC: The Reprint Company, 1978.

Hayne, Rob Y. "Letters on the Nullification Movement in South Carolina, 1830–1834." *American Historical Review* 6, no. 4 (1901): 736–765.

Hechter, Michael. "The Dynamics of Secession." *Acta Sociologica* 35, No. 4 (1992): 367–373.

Hechter, Michael and Dina Okamoto. "Political Consequences of Minority Group Formation." *Annual Review of Political Science* 4 (2001): 189–215.

Helper, Hinton Rowan. *The Impending Crisis of the South, How to Meet it.* Cambridge, MA: The Belknap Press of Harvard University Press, 1968.

Hofstadter, Richard. *The American Political Tradition.* New York: Knopf, 1962.

Holt, Michael F. *The Political Crisis of the 1850s.* New York: John Wiley and Sons, 1978.

Holt, Michael F. *The Rise and Fall of the American Whig Party.* New York and Oxford: Oxford University Press, 1999.

Horowitz, Donald L. *Ethnic Groups in Conflict.* Berkeley: University of California Press, 1985.

Jervis, Robert. "Political Implications of Loss Aversion." *Political Psychology* 13, no. 2 (1992): 187–204.

Jessop, Bob. *State Theory: Putting States in their Place.* University Park, PA: Pennsylvania State University Press, 1990.

Jessup, John E., editor in chief and Louise B. Ketz, executive editor. *Encyclopedia of the American Military* 3 vols. 1994.

Jillson, Calvin C. *Constitution Making: Conflict and Consensus in the Federal Convention of 1787.* New York: Agathon Press, 1988.

Kaplanoff, Mark D. "Charles Pinckney and the American Republican Tradition." In *Intellectual Life in Antebellum Charleston*, edited by Michael O'Brien and David Moltke-Hansen, 85–122. Knoxville, TN: University of Tennessee Press, 1986.

Kato, Junko. "Review Article: Institutions and Rationality in Politics—Three Varieties of New-Institutionalists." *British Journal of Political Science* 26, no. 4 (1996): 553–582.

Keohane, Robert. "Associative American Development, 1776–1860: Economic Growth and Political Disintegration." In *The Antinomies of Interdependence: National Welfare and the International Division of Labor*, edited by John Gerard Ruggie, 43–90. New York: Columbia University Press, 1983.

Kibler, Lillian. 1938. "Unionist Sentiment in South Carolina in 1860." *Journal of Southern History* 4 (1938): 346–366.
Kibler, Lillian. *Benjamin F. Perry: South Carolina Unionist*. Durham, NC: Duke University Press, 1946.
Knight, Jack and Lee Epstein. "On the Struggle for Judicial Supremacy." *Law and Society Review* 30, no. 1 (1996): 87–120.
Knupfer, Peter B. *The Union as It Is: Constitutional Unionism and Sectional Compromise, 1787–1861*. Chapel Hill, NC: University of North Carolina Press, 1991.
Kuic, Vukan. "John C. Calhoun's Theory of the 'Concurrent Majority.'" *American Bar Association Journal* 69 (1983): 482–486.
Leff, Carol Skalnik. "Democratization and Disintegration: Federalism and the Break-up of the Communist Federal States." *World Politics* 51 (1999): 205–235.
Lence, Ross M., ed. *Union and Liberty: The Political Philosophy of John C. Calhoun*. Indianapolis: Liberty Fund, 1992.
Lesesne, Henry. *The Making of a Southern Research University: The University of South Carolina, 1940–1990*. Ph.D. diss. University of South Carolina, 1998.
Lipset, Seymour Martin. *Political Man: The Social Bases of Politics*. Garden City, New York: Doubleday & Company, Inc, 1959.
Livingston, Donald. "The Secession Tradition in America." In *Secession, State and Liberty*, edited by David Gordon, 1–34. New Brunswick, NJ: Transaction Publishers, 1998.
Lowi, Theordore. *The End of Liberalism: The Second Republic of the United States*, second edition. New York: W.W. Norton & Company, 1979.
Maier, Pauline. "The Road Not Taken: Nullification, John C. Calhoun, and the Revolutionary Tradition in South Carolina." *The South Carolina Historical Magazine* 82, no. 1 (1981): 1–19.
Mann, Michael. "The Autonomous Power of the State: Its Origins, Mechanisms and Results." *European Journal of Sociology* 25, no. 2 (1984): 185–213.
Mann, Michael. "Nation-States in Europe and Other Continents: Diversifying, Developing, Not Dying." *Daedalus* 122, no. 3 (1993): 115–140
Mann, Michael. *Sources of Social Power, Volume 2*. Cambridge and New York: Cambridge University Press, 1993.
March, James G. and Johan P. Olsen. "The New Institutionalism: Organizational Factors in Political Life." *American Political Science Review* 78, no. 3 (1984): 734–749.
Marx, Karl and Friedrick Engels. *The Civil War in the United States*. New York: International Publishers, 1961.
McCormick, Richard P. *The Second American Party System: Party Formation in the Jacksonian Era*. Chapel Hill, NC: University of North Carolina Press, 1966.
McCrary, Peyton, Clark Miller, and Dale Baum. "Class and Party in the Secession Crisis: Voting Behavior in the Deep South, 1859–1861." *Journal of Interdisciplinary History* 8, no. 3 (1978): 429–457.
McCurry, Stephanie. *Masters of Small Worlds: Yeoman Households, Gender Relations, and the Political Culture of the Antebellum South Carolina Low Country*. New York: Oxford University Press, 1995.
McCurry, Stephanie. "The Politics of Yeoman Households in South Carolina." In *Divided Houses: Gender and the Civil War*, edited by Catherine Clinton and Nina Silber, 22–42. New York: Oxford University Press, 1992.
McDonnell, Lawrence T. "Struggle Against Suicide: James Henry Hammond and the Secession of South Carolina." *Southern Studies* 22, no. 2 (1983): 109–137.

McGarry, John and Brendan O'Leary. *The Politics of Ethnic Conflict Regulation.* London and New York: Routledge, 1993.

McPherson, Edward. *The Political History of the United States of America During the Great Rebellion, 1860–1865.* New York: Da Capo Press, 1972.

McPherson, James M. *Battle Cry of Freedom: The Civil War Era.* New York: Oxford University Press, 1988.

Meadwell, Hudson and Lawrence Anderson. "Sequence and Strategy in the Secession of the American South." *Theory and Society* 37 (2008): 199–227.

Meadwell, Hudson. "The Politics of Nationalism in Quebec." *World Politics* 45, no. 2 (1993): 203–241.

Meadwell, Hudson. "Breaking the Mould? Quebec Independence and Secession in the Developed West." In *Notions of Nationalism*, edited by Sukumar Periwal, 129–152. Budapest and New York: Central European University Press, 1995.

Meadwell, Hudson. "Secession, States and International Society." *Review of International Studies* 25, no. 3 (1999): 371–387.

Meadwell, Hudson. "Institutional Design and State-breaking in North America." In *The International Politics of Quebec Secession. State-making and State-breaking in North America*, edited by David Carment, John F. Stack Jr, and Frank Harvey, 11–32. Westport, CT and London: Praeger Publishers, 2001.

Memminger, C.G. Doc. No. LVIII. *Address of the Hon. C.G. Memminger, Special Commissioner from the State of South Carolina, before the Assembled Authorities of the State of Virginia, January 19, 1860.* 1860.

Millett, Allan R. and Peter Maslowski. *For the Common Defense: A Military History of the United States of America.* New York and London: The Free Press, 1984.

Mills, Walter. *Arms and Men: A Study in American Military History.* New York: G.P. Putnam's Sons, 1956.

Moore, Barrington. *Social Origins of Dictatorship and Democracy: Lord and Peasant in the Making of the Modern World.* Boston: Beacon Press, 1966.

Moore, John Basset, ed. *The Works of James Buchanan*, Vol. 11. Philadelphia and London: J.B. Lippincott Company, 1910.

Nettl, J.P. "The State as a Conceptual Variable." *World Politics* 20, no. 4 (1968): 559–592.

Nichols, Roy Franklin. *The Disruption of American Democracy.* New York: The Free Press, 1948.

Nicolay, John G. and John Hay. *Abraham Lincoln: A History Volume Two.* New York: The Century Co, 1890.

Nordlinger, Eric. *On the Autonomy of the Democratic State.* Cambridge, MA and London: Harvard University Press, 1981.

North, Douglass. *The Economic Growth of the United States, 1790–1860.* New York: W.W. Norton and Company, 1966.

North, Douglass. *Structure and Change in Economic History.* New York: Norton, 1981.

O'Neill, Charles Edwards. *Louisiana, A History.* Arlington Heights, IL: Forum Press, 1984.

Ochenkowski, J.P. "The Origins of Nullification in South Carolina." *The South Carolina Historical Magazine* 83, no. 2 (1982): 121–153.

Paskoff, Paul F. and Daniel J. Wilson. *The Cause of the South: Selections from De Bow's Review, 1846–1867.* Baton Rouge and London: Louisiana State University Press, 1982.

Perritt, Henry Hardy. *Robert Barnwell Rhett: South Carolina Secession Spokesman.* Ph.D. diss. University of Florida, 1954.

Pierson, Paul. *Politics in Time.* Princeton, NJ: Princeton University Press, 2004.

Poole, Keith T. and Howard Rosenthal. *Congress: A Political-Economic History of Roll Call Voting.* New York and Oxford: Oxford University Press, 1997.
Potter, David M. *The Impending Crisis: 1848–1861.* New York: Harper and Rowe, 1976.
Potter, David M. *The South and the Sectional Conflict.* Baton Rouge: Louisiana State University Press, 1968.
Premdas, Ralph R. "Secessionist Movements in Comparative Perspective." In *Secessionist Movements in Comparative Perspective*, edited by Ralph R. Premdas, S.W.R. Samarasinghe, and Alan B. Anderson, 12–31. New York: St. Martin's Press, 1990.
Procter, Ben H. *Not Without Honor: The Life of John H. Reagan.* Austin: University of Texas Press, 1962.
Rainwater, Percy Lee. *Mississippi: Storm Center of Secession.* Baton Rouge: Otto Claitor, 1938.
Rhodes, James Ford. *History of the United States from the Compromise of 1850.* New York: The Macmillan Company, 1953.
Riccards, Michael P. "Lincoln and the Political Question: The Creation of the State of West Virginia." *Presidential Studies Quarterly* 27, no. 3 (Summer, 1997): 549–564.
Riker, William. *Federalism: Origin, Operation, Significance.* Boston and Toronto: Little, Brown and Company, 1964.
Riker, William. *Soldiers of the States.* Washington, DC: Public Affairs Press, 1979.
Riker, William. *The Strategy of Rhetoric: Campaigning for the American Constitution.* New Haven: Yale University Press, 1996.
Ringold, May Spencer. "Robert Newman Gourdin and the '1860 Association'." *Georgia Historical Quarterly* 55, no. 4 (1971): 501–509.
Roeder, Philip G. "Soviet Federalism and Ethnic Mobilization." *World Politics* 43 (1991): 196–232.
Rogers, George C. "South Carolina Federalists and the Origins of the Nullification Movement." *South Carolina Historical Magazine* 71, no. 1 (1970): 17–32.
Rogers, George C. *Generations of Lawyers: A History of the South Carolina Bar.* Columbia, SC: The South Carolina Bar Foundation, 1992.
Rogers, William Warren, ed. *Alabama: The History of a Deep South State.* Tuscaloosa: University of Alabama Press, 1994.
Romney, Paul. "Provincial Equality, Special Status and the Compact Theory of Canadian Confederation." *Canadian Journal of Political Science* 32 (1999): 21–40.
Ryle, Walter Harrington. *Missouri: Union or Secession.* Nashville, TN: George Peabody College for Teachers, 1931.
Scarborough, William Kauffman, ed. *The Diary of Edmund Ruffin, Volume 1 Toward Independence October, 1856–April 1861.* Baton Rouge and London: Louisiana State University Press, 1972.
Schaper, William A. *Sectionalism and Representation in South Carolina.* Washington, DC: American Historical Association, 1901.
Scharf, John Thomas. *History of Delaware: 1609–1888.* Philadelphia: L.J. Richards, 1888.
Schrader, Charles Reginald, ed. *Reference Guide to the United States Military History* vol. 2. New York: Facts on File, 1993.
Schultz, Harold S. *Nationalism and Sectionalism in South Carolina 1852–1860.* Durham, NC: Duke University Press, 1950.
Shanks, Henry T. *The Secession Movement in Virginia, 1847–1861.* Richmond, VA: Garrett and Massie Publishers, 1934.

Sitterson, Joseph C. *The Secession Movement in North Carolina.* Chapel Hill, NC: University of North Carolina Press, 1939.

Skocpol, Theda. "State Formation and Social Policy in the United States." *American Behavioral Scientist* 35, no. 4/5 (1992): 559–584.

Skocpol, Theda. "Why I am an Historical Institutionalist." *Polity* 28, no. 1 (1995): 103–106.

Skowronek, Stephen. *Building a New American State.* New York: Cambridge University Press, 1982.

Small, Melvin and J. David Singer. *Resort to Arms: International and Civil Wars, 1816–1980.* Beverly Hills, CA: Sage Publications, 1982.

Spruyt, Hendrik. *The Sovereign State and its Competitors: An Analysis of Systems Change.* Princeton, NJ: Princeton University Press, 1994.

Stampp, Kenneth M. *The Peculiar Institution: Negro Slavery in the American South.* London: Eyre and Spottiswoode 1956.

Stavisky, Leonard Price. "Industrialism in Ante Bellum Charleston." *Journal of Negro History* 36, no. 3 (1951): 302–322.

Steinmo, Sven, Kathleen Thelen, and Frank Longstreth, eds. *Structuring Politics: Historical Institutionalism in Comparative Analysis.* Cambridge and New York: Cambridge University Press, 1992.

Taubman, Geoffry. "Nationalism, Loss-Gain Framing and the Confederate States of America." *Nations and Nationalism* 3, no. 2 (1994): 251–271.

Taussig, F.W. *The Tariff History of the United States.* New York: Capricorn, 1962.

Taylor, Rosser, H., ed. "Boyce-Hammond Correspondence." *Journal of Southern History* 3, no. 3 (1937): 348–354.

Tebeau, Charlton W. *A History of Florida.* Coral Gables, FL: University of Miami Press, 1971.

Thelen, Kathleen. "Historical Institutionalism in Comparative Politics." *Annual Review of Political Science* 2 (1999): 369–404.

Thomas, David Y. "Southern Non-Slaveholders in the Election of 1860." *Political Science Quarterly* 26, no. 2 (1911): 222–237.

Thomas, Emory M. *The Dogs of War: 1861.* New York: Oxford University Press, 2011.

Thorpe, Francis Newton. *The Federal and State Constitutions, Colonial Charters, and other Organic Laws of the States, Territories, and Colonies Now or Heretofore Forming The United States of America.* Washington, DC: Government Printing Office, 1909.

Tilly, Charles ed. *The Formation of National States in Western Europe.* Princeton, NJ: Princeton University Press, 1975.

Treisman, Daniel S. "Russia's 'Ethnic Revival': The Separatist Activism of Regional Leaders in Postcommunist Order." *World Politics* 49 (1997): 212–249.

United States Department of Commerce. Bureau of the Census. *The Statistical History of the United States: From Colonial Times to the Present.* New York: Basic Books, Inc., Publishers, 1975.

Van Deusen, John G. *Economic Bases of Disunion in South Carolina.* New York: Columbia University Press, 1928.

Varon, Elizabeth R. *Disunion! The Coming of the American Civil War, 1789–1859.* Chapel Hill, NC: University of North Carolina Press, 2008.

Venable, Austin L. "The Conflict Between the Douglas and Yancey Forces in the Charleston Convention." *Journal of Southern History* 8, no. 2 (1942): 226–241.

Vincent, Andrew. *Theories of the State.* Oxford and New York: Basil Blackwell, 1987.

Vipperman, Carl J. *William Lowndes and the Transition of Southern Politics: 1782–1822.* Chapel Hill, NC: University of North Carolina, 1989.

Wakelyn, Jon L. "The Changing Loyalties of James Henry Hammond: A Reconsideration." *South Carolina Historical Magazine* 75 (1974): 1–13.

Wallace, David Duncan. *The History of South Carolina* 3 vols. New York: The American Historical Society, 1934.

Walther, Eric H. *The Fire-Eaters.* Baton Rouge and London: Louisiana State University Press, 1992.

Weber, Max. *Economy and Society* 3 vols. New York: Bedminster Press, 1968.

Weingast, Barry. *Institutions and Political Commitment: A New Political Economy of the American Civil War Era.* Unpublished Manuscript, Hoover Institution, Stanford University, 1996.

Weingast, Barry. "Political Stability and Civil War: Institutions, Commitment and American Democracy." In *Analytic Narratives*, edited by Robert H. Bates, Avner Greif, Margaret Levi, Jean-Laurent Rosenthal, and Barry R. Weingast, 148–193. Princeton, NJ: Princeton University Press, 1998.

Weir, Robert M. "'The Harmony We Were Famous For': An Interpretation of Pre-Revolutionary South Carolina Politics." *William and Mary Quarterly* 26, no. 4 (1969): 473–501.

White, Laura A. *Robert Barnwell Rhett: Father of Secession.* Gloucester, MA: Peter Smith, 1931.

Wickwar, W. Hardy. *300 Years of Development Administration in South Carolina.* Columbia, SC: University of South Carolina Bureau of Governmental Research and Service, 1970.

Woods, James M. *Rebellion and Realignment: Arkansas's Road to Secession.* Fayetteville, AR: University of Arkansas Press, 1987.

Wood, John R. "Secession: A Comparative Analytical Framework." *Canadian Journal of Political Science* 14, no. 1 (1981): 107–134.

Wooster, Ralph. *The Secession Conventions of the South.* Princeton, NJ: Princeton University Press, 1962.

Wooster, Ralph. *The People in Power: Courthouse and Statehouse in the Lower South, 1850–1860.* Knoxville, TN: University of Tennessee Press, 1969.

Yarbrough, Beth V. and Robert M. "Unification and Secession: Group Size and 'Escape from Lock-In'." *Kyklos* 51, no. 2 (1998): 171–195.

Yarwood, Dean. "A Failure in Coalition Maintenance: The Defection of the South Prior to the Civil War." In *The Study of Coalition Behavior: Theoretical Perspectives and Cases from Four Continents*, edited by Sven Groennings, E.W. Kelley, and Michael Leiserson, 226–234. New York: Holt, Rinehart and Winston, Inc., 1970.

Index

A

Abandonment memories, 83, 85
Abolition, 61, 62. *See also* John Brown's raid
Agriculturalism, 2
Alabama, delegation withdrawal from Democratic convention of 1860, 69; early secession, 111–113; move toward secession, 66–67; Nullification doctrine as revolutionary and subversive, 39
Alabama platform, 68. *See also* Democratic convention of 1860
Alden, J. R., 145n26
Aldrich, A. P., 49, 86–87
Alexander, T. B., 149n65, 154n42
Alien and Sedition Acts, 18, 117
American Federalism. *See* Federalism
American people, sovereignty, 14
American State, early challenges to central state authority, 9–11, 17–20; European and American states, 12–17; federalism as defining feature, 22; stalemated, 13
American Union. *See* Union
Ames, H. V., 145n29, n30, n31, n33, 149n71, n72, n73
Amoretti, U., 142n9
Anderson, A. B., 141n4
Anderson, L.M., 142n11, n12, 151n114, 163n2
Anti-partyism, South Carolina, 27
Anti-slavery activation, 29. *See also* Slavery
Anti-slavery legislation, 13. *See also* Slavery
Anti-statist principles, 19
Anti-system movements, 11
Aranson, P., 150n74
Arkansas, secession, 120–122
Articles of Confederation, 14, 15, 17
Ashworth, J., 141n3
Ayer, L. M., Jr., 151n106
Ayer, Lewis Malone, 50, 51

B

Balance, centralization and decentralization, 140
Balance of power, 99
Balance rule, 13, 127
Ballots, 27
Baltimore, Maryland, 69
Bancroft, F., 146n28
Banner, J. M., Jr., 145n11, 146n16
Barker, E., 143n5
Barney, W. L., 150n76, n83, 151n113, 159n145
Barnswell, J., 147n33, 150n95, 151n99, n102, 155n61
Basch, N., 159n137
Bates, R. H., 145n32
Baum, D., 160n5
Beard, C. A., 141n3
Beard, M. R., 141n3
Beer, S. H., 145n22, n23
Bennett, A., 142n13
Bensel, R. F., 141n3, 144n18, 145n36
Bermeo, N., 142n9
Beunger, W., 161n42
Birnbaum, P., 144n13
Black seaman, 28
Blank space, Constitution, 15
Bleeding Kansas, 61
Bleser, C., 151n111, 157n87
Bluffton movement, 40–48
Border South, 1, 106–107, 137

Boucher, C. S., 146n28, 149n69, 150n75, 151n96, 152n117, 159n143, 162n67
Bowman, S. D., 141n1
Boyce, Congressman William, 51, 95
Boyce, W. W., 151n110
Brancati, D., 142n11
Breckenridge, John C., Alabama support, 112; Arkansas support, 121; election data, 108; Florida support, 111; Georgia support, 114; Louisiana support, 115; North Carolina support, 124; Maryland support, 129; Mississippi support, 109; plurality of votes in Delaware, 130; Texas vote, 115
Bright, C., 144n15
Brown, Governor Joseph E. (Georgia), 72
Buchanan, A., 141n4
Burnham, W. D., 145n11
Burt, A., 151n107

C

Calhoun, Congressman, Senator, Vice President John C., 7, 29, 32
California, 43, 44–45, 102
Canada, adoption of federalism, 137
Capers, Henry D., 153n20, n21, n22
Catton, B., 162n84
Cauthen, C. E., 156n71, n80, 158n112
Central state authority, challenges and the south, 10; early challenges, 17–20; state challenges and right to secede, 135. *See also* Federal government
Central states, secession, 1
Chambers, W. N., 145n11
Channing, S., 152n17, 154n40
Charleston Harbor forts, 88
Charleston *Mercury*, election convention and secession responses in Charleston, 91–92; Plan, 74–76; pro-secessionist opinion, 7; South Carolina radicalism, 27
Charleston *Standard*, article on slavery, 97
Charleston, South Carolina, 67
Chesnut, M. B., 156n69, 158n110
Chesnut, U.S. Senator James, 86
Citizens, vote in Mississippi, 109
Civil War, 2
Clark, T. D., 162n79

Clashes, Québec, 138–139
Clay, Henry, 44
Cobb, Secretary Howell, 87
Coercion (by Lincoln administration), Arkansas and Tennessee, 122; Missouri, 128; North Carolina, 124; seceded states, 106; Texas, 116; Virginia, 118
Cole, A. C., 155n64, 163n1
Coleman, K., 160n28
Collective policies, 138
Commager, H. S., 145n27, n28, 149n57, 150n94, 154n38, n39, 155n58, n59, 161n51
Commerce, regulation, 15
Commercial ties, North, 114, 127
Compact theory, 15, 19, 137
Compromise of 1850, Alabama support, 111; ambivalence in Virginia, 117; Calhoun address to Senate, 43; California admittance to Union as free state, 45, 46, 47–48; Florida support, 110; Georgia support, 113; Kentucky support, 128; Mississippi commitment, 109; Tennessee support, 122; Texas support, 115
Compromise Tariff of 1833, 6, 37
Concurrent majority concept, 37–38
Confederate States of America, 1–2, 119
Conflicts, 34–35, 135
Conger, J. L., 150n74
Congress, 42–43
Congressional election, 1858, 59
Conner, District Attorney James, 80
Conquest, neighboring states in Europe, 11
Consensus system, 26
Conservatism, 113, 127
Conservative candidates, 114. *See also* Georgia
Conservative speeches, 84
Consolidated political power, 35
Constitution, 17, 95, 125
Constitution compact, 36
Constitutional Union Party, 111
Convention, election and nullifiers win over unionists in South Carolina, 35–36; campaign in South Carolina, 90–91; effects of delay and passage of bill for later convention date, 82; election in Charleston, 91–93; Houston

stalling efforts, 115–116; secession accomplished, 95–98; South Carolina to secede or nullify in 1844, 40; Southern-wide convention and cooperative secession, 48. *See also* Cooperative secession; Secession; Unilateral secession
Cooper, Thomas, 28
Cooperative secession, second referendum on secession in South Carolina, 102; failure by South Carolina, 136; Senator Hammond, 85; South Carolina attempt, 48–53; Up country, 84. *See also* Unilateral secession
Corlew, R. E., 162n63, n64
Cotton, 29
Craven, A. O., 161n45
Craven, G., 152n118
Creel, G., 161n42
Crenshaw, O., 153n26
Crittenden Compromise, 119, 128
Crofts, D. W., 161n55, n65
Cullinan, G., 155n67
Cultural domination, 3
Cultural survival, 139
Cunningham, Representative John, 83, 84

D

Davidson, C. G., 145n5, 146n23
Day, D., 161n42
de Roulhac, J. G., 155n62
De Tocqueville, A., 144n13
Decentralization, 9
Declaration of Immediate Causes, 96
Declaration of Independence, 78
Deep South states, 1, 69
Delaware, 19, 130–131
Democratic convention(s) of 1860, 67–70
Democratic Party, 13, 70, 77, 136
Democratization, 109, 110
Denman, C. P., 153n33, 154n34, 158n127, n128, 160n25
Denton, L. M., 162n81, n83
Deudney, D. H., 144n11, n13, n17
Devolution, 139
Dion, S., 141n6
Disquisition on Government, 38. *See also* Calhoun
District of Columbia, 44, 52
Disunion, 10

Domestic industries, 29
Domestic policy, 89–90
Donnelly, W. J., 161n41
Doran, C. F., 163n5
Dorman, L., 160n21, n22
Douglas, Senator Steven, 44, 67, 127
Dred Scott decision, 54. *See also* Slavery
Dual executive, 38
Dumond, D. L., 142n12, 155n62, 160n14, n34, 162n74

E

Early convention bill, 80–84
Early seceders, 106
Eaton, C., 144n20, 155n66
Economic exploitation, 3
Economic prosperity, 29, 79
Edgar, W. B., 145n1, 147n34, n41, 149n49, n68, 151n97, 159n136
Edgefield *Advertiser*, 50
Educational institutions, 27
1860 Association of South Carolina, 7, 92–93
Election, Lincoln and secession, 84
Election of 1800, 19
Elections, data, 107
Electoral College, 70, 76, 80, 110
Ellis, Governor John (North Carolina), 71
Elmore, John, 95
Emizet, K. N., 141n6
Engels, F., 145n32
Engerman, S. L., 155n63
Entrepreneurs, secessionist, 6
Epstein, L., 142n14
Erk, J., 141n7, n11
Ertman, T., 143n5
Europe, state formation versus America, 9, 11
Executive authority, 25
Export economy, 33
Exposition and Protest, 33. *See also* Calhoun
Eysturlid, L. W., 144n19

F

Failed mission, 64. *See also* Southern Confederacy
Faust, D. G., 146n32
Federal design of American state, secession, 103
Federal government, Canada and Québec secession, 138; expanding

power and nullification support in South Carolina, 29, 31–32; participation in Union states, 12; powers and American people, 14; protectionist tariff and crisis in South Carolina in 1832, 135; weaknesses, 134
Federalism, political union and secession of South Carolina, 3; paradoxical impact, 138; past and future, 134–140; stability of institutions over time, 4; United States and locus of sovereignty, 135
Federalist 10, 93
Federalist 62, 15–16
Federalist Papers, 19
Federalist Party, 18, 19
Federalist-nationalist alternative, 138. *See also* Québec
Fehrenbacher, D. E., 160n30
Filippov, M., 142n8
First secession crisis, 40–48. *See also* Secession of South Carolina
Fish, C. R., 155n65
Fite, E. D., 150n82, 154n41
Florida, 110–111
Floyd, Secretary of War John B., 89
Flynn, J. M., 144n19
Fogel, R. W., 149n61, 155n63
Foote, Governor Henry (Mississippi), 109
Force Bill, 37
Ford, L. K., 146n17, 158n111, n123, n125, 159n139
Foreign policy, 59–60
Foreign slave trade, 100. *See also* Slavery
Fornell, E. W., 161n38, n39
Fort Sumter, secession link, 106, 120, 121, 123, 137
Founding Fathers, 9, 17
Free soilers, 45
Free States, 13f, 45t. *See also* Union
Freehling, W. W., 142n12, 145n2, 146n25, 146n32, 147n47, 149n60, 152n15, 159 n1, n135, n144, 160n7, n19, n27, n32, 161n44
Frémont, John, 59

G
Genovese, E., 146n29
George, A., 142n13

Georgia Platform, adherence to Compromise of 1850, 136; Alabama 111; elimination of the threat of secession, 47–48, 52, 55; Georgia, 113; Mississippi, 109; North Carolina support, 124. *See also* Compromise of 1850
Georgia, 39, 113–114, 136
Gettys, J. W., 158n109
Gibbes, R. W., 159n129
Gist, Governor William Henry (South Carolina), advise to Mississippi to secede, 110; leading actor in strategy for secession, 7; mobilizing support by letter writing to Deep South governors in 1860, 70–74; threat and counter-revolution, 87–88. *See also* Secession of South Carolina
Goldstein, E., 144n10, 146n24
Goldstein, L. F., 144n14
Great Britain, secession potential, 139
Greenberg, K. S., 145n6, 146n20, n21, n22, 159n1
Grief, A., 145n32
Grievances, failure of federal government and protect New England states, 19–20; remedial action, 134; Rhett's July 4 speech, 60; secession from American Union, 2, 52–53; secession in Canada, 138, 139; South Carolina outcomes, 49, 102; structure and secession, 3–5

H
Hale, H. E., 142n10
Hall, P., 142n15
Hamer, P. M., 159n147
Hamilton, A., 145n24
Hamilton, D. H., 151n103
Hammond, J. H., 156n86
Hammond, U.S. Senator James Henry, 7, 49, 51, 84–87
Hanly Plan, 121
Harding, S., 144n15
Harper's Ferry, Virginia, 61. *See also* John Brown's raid
Hartford Convention, 19–20
Hay, J., 157n100, n102
Hayne, R. Y., 149n50
Hechter, M., 141n6, 142n10
Helper, H. R., 159n133

Index 183

Hesli, V., 141n6
Hicks, Governor Thomas (Maryland), 130
Historical debate, Georgia secession, 114
Hofstadter, R., 147n39
Holt, M. F., 145n11, 150n93
Hooker, C. E., 95
Horowitz, D. L., 141n4
House of Representatives, elections, 16, 77, 59
Houston, Governor Sam (Texas), 115

I

Imported goods, 29
Imprisonment, 130
Industry protection, 32
Institutional design, 11, 134
Institutional explanations, radicalism, 22–28
International trade, 28
Interstate competition, 11

J

Jackson, President Andrew, 33, 36–37
January convention date, 82
Jay, J. J., 145n24
Jeffersonian Republicans, 19
Jervis, R., 141n5
Jessop, B., 143n3
Jessup, J. E., 144n19
Jillson, C. C., 142n14
John Brown's raid, 61–63, 136
Johnston, A. S., 147n46

K

Kansas, 46
Kansas–Nebraska Act, 54
Kaplanoff, M. D., 158n123
Kato, J., 142n15
Kentucky and Virginian Resolutions of 1798/1799, 18. *See also* Alien and Sedition Acts
Kentucky, 128–129
Keohane, R., 144n12, 146n30
Ketz, L. B., 144n19
Kibler, L., 147n48, 158n107, 158n109
Knight, J., 142n14
Knupfer, P. B., 144n16
Kuic, V., 149n64

L

Late conventioneers, 82
Late seceders, 117–118

Laws, constitutionality, 36–37. *See also* Ordinance of Nullification
Lecompton Constitution, 46, 67
Lence, R. M., 147n40, 149n63, n66
Lesene, H., 146n23
Levi, M., 145n32
Limited government, 16
Lincoln, President Abraham, election and Arkansas, 121; election and early seceders, 108; election ramifications, 76–78; Moore's reluctance to secede, 67; quelling rebellion at Fort Sumter, 106; secession, 2, 6, 112; sectional conflicts, 136; southerners fearful of, 79
Lipset, S. M., 154n43, 160n5
Livingston, D., 143n2
Longstreth, F., 142n15
Louisiana, 114–115
Low Country, 23, 25, 26
Lowi, T., 144n18

M

Madison, J., 145n24
Magrath, Judge A. J., 80, 92
Maier, P., 147n40
Mail, delivery, 15
Majority platform, 68
Mann, M., 143n3, n8
Manufactured goods, per capita value, 126t
March, J. G., 142n15
Marriage, South, 98
Marx, K., 145n32
Maryland, 129–130
Maslowski, P., 144n19
McCormick, R. P., 145n11, 160n11
McCrary, P., 160n5
McCulloch v. Maryland, 12
McCurry, S., 147n48, 158n107, 159n137
McDonnell, L. T., 157n92
McGarry, J., 141n4
McPherson, E., 156n79, 161n36, 162n80
Meadwell, H., 143n5, 151n114, 163n4
Memminger, Christopher G., 63–65, 92, 96, 98
Middle country, 26
Miles, William Porcher, 65–66
Military defense, power of American State, 15
Miller, C., 160n5

Millet, A. R., 144n19
Mills, W., 144n19
Minnesota, 46
Mississippi, 108–110
Mississippi River, 127
Missouri Compromise, 43, 45
Missouri, 127–128
Missouri River, 127
Moore, J. B., 141n3, 157n103, n104, 158n105, n106
Moore, Governor A. B. (Alabama), 67, 72–73
Moore, Governor Thomas O. (Louisiana), 72
Moses, F. J., 158n117

N
Nashville Convention, 46, 49, 108, 135. *See also* Convention
National self-determination, 1
Nettl, 143n6, n7, 144n12
New institutionalism, 6
Nichols, R. F., 154n40, 157n100
Nicolay, J. G., 157n100, n102
Nomination, presidential candidates, 69
Non-coercion, 89, 90, 94
Non-seceders, 125–127
Non-slaveholders, 97, 98–100
Nordlinger, E., 144n13
North Carolina, 39, 123–125
North, D., 143n3, 146n30, 155n57
North, dominance in Union and unilateral secession of South Carolina, 102; interference with domestic policy of individual states, 89–90; king cotton and international trade with Great Britain, 28; strength in Union, 20; threat to slavery, 10
North–South incompatibility, 96–97
Northern manufacturers, 28
Northwest Ordinance of 1787, 41
Nullification, laws, 18. *See also* Constitution
Nullification controversy, 37, 38

O
O'Leary, B., 141n4
O'Neill, C. E., 160n33
Ochenkowski, J. P., 147n33
Ohio River, 129
Okamoto, D., 142n10
Olsen, J. P., 142n15

Opinion leader, 74. *See also* Charleston *Mercury*
Ordeshook, P. C., 142n8
Ordinance of Nullification, 36
Oregon, 46

P
Pamphlets, secessionist, 92–93
Party patronage positions, 79–80
Paskoff, P. F., 159n138
Passive office seeking, 27
Paternalistic domination, 98
Perritt, H. H., 152n5
Perry, Benjamin Franklin, 54, 90–91
Perry, Governor M. S. (Florida), 73
Petigru, James Louis, 91
Pettus, John J., 72
Pierson, P., 142n13
Planters, 23, 24t, 25t, 52
Political elite, South Carolina, 1, 26
Political mobilization, 4, 5
Political power, South and Lincoln election, 2, 3
Political revolution, South Carolina, 1
Political voice, 5
Poole, K. T., 152n3
Poor whites, 99
Populace, vote for Lincoln, 75t
Porter, W. D., 142n15
Postmasters general, 79
Potter, D. M., 142n12, 145n35, 150n87, n91, 152n13, n14, 154n40, 156n75, n78, 158n108, n126, 160n8, n9, n10, n12, n16, n18, n31, 162n86
Power, limitations and federal government, 14–15, Tariff of 1828, 33–34
Premdas, R. R., 141n4
Presidential election, 58t
Presidential electors, South Carolina, 26
Presidential nominating conventions, 27
Proctor, B. H., 160n34
Property, definitions in different states, 77
Pro-secessionist newspapers/pamphlets, 7
Pro-slavery, 14, 32. *See also* Slavery
Protectionist tariffs, 22, 29
Protective action, slavery and secession, 80
Public opinion, 48

Q

Quality of life, poor whites in South, 100
Québec, secession, 137

R

Radical abolitionism, 63
Radical actions, South Carolina, 39, 101. *See also* Secession of South Carolina
Rainwater, P. L., 160n13
Regional conflict, 137
Remediation strategy, 4
Republican Party, arising from ashes of Whig Party, 59; dominance during Civil War and reconstruction, 77; formation in north, 14; political preferences and platform, 77–78; presidential election of 1856, 59
Republican Presidency, impetus for secession, 7, 137
Resources, extraction from population, 9
Revolution, 17, 125
Rhett, Senator Robert Barwell, election convention in Charleston, 92; July 4 speech, 59–61; jump-starting secessionist movement, 40–41, 43; leading actor in strategy for secession, 7; secession document for South Carolina, 96, 97–98; unilateral secessionists, 49, 50–51, 53
Rhode Island, 19
Rhodes, J. F., 162n61
Riccards, M. P., 161n50
Richmond, Virginia, 69
Riker, W., 142n14, 144n10, 144n19
Ringold, M. S., 158n118, n119
Rogers, G. C., 146n22, n23, 149n67, 156n69, 158n120, n121. 160n20, n22, n24
Romney, P., 163n3
Rosenthal, H., 152n3
Rosenthal, J-L., 145n32
Ruffin, Edmund, 81, 82
Ruggie, J. G., 144n13
Rump convention, 70
Rutledge (pen name), 50, 152n16
Ryle, W. H., 162n77

S

Samarasinghe, S. W. R., 141n4
Scarborough, W. K., 156n70, n74, 158n107
Schaper, W. A., 145n7
Scharf, J. T., 162n85
Schrader, W., 144n19
Schulz, H. S., 153n29
Secession banner, 132f
Secession convention of 1852, 50, 51
Secession, path and three Souths, Alabama, 111–113; Arkansas, 120–122; Delaware, 130–131; early seceders, 108; Florida, 110–111; Georgia, 113–114; Kentucky, 128–129; late seceders, 117–118; Louisiana, 114–115; Maryland, 129–130; Mississippi, 108–110; Missouri, 127–128; non-seceders: border states look North, 125–127; North Carolina, 123–125; overview, 105–108; Tennessee, 122–123; Texas, 115–116; Virginia, 118–120
Secession of South Carolina, Alabama makes a move and an issue, 66–67; beginnings, 57–59; case in perspective, 102–103; convention campaign, 90–91; convention and accomplishment, 95–98; convention election in Charleston, 91–93; counter-revolution? Gist's threat, 87–88; Democratic convention(s) of 1860, 67–70; early convention bill passed, 80–84; election of Lincoln, 76–80; explaining non-slaveholder's support, 98–100; Governor Gist and depth of southern sentiment, 70–74; "Hammond's defection" and paradoxical position of South, 84–87; 116-day window of opportunity: Buchanan's guarantee, 88–90; John Brown's raid, 61–63; making Virginia take the lead, 63–66; *Mercury* plan, 74–76; Rhett's fourth of July speech, 59–61; strategy of unilateral, 93–95; ultimate challenge to central state authority, 10
Secessionism, as paradox of federalism, 2
Secessionist entrepreneurs, 80, 101

186 *Index*

Secessionist sentiment, 92–93
Secessionists, unilateral versus cooperative, 35
Second American Revolution, 134
Second-party system, 13
Sectional domination, 60
Sectional political parties, 16
Sectional victory, Lincoln election, 76, 105
Senate, 59
Shanks, H. A., 161n46, n47, n48, n49, n53
Shvetsova, O., 142n8
Simpson, C. M., 160n32
Singer, J. D., 144n10
Sitterson, J. C., 162n66, n68, n69, n70, n71, n72
Skocpol, T., 142n15, 143n4
Skowronek, S., 144n18
Slave states, admission to union, 45t; free state balance, 13; states not seceding, 106–107
Slaveholders, large-scale and political dominance in South Carolina, 23, 26; non-seceding Border South states, 107; number in Upper South, 117; percentage in states, 24t; secession, 105
Slave-owning class, aspiration of non-slaveholders, 100
Slavery, abolishment and Northern super-majority, 46; as immoral institution and North, 55; decimation of Whig Party, 59; extinction and *Mercury* call for convention and secession, 74; future of institution in territorial addition from Mexican War, 41–42; importance to Deep versus Upper South, 117; institution role in bonding of later seceders to early seceders, 106; key issue in Democratic convention of 1860, 68; moderate position by northern Democratic versus southern Democratic Party, 13–14; perception of serious threat and secession from Union by South Carolina, 2; political protection and Deep South, 77; protection and nullification support in South Carolina, 23, 29, 29t, 136; protection and secession of Mississippi, 110; protection by North or secession, 93; protection by the South and the increasing monolithic North, 22; survival and and Congressional proscription, 42–43; Texas, 41
Slaves, as percentage of population in state, 23, 24t; insurrection and non-slaveholders support in South, 99; rebellion in South Carolina attempts to inhibit in 1820s, 28
Small republics, James Madison, 93
Small, M., 144n10
Social institution, slavery as primary, 23
Social revolution, avoiding, 1
Society, attitudes and slavery prohibition, 43
Society of Ernest Men. *See* 1860 Association of South Carolina
South, contribution to Mexican War and territorial addition to Union, 41–42; following lead of South Carolina, 104. *See also* South Carolina
South Carolina, acting alone in unilateral secession, 65; attempt at cooperative secession, 48–53; attitudes toward federal government and state's versus federal rights, 19; Bluffton movement and origin of the first secession crisis, 40–48; institutional explanations for radicalism, 22–28; movement of secession, 5; nullification, 28–40; unilateral right to secede and later events preventing, 46–47; willingness to secede alone, 1, 71, 74. *See also* Secession of South Carolina
South Carolina College, 27
Southern apprehensions, balance in Senate, 16–17
Southern Confederacy, creation and unilateral secessionists, 51; effect of conservative Georgia, 113; establishment and South Carolina willingness to secede, 2, 71; mobilization for and Rhett's July 4 speech, 60; multi-step and multi-stage process, 5;

need for formation and Southern safety, 64; protection of slavery, 93; unilateral secession by South Carolina and Deep South, 136
Southern institutions, risk to staying in Union, 16, 103
Southern Patriot, 48
Southern rights, 55, 135
Sovereign status, individual states, 134
Sovereignty, 12, 17
Spratt, I. W., 97
Spruyt, H., 143n5
Squatter sovereignty, 42
Stampp, K. M., 159n132
State, American versus Europe, 14; definition, 11; formation in West versus East, 11; interposition, 36, 135; legislature, 16, 25, 83, 122; purpose and protection of property, 77; referendum, 121; rights, 20, 31, 59
State sovereignty, 14, 17, 34, 103
Statelessness, 12
States election of 1832, 35
Stavisky, L. P., 159n3
Steinmo, S., 142n15
Supremacy clause, 12
Supreme Court, 69
Swenden, W., 142n7

T
Tariff Act of 1828, South Carolina reaction, 29, 32, 33–34
Tariff Act of 1832, South Carolina reaction, 29, 30, 34
Tariff Act of 1844, Bluffton movement in South Carolina, 40
Tariff bill of 1816, support, 29
Tariff of Abomination. See Tariff of 1928
Tariff reduction, 135
Taubman, J., 141n5
Taussig, F. W., 147n36, n37, n41, n44
Taylor, R. H., 157n93
Tebeau, C. W., 160n15
Tennessee, 122–123
Tenth Amendment, 15
Territorial legislature, 42
Territorial reach, 11–12
Territories, Union and slavery versus non-slavery issue, 43–44, 102. See also Union
Texas, 115–116

Texas annexation, 40
The Plan, 49
Thelen, K., 142n15, 142n16
Theory of State interposition (or nullification), 18
Theory of state's sovereignty, 54
Thomas, D. Y., 159n134, n141
Thorp, F. N., 145n2, 146n9
Tilly, C., 143n5, n8
Timing, secession, 2, 52, 136
Toombs, Senator Robert, 83
Townsend, 158n122
Trenholm, George A., 81, 84
Tucker, Nathaniel Beverley, 46, 85
Two-party competition, Alabama, 112; Florida, 110–111; lack and political power in South Carolina, 23, 26; Mississippi, 109; Virginia, 117

U
Ullom, H. H., 161n42
Unification, South and bipartisan convention in Jackson Mississippi, 44
Unilateral secession, Alabama, 112–113; Bluffton movement, 40; Georgia, 114; Louisiana, 115; *Mercury* plan, 76; North Carolina, 125; South Carolina, 26–27, 84, 90–91, 93–99, 136; Tennessee, 123; Texas, 116; Virginia, 120
Union, balancing with free and slave states, 46; confrontations, 39–40; free state of California, 43; inhospitable to slavery, 4; instability of territorial addition from Mexican War, 41; maintaining and slavery, 57; shifting powers toward nationalism point of view, 20; threats to scope of federal government and territorial integrity, 9; value of and South Carolinian nullifiers, 39
Unionism, support in Alabama, 111; support in North Carolina, 124; support in Tennessee, 123; support in Virginia, 118; support of Governor Sam Houston of Texas, 116
Up country, 26, 83. See also Upper South

Upper South, convincing to form a Southern Confederacy, 64; entrenchment and effect on unilateral secession, 66; John Brown's raid on Harper's Ferry, 62l; late seceders, 117; seceding states and Virginia, 119; South secession from Union, 1

V

Van Deusen, J. G., 155n64
Varon, E. R., 143n1
Venable, A. L., 154n35
Vincent, A., 144n13
Vipperman, C. J., 145n32
Virginia, 63–66, 118–120
Voting, male non-slaveholders, 99

W

Wakelyn, J. L., 157n92
Walker, Governor Joseph Walker (Louisiana), 115
Wallace, D. D., 147n34, 150n81, 152n6, n7, n8, n9, n10
Walther, E. H., 150n77
War making, Europe, 11
War, 9, 136
War of 1812, 19
Washington Peace Conference, 124, 131
Weber, M., 143n3
Weingast, B., 142n14, 145n32, 162n75
Weir, R. M., 146n15
West Virginia, 119
Whig Party, 13
White, L. A., 151n108, 159n142, 160n9
Wickwar, W. H., 146n31
Wilmot Proviso, 41, 69
Wilmot, David, 41
Wilson, D. J., 159n138
Window of opportunity, 88–90
Wood, J. R., 141n6
Woods, J. M., 161n58, n59
Wooster, R., 158n109, 160n6, n17, n26, 161n37, n40, n43, n52, n57, n60, n61, 162n73, n76, n78, n80, n87, n89, n90

Y

Yancey, William, 69, 111
Yarbrough, B. V., 163n6
Yarbrough, R. M., 163n6
Yarwood, D., 154n35

CPSIA information can be obtained
at www.ICGtesting.com
Printed in the USA
LVHW02s1924040318
568600LV00042B/2729/P